100 MOST BEAUTIFUL SONGS EVER
FOR FINGERSTYLE UKULELE

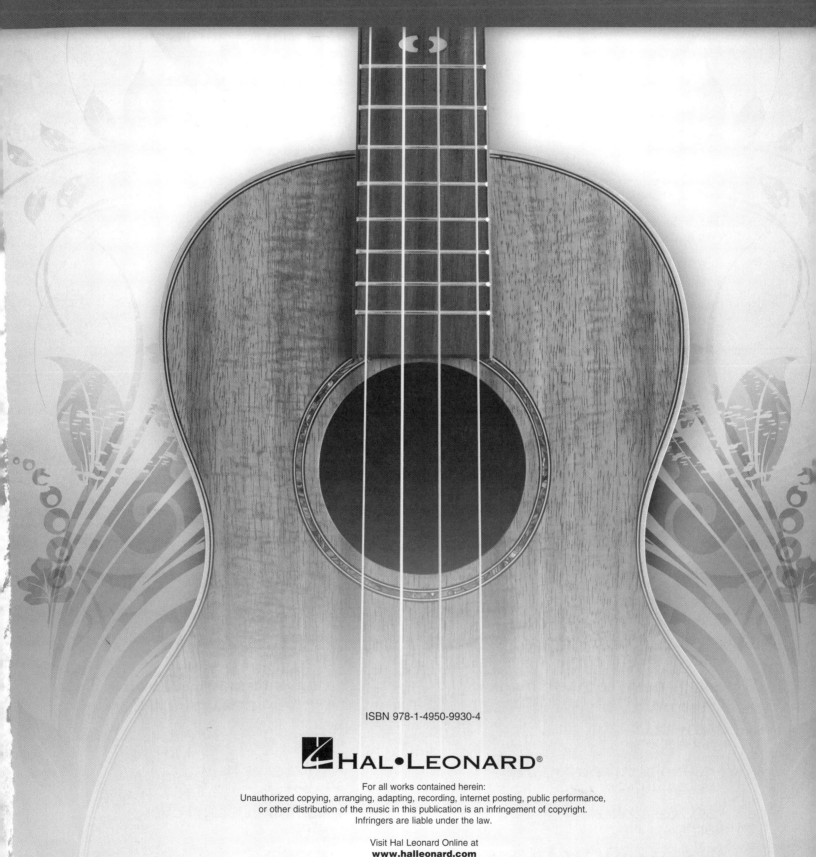

ISBN 978-1-4950-9930-4

HAL•LEONARD®

Visit Hal Leonard Online at
www.halleonard.com

Contact us:
Hal Leonard
7777 West Bluemound Road
Milwaukee, WI 53213
Email: info@halleonard.com

In Europe, contact:
Hal Leonard Europe Limited
42 Wigmore Street
Marylebone, London, W1U 2RN
Email: info@halleonardeurope.com

In Australia, contact:
Hal Leonard Australia Pty. Ltd.
4 Lentara Court
Cheltenham, Victoria, 3192 Australia
Email: info@halleonard.com.au

C000060154

After the Love Has Gone

Words and Music by David Foster, Jay Graydon and Bill Champlin

Verse

Slow, in 2

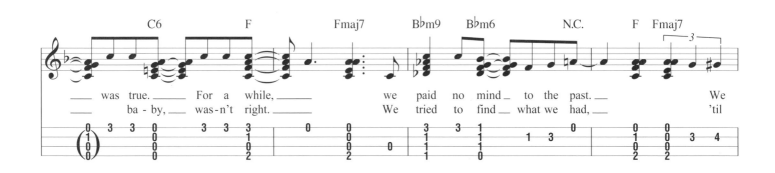

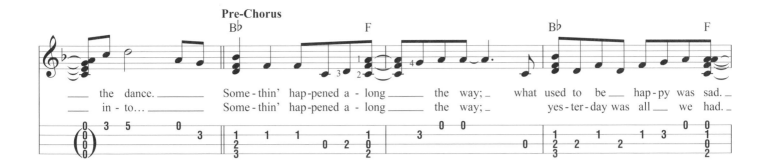

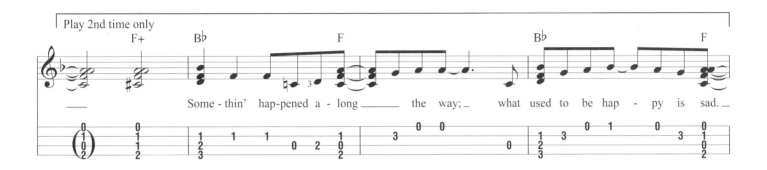

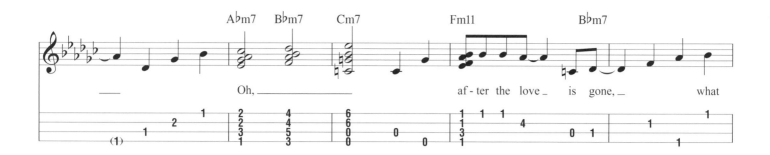

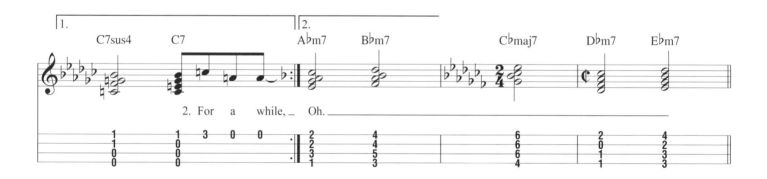

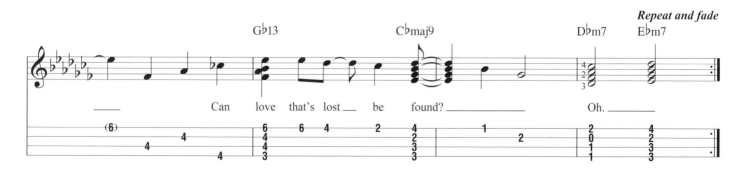

Against All Odds
(Take a Look at Me Now)

from AGAINST ALL ODDS

Words and Music by Phil Collins

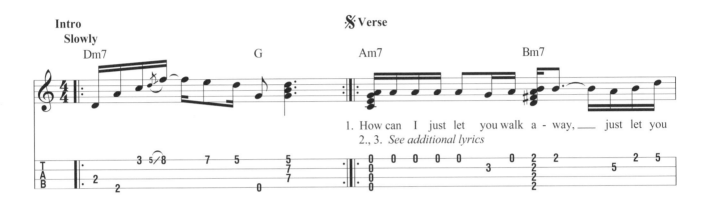

1. How can I just let you walk a-way,___ just let you
2., 3. *See additional lyrics*

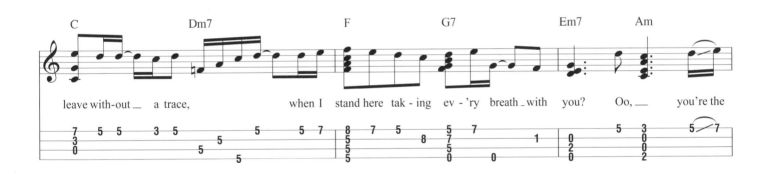

leave with-out ___ a trace, when I stand here tak-ing ev-'ry breath _ with you? Oo, ___ you're the

on-ly one who real-ly knew me _ at all. ___   So take a look at me

Chorus

now, _ well, there's just an emp-ty space. And there's noth-ing left _ here _ to re-mind _ me, _ just the

mem-'ry of ___ your face. _

1. Well, take a look at me now, ___ well, there's just an
2. Now, take a look at me now, ___ 'cause there's just an

1.

emp-ty space. And you com-in' back to me ___ is a-gainst the odds, ___ and that's
emp-ty space. But to

what I've got ___ to face. ___

3. I

2.

wait for you _ is all I can do, _ and that's what I've got _ to face. _ Take a good look at me

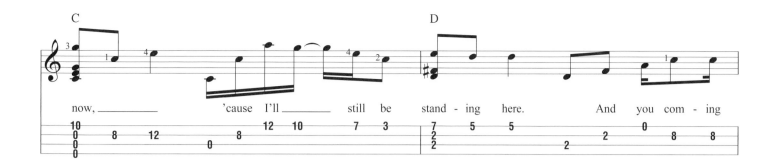

now, _____ 'cause I'll _____ still be stand - ing here. And you com - ing

back to me ___ is a - gainst all odds, _ it's the chance I've got _ to take. _____

Outro

Take a look at me now.

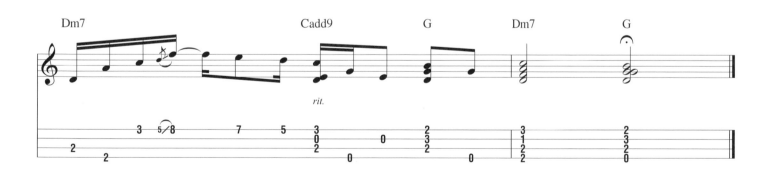

rit.

Additional Lyrics

2. How can you just walk away from me,
   When all I can do is watch you leave?
   'Cause we shared the laughter and the pain,
   And even shared the tears.
   You're the only one who really knew me at all.

3. I wish I could just make you turn around,
   Turn around and see me cry.
   There's so much I need to say to you,
   So many reasons why.
   You're the only one who really knew me at all.

All by Myself

Music by Sergei Rachmaninoff
Words and Additional Music by Eric Carmen

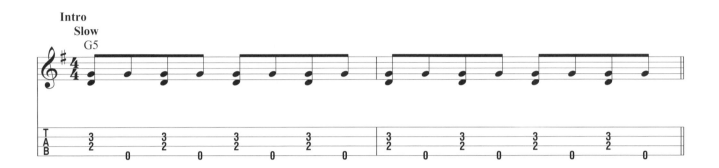

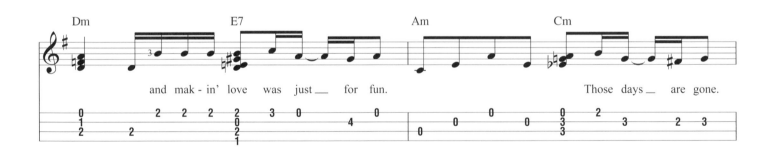

1., 4. When I was young ___ I nev-er need-ed an-y-one,
2., 3. *See additional lyrics*

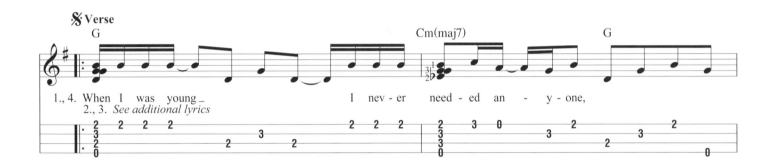

and mak-in' love was just ___ for fun. Those days ___ are gone.

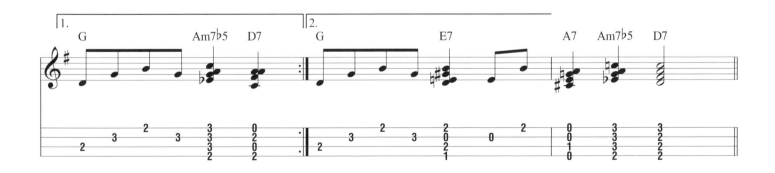

Chorus

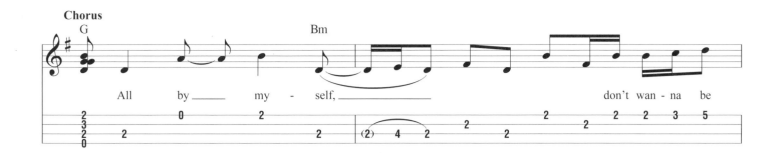

All by _____ my - self, _____ don't wan - na be

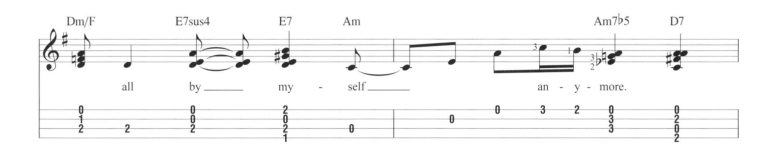

all by _____ my - self _____ an - y - more.

All by _____ my - self, _____ don't wan - na be

To Coda ⊕

D.S. al Coda
(take repeat)

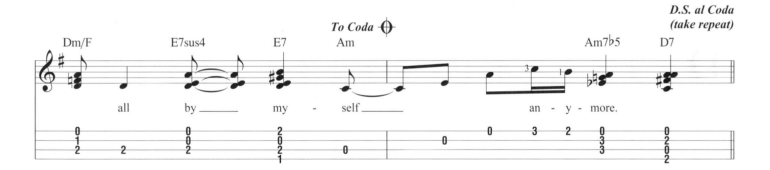

all by _____ my - self _____ an - y - more.

⊕ **Coda**

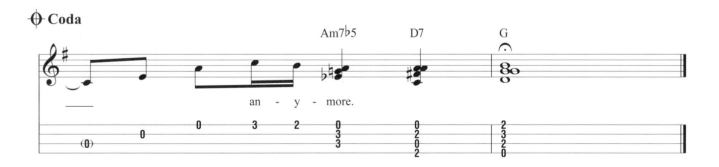

_____ an - y - more.

Additional Lyrics

2. Livin' alone, I think of all the friends I've known,
But when I dial the telephone
Nobody's home.

3. Hard to be sure, sometimes I feel so insecure,
And love so distant and obscure,
Remains the cure.

Almost Paradise

Love Theme from the Paramount Motion Picture FOOTLOOSE

Words by Dean Pitchford
Music by Eric Carmen

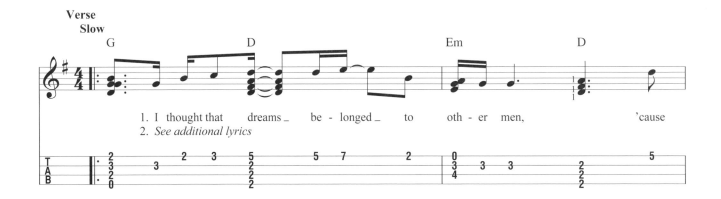

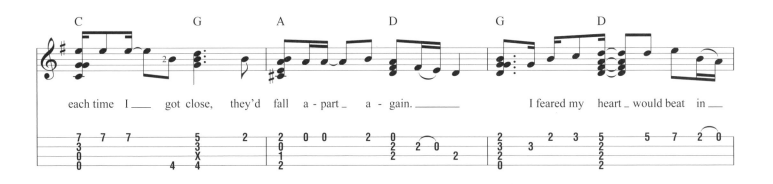

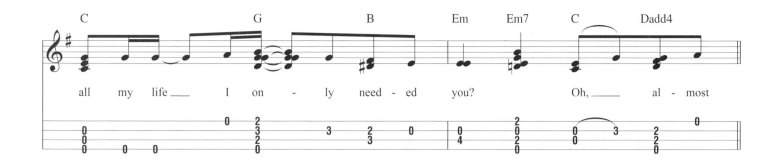

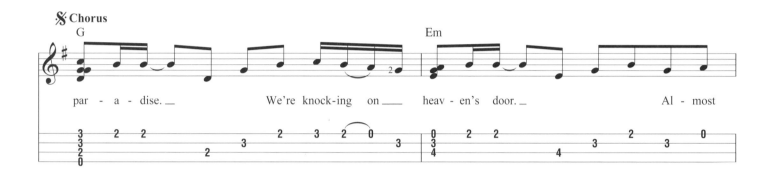

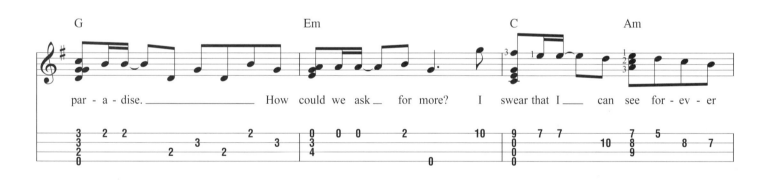

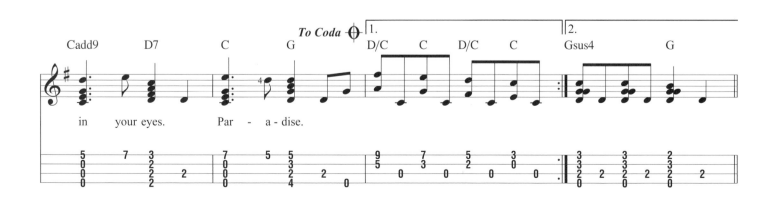

Bridge

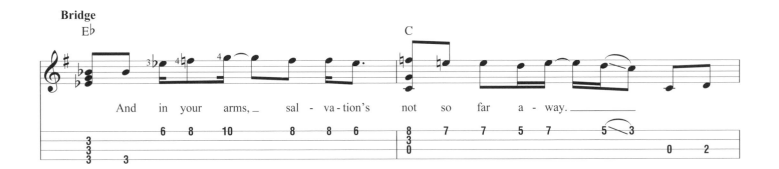

And in your arms, ___ sal - va - tion's not so far a - way. ___

D.S. al Coda

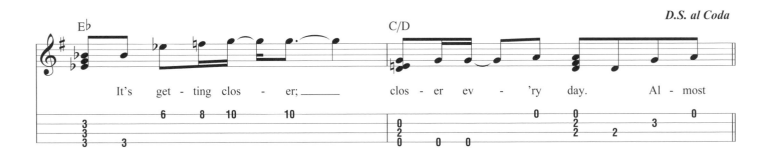

It's get - ting clos - er; ___ clos - er ev - 'ry day. Al - most

⊕ Coda

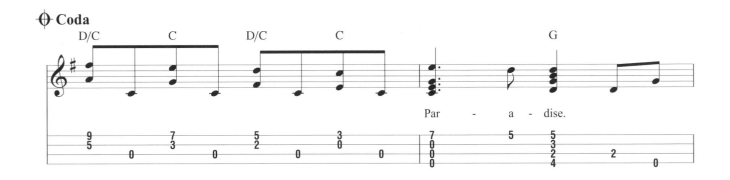

Par - a - dise.

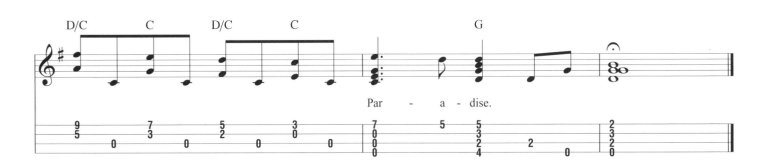

Par - a - dise.

Additional Lyrics

2. It seems like perfect love's so hard to find.
I'd almost given up. You must have read my mind.
And all these dreams I saved for a rainy day,
They're finally coming true.
I'd share them all with you,
'Cause now we hold the future in our hands.

And I Love You So

Words and Music by Don McLean

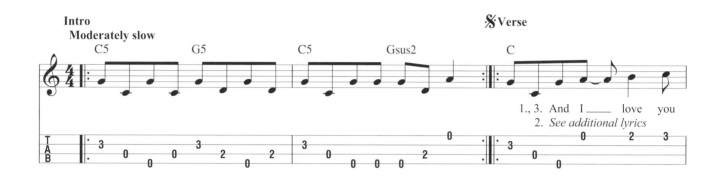

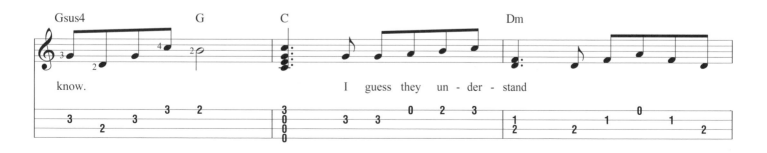

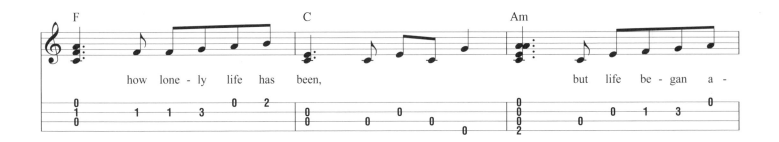

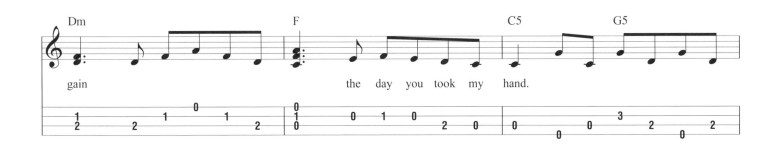

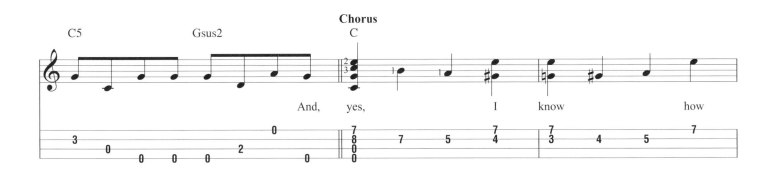

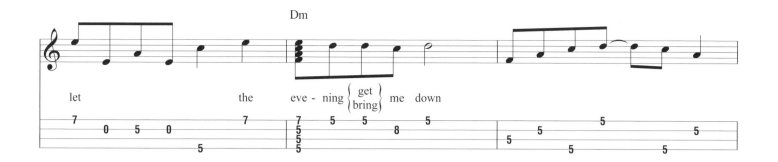

let   the   eve - ning ⎧ get ⎫ me down
                                   ⎩ bring ⎭

now that you're a - round   me.

2nd time, D.S. al Coda

⊕ **Coda**

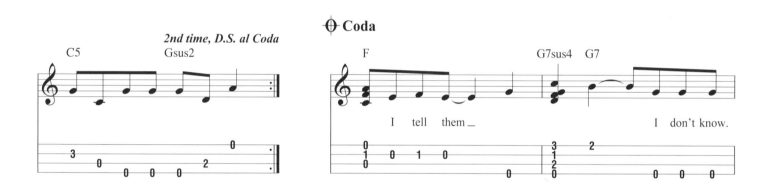

I tell them __   I don't know.

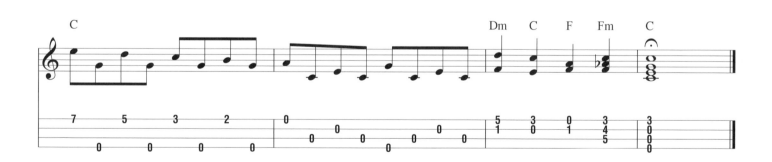

Additional Lyrics

2. And you love me, too;
   Your thoughts are just for me.
   You set my spirit free;
   I'm happy that you do.
   The book of life is brief,
   And once a page is read,
   All but love is dead.
   That is my belief.

Angel

Words and Music by Sarah McLachlan

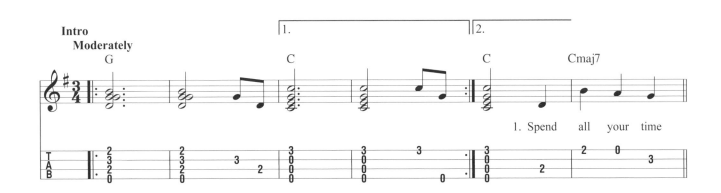

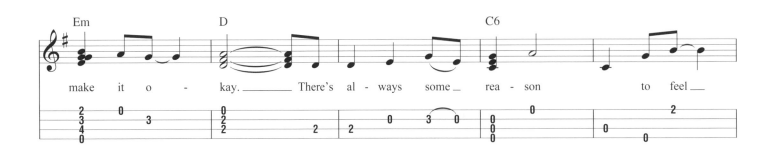

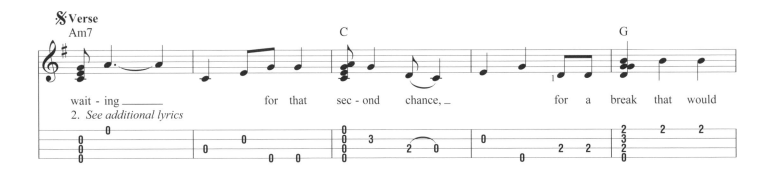

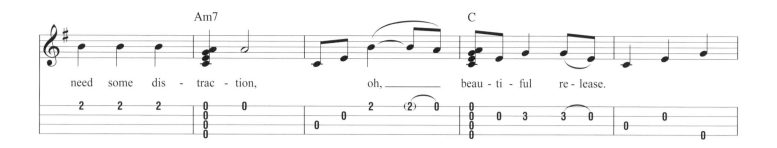

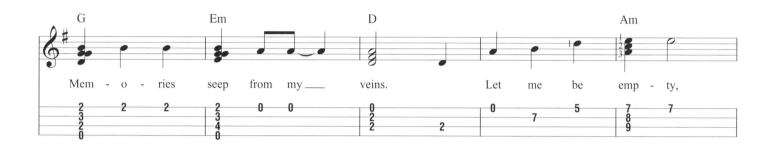

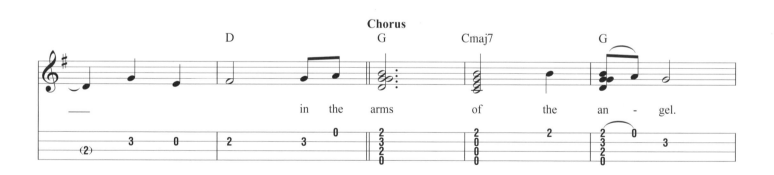

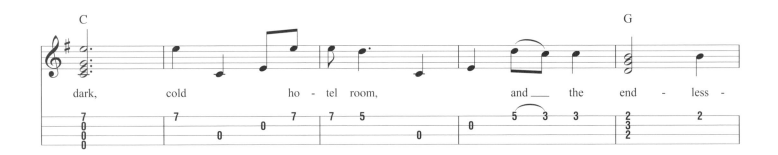

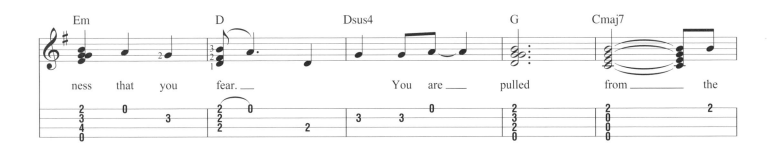

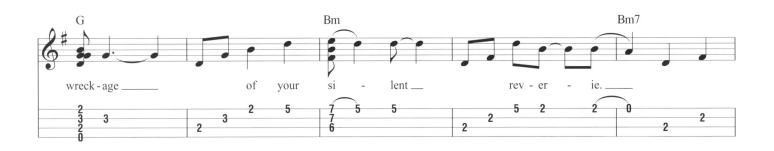

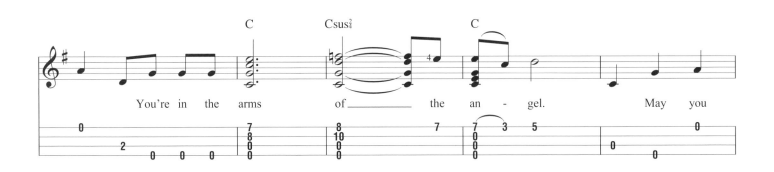

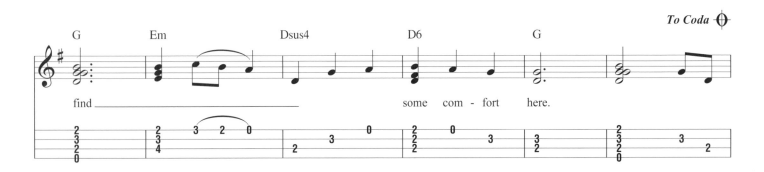

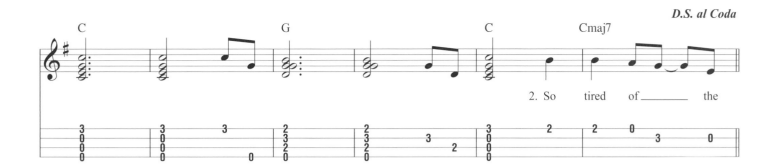

2. So tired of _____ the

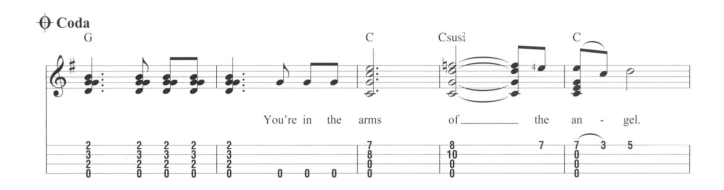

You're in the arms of _____ the an - gel.

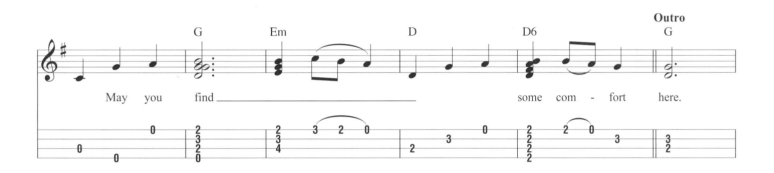

May you find _____ some com - fort here.

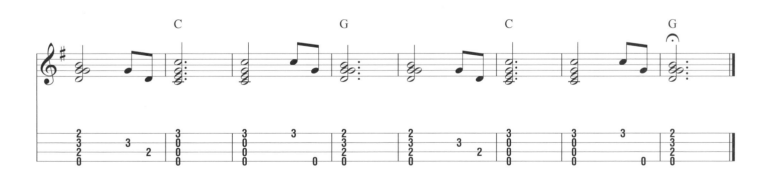

Additional Lyrics

2. So tired of the straight line, and everywhere you turn
   There's vultures and thieves at your back.
   The storm keeps on twisting.
   Keep on building the lies that you make up for all that you lack.
   It don't make no difference escaping one last time.
   It's easier to believe in this sweet madness;
   Oh, this glorious sadness that brings me to my knees…

Annie's Song

Words and Music by John Denver

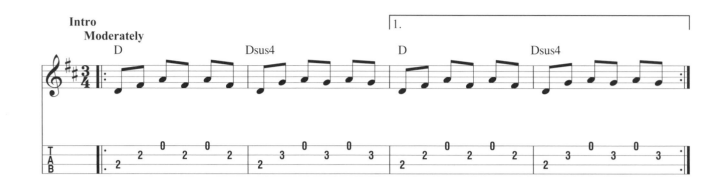

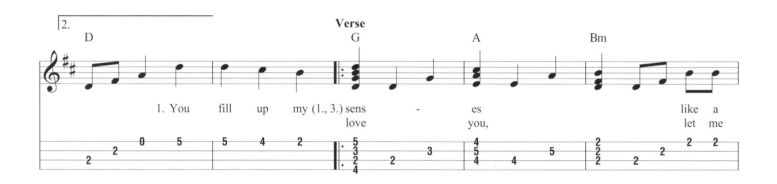

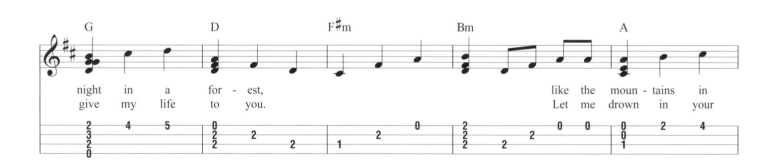

like a storm in the des - ert,
Let me lay down be - side you,

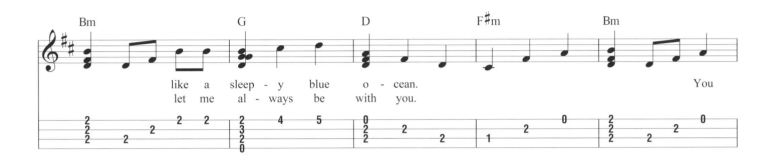

like a sleep - y blue o - cean.
let me al - ways be with you.

You

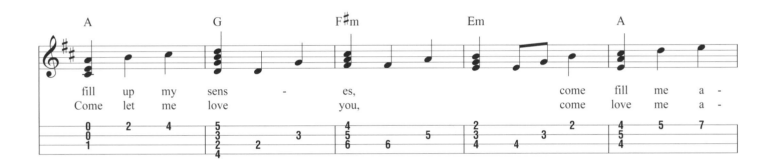

fill up my sens - es,
Come let me love you,

come fill me a -
come love me a -

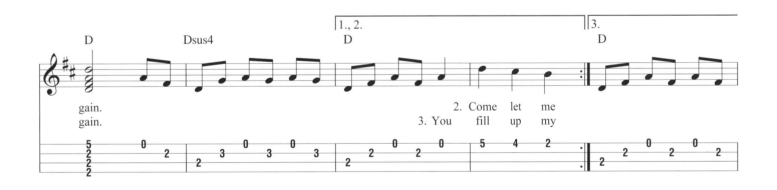

gain.
gain.

2. Come let me
3. You fill up my

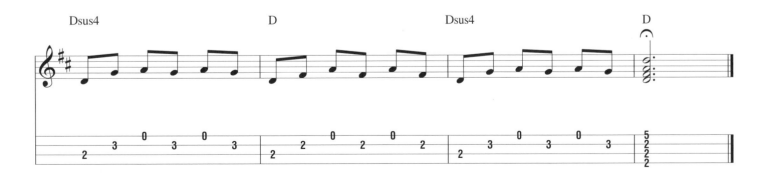

Believe

from Warner Bros. Pictures' THE POLAR EXPRESS

Words and Music by Glen Ballard and Alan Silvestri

Best of My Love

Words and Music by Don Henley, Glenn Frey and John David Souther

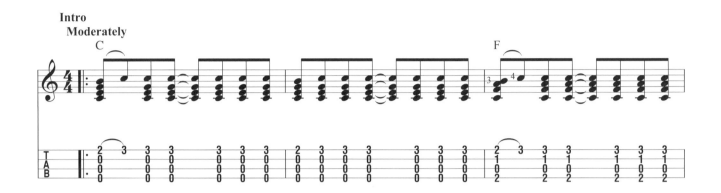

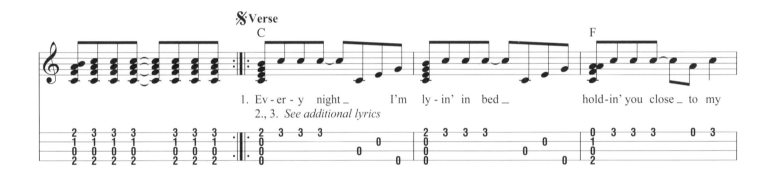

1. Ev - er - y night ___ I'm ly - in' in bed ___ hold - in' you close ___ to my dreams. ___
2., 3. *See additional lyrics*

Think - in' a - bout ___ all the things that we ___ said and com - in' a - part ___ at the seams. ___

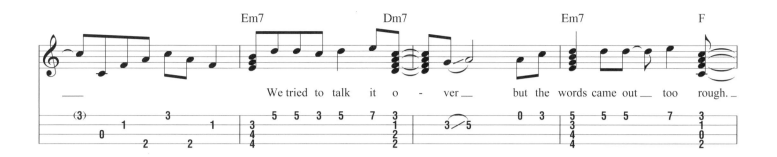

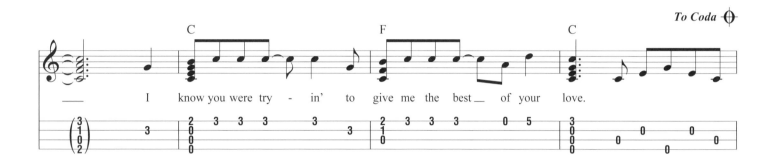

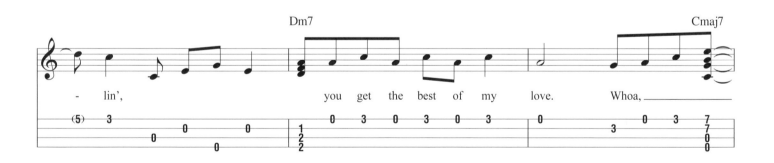

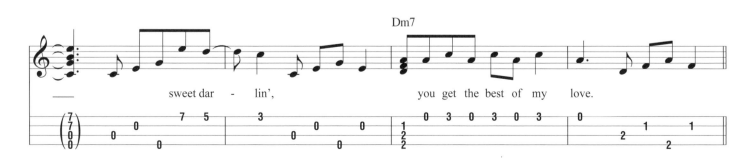

Bridge

I'm go-in' back in time_ and it's a sweet dream._ It was a

D.S. al Coda

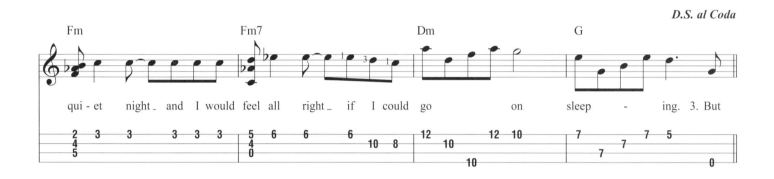

qui - et night_ and I would feel all right_ if I could go on sleep - ing. 3. But

⊕ Coda

Outro-Chorus

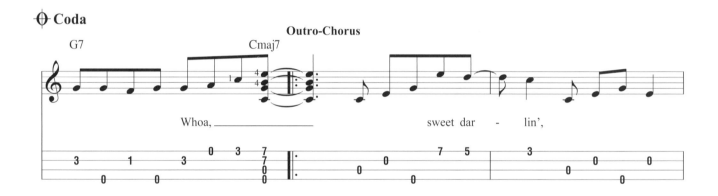

Whoa,_____ sweet dar - lin',

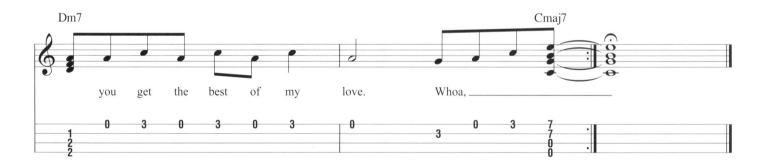

you get the best of my love. Whoa,_____

Additional Lyrics

2. Beautiful faces and loud empty places, look at the way that we live.
   Wastin' our time on cheap talk and wine, left us so little to give.
   That same old crowd was like a cold, dark cloud that we could never rise above.
   But here in my heart, I give you the best of my love.

3. But every morning I wake up and worry what's gonna happen today.
   You see it your way and I see it mine but we both see it slippin' away.
   You know we always had each other, baby. I guess that wasn't enough.
   Oh, oh, but here in my heart, I give you the best of my love.

Can't Help Falling in Love

from the Paramount Picture BLUE HAWAII

Words and Music by George David Weiss, Hugo Peretti and Luigi Creatore

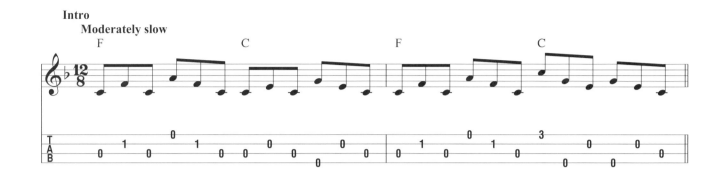

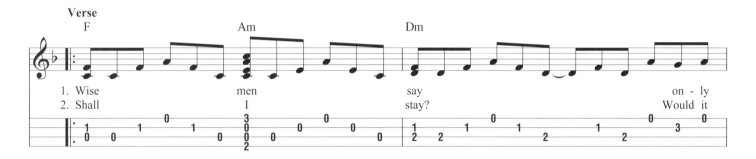

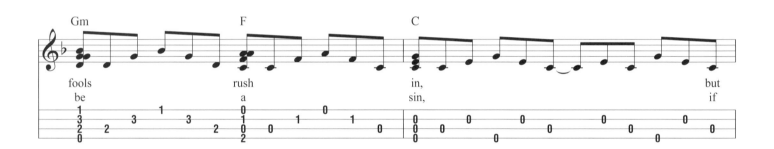

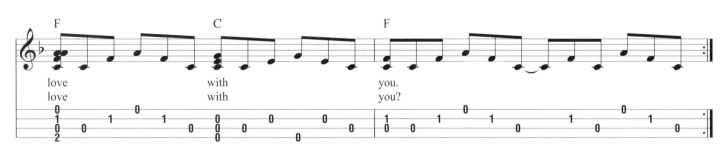

Bridge

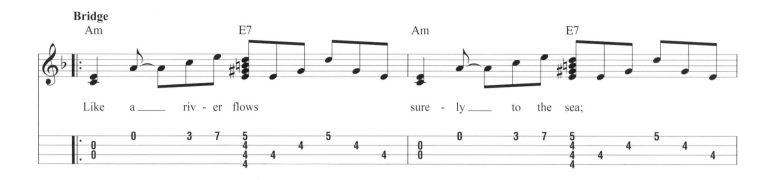

Like a _____ riv - er flows   sure - ly _____ to the sea;

dar - ling, ___ so it goes.   Some things _ are ___ meant to

Verse

be.   3., 4. Take my

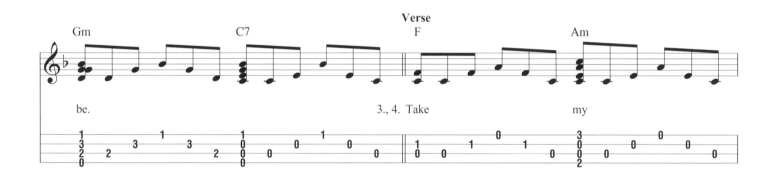

hand,   take my whole   life

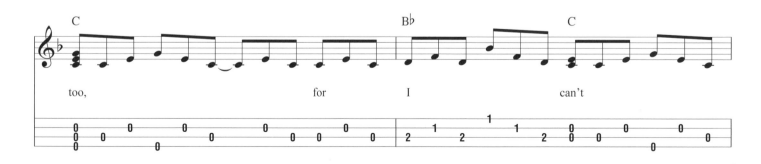

too,   for   I   can't

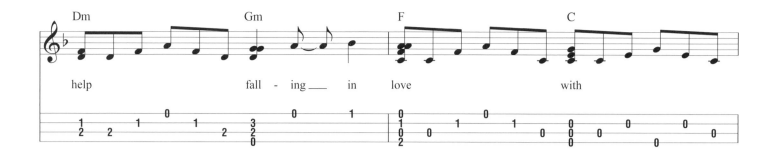

help   fall - ing ___ in   love   with

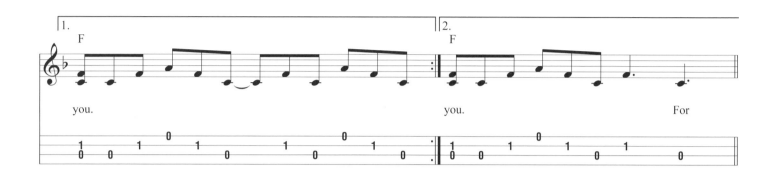

you.   you.   For

Outro

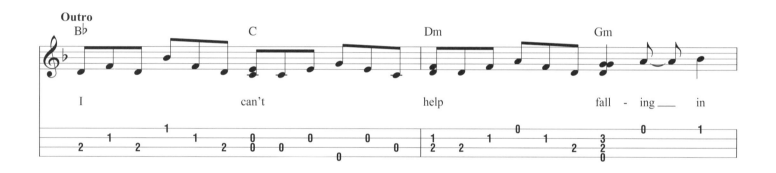

I   can't   help   fall - ing ___ in

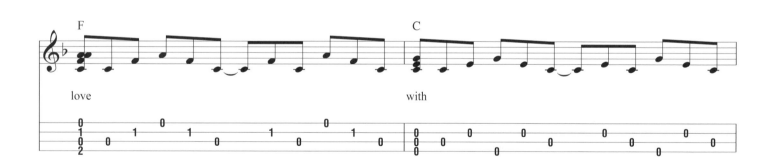

love   with

you.   *rit.*

Bless the Broken Road

Words and Music by Marcus Hummon, Bobby Boyd and Jeff Hanna

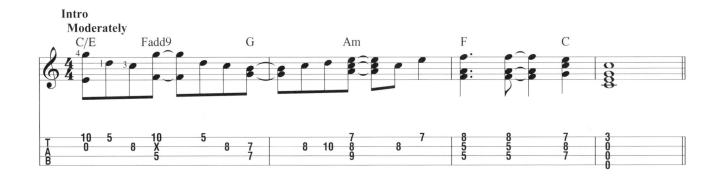

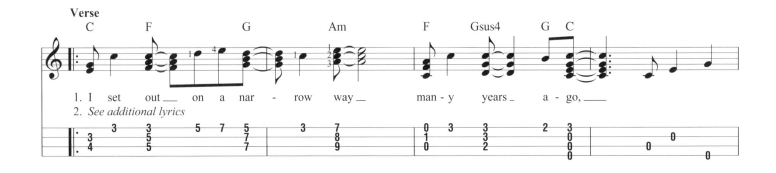

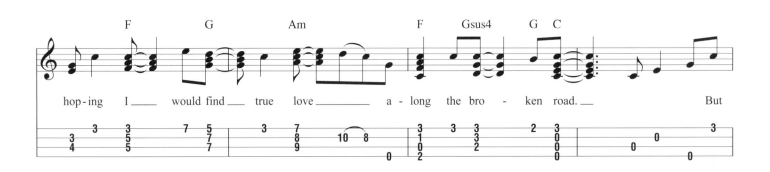

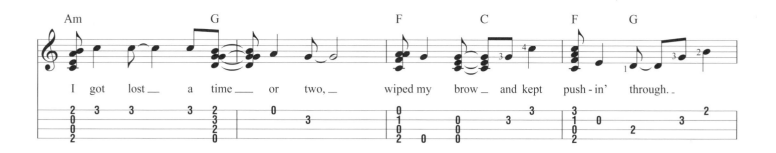

I got lost __ a time __ or two, __ wiped my brow __ and kept push-in' through. _

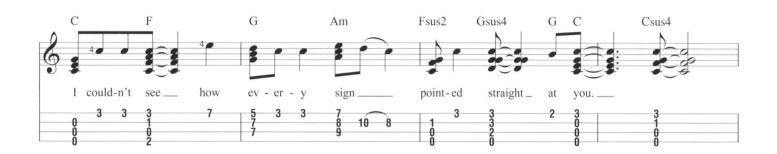

I could-n't see __ how ev-er-y sign _____ point-ed straight _ at you. __

Chorus

But ev-er-y long lost __ dream _____ led me to where you __ are. __

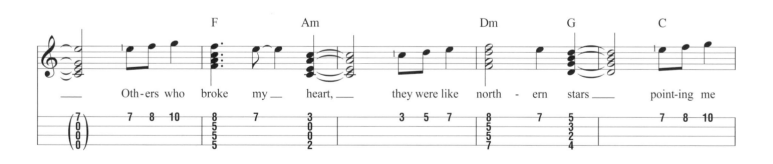

Oth-ers who broke my __ heart, ___ they were like north-ern stars ___ point-ing me

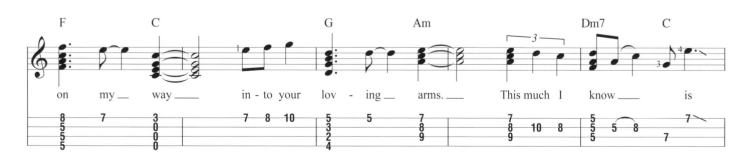

on my __ way ___ in-to your lov-ing __ arms. __ This much I know ___ is

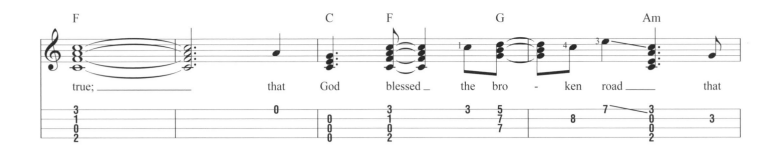

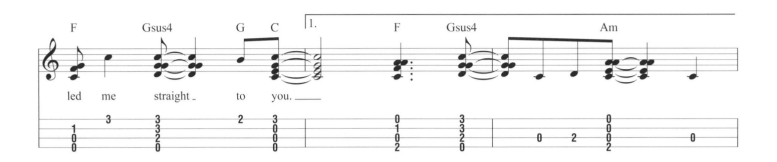

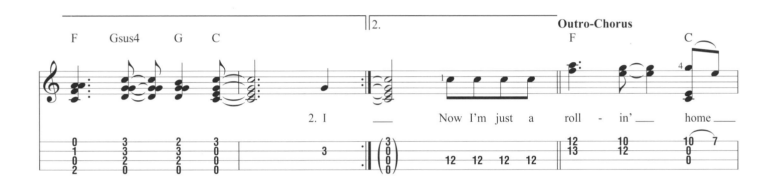

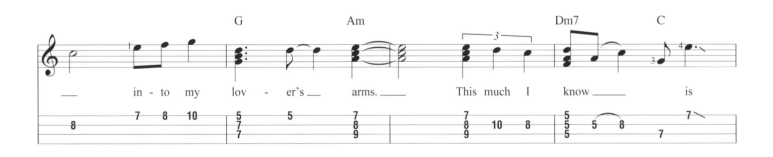

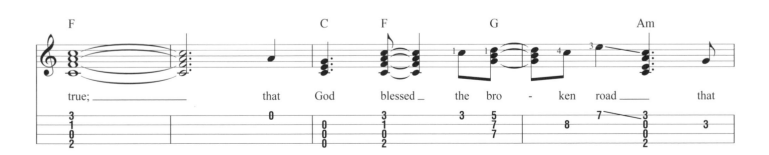

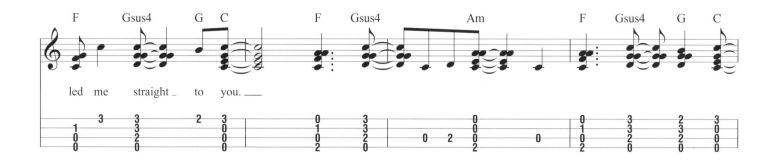

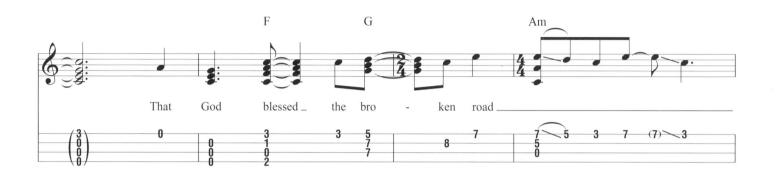

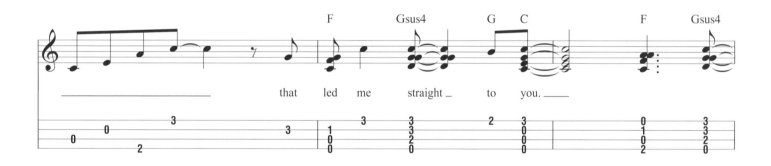

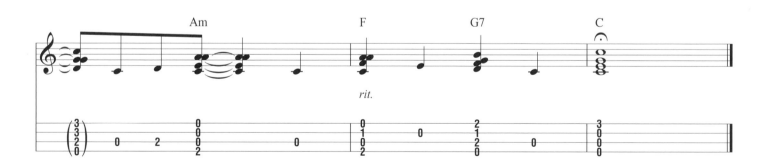

Additional Lyrics

2. I think about the years I've spent just passing through.
   I'd like to have the time I lost and give it back to you.
   But you just smile and take my hand.
   You've been there, you understand,
   It's all part of a grander plan that is comin' true.

Candle in the Wind

Words and Music by Elton John and Bernie Taupin

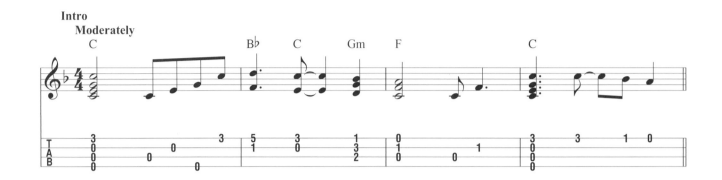

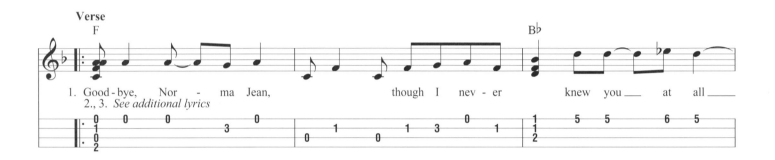

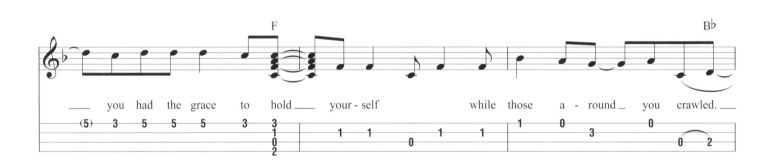

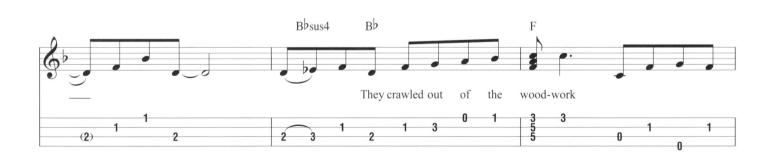

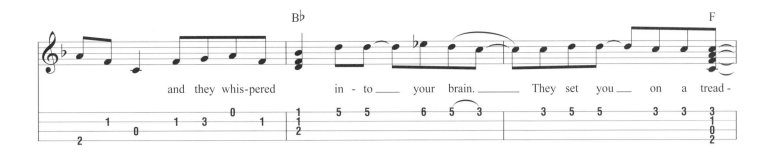

and they whis-pered in - to ___ your brain. ___ They set you ___ on a tread -

- mill and they made you change ___ your name. ___

And it seems to me ___ you lived your life ___ like a

can - dle in ___ the wind, ___ nev - er know - ing who ___ to cling ___

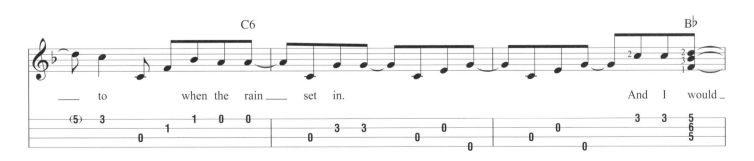

___ to when the rain ___ set in. And I would ___

have liked to've known you, but I was just a kid. Your

candle burned out long before your legend ever did.

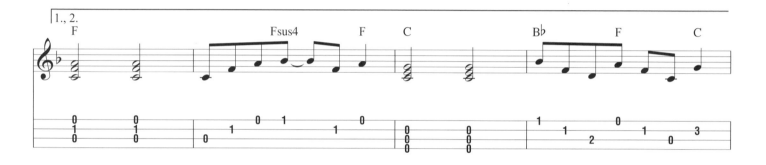

Your candle burned out

long before your legend ever did.

Additional Lyrics

2. Loneliness was tough, the toughest role you ever played.
Hollywood created a superstar, and pain was the price you paid.
Even when you died, oh, the press still hounded you.
All the papers had to say was that Marilyn was found in the nude.

3. Goodbye, Norma Jean, though I never knew you at all.
You had the grace to hold yourself while those around you crawled.
Goodbye, Norma Jean, from the young man in the twenty-second row
Who sees you as something more than sexual,
More than just our Marilyn Monroe.

(They Long to Be) Close to You

Lyrics by Hal David
Music by Burt Bacharach

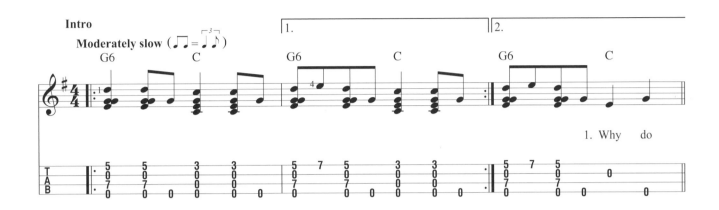

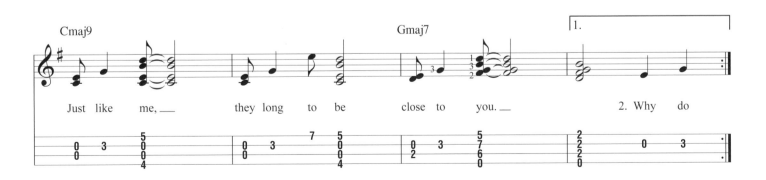

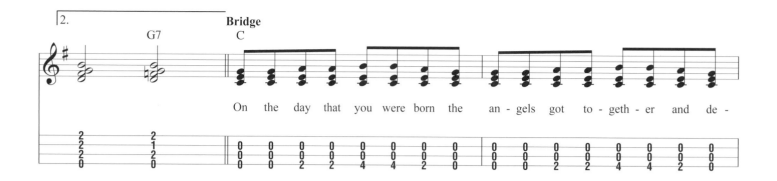

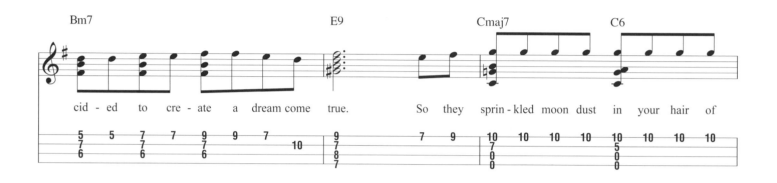

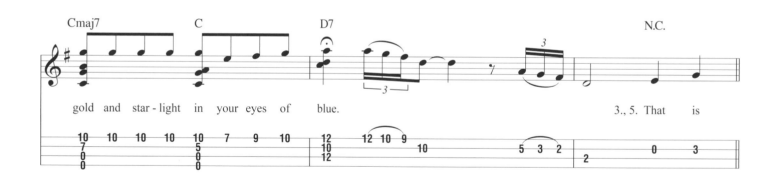

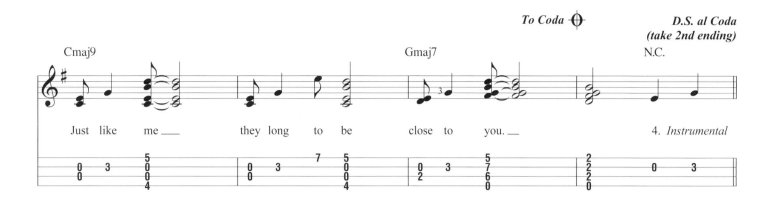

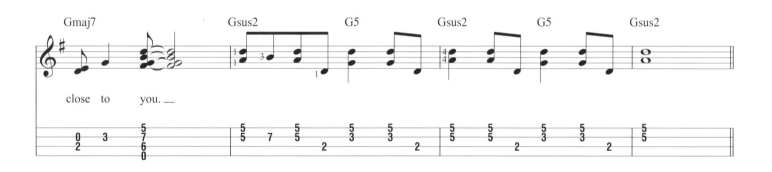

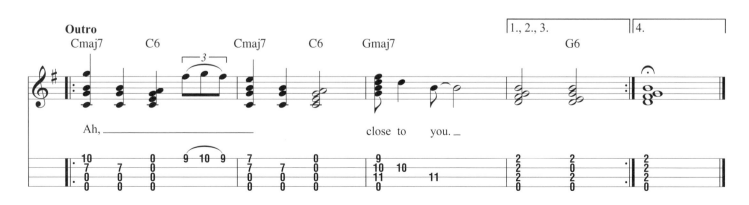

Cherish

Words and Music by Terry Kirkman

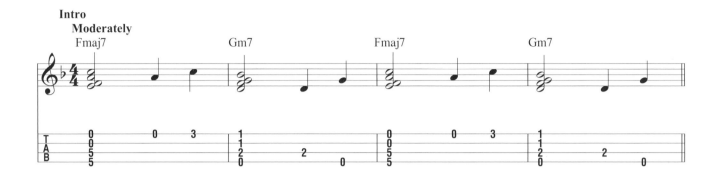

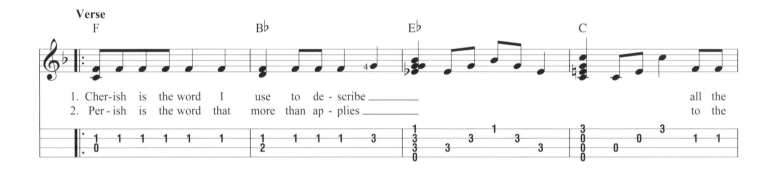

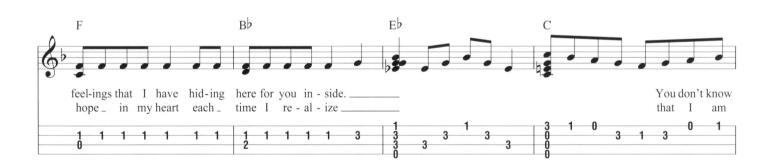

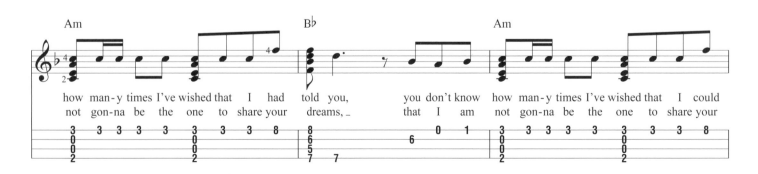

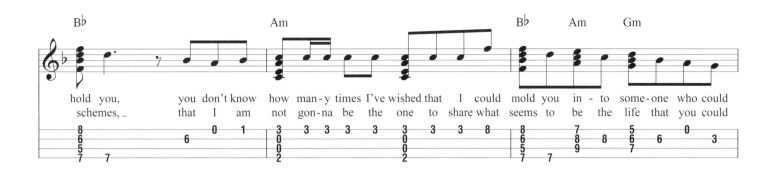

hold you,   you don't know how man-y times I've wished that   I could mold you in - to some-one who could
schemes, _   that   I   am   not gon-na be the one to share what seems to   be   the   life that you could

cher-ish me as much as   I   cher-ish you.
cher-ish me as much as   I   do ___ you.

Oh, I'm be - gin-ning to think that man has nev-er found the

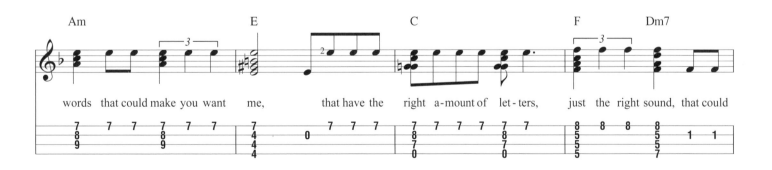

words that could make you want   me,   that have the   right a-mount of let-ters,   just the right sound, that could

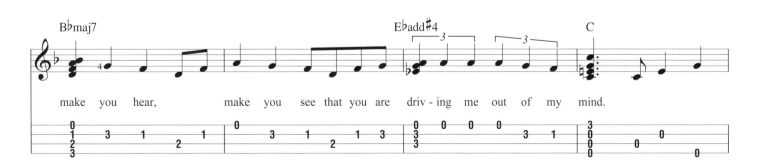

make   you   hear,   make   you   see that you are driv - ing me out of my mind.

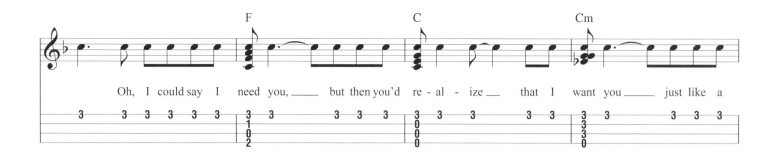

Oh, I could say I need you, ____ but then you'd re-al-ize that I want you ____ just like a

thou-sand oth-er guys who'd say they loved you ____ with all the rest of their lies, ___ when all they

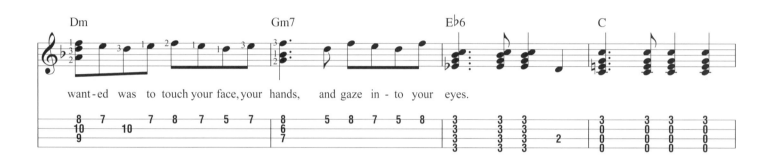

want-ed was to touch your face, your hands, and gaze in-to your eyes.

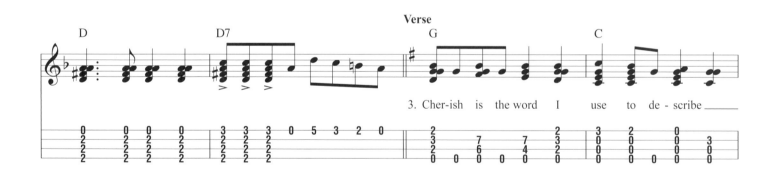

Verse

3. Cher-ish is the word I use to de-scribe ____

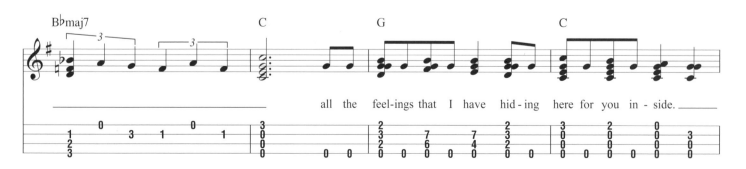

all the feel-ings that I have hid-ing here for you in-side. _____

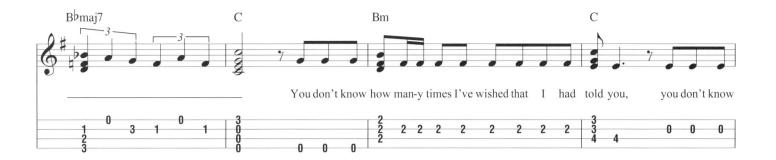

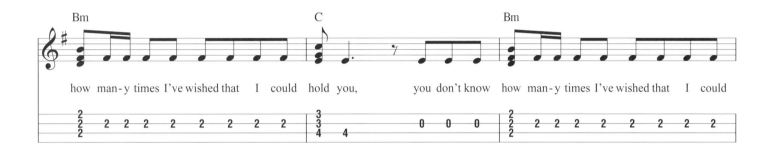

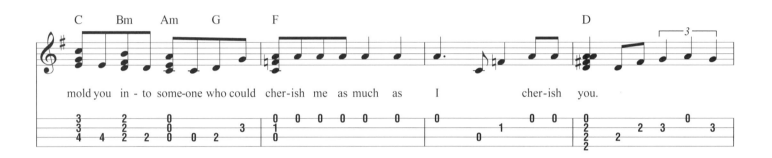

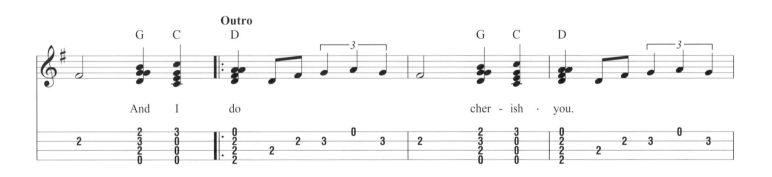

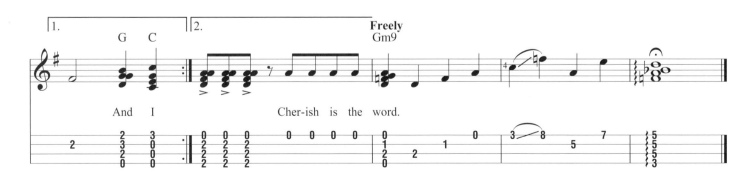

The Colour of My Love

Words and Music by David Foster and Arthur Janov

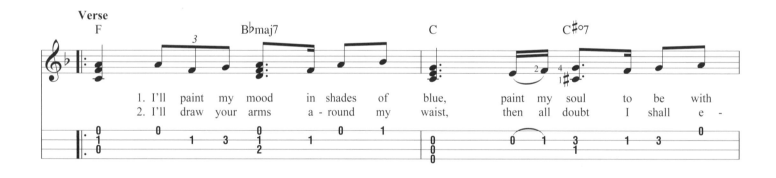

1. I'll paint my mood in shades of blue, paint my soul to be with
2. I'll draw your arms a-round my waist, then all doubt I shall e -

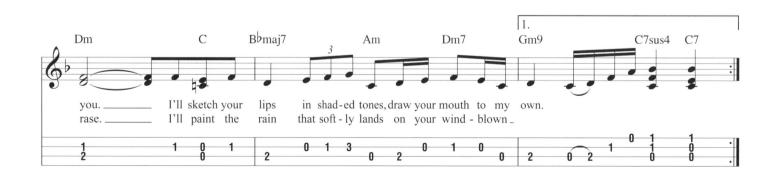

you. _____ I'll sketch your lips in shad-ed tones, draw your mouth to my own.
rase. _____ I'll paint the rain that soft-ly lands on your wind - blown _

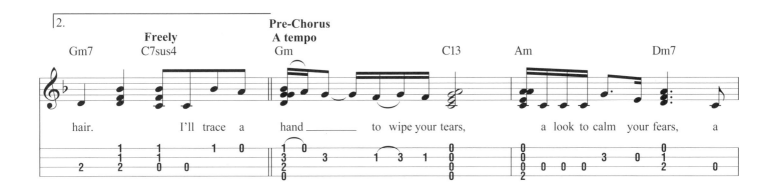

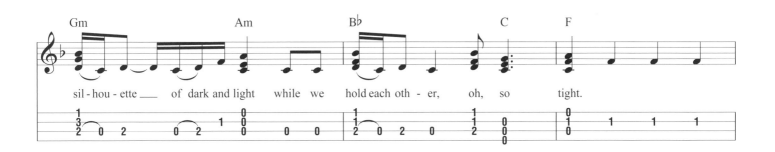

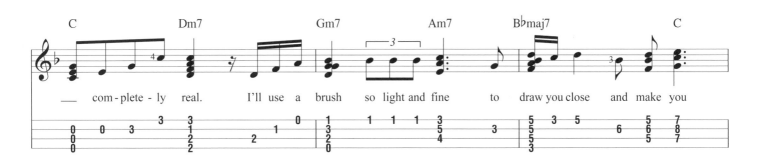

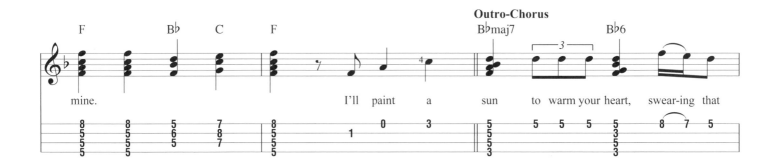

mine. I'll paint a sun to warm your heart, swear-ing that

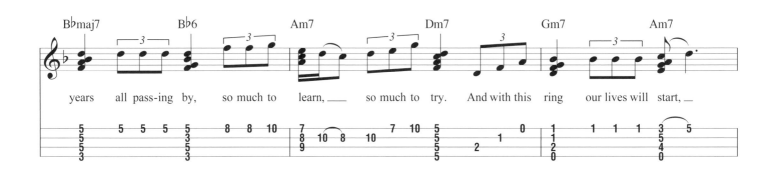

we'll nev-er, ev-er part. That's the col-our of_____ my love._____ I'll draw the

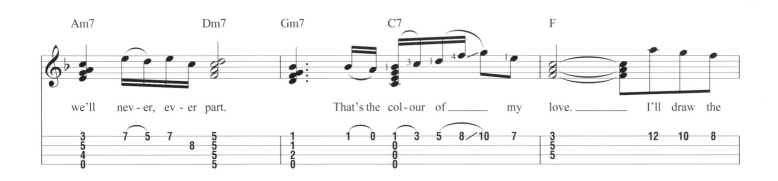

years all pass-ing by, so much to learn,___ so much to try. And with this ring our lives will start,___

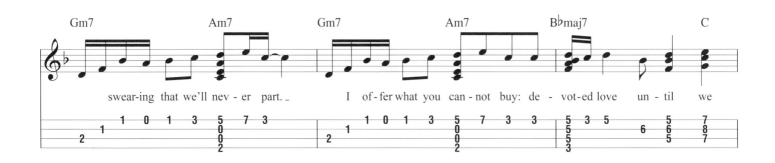

swear-ing that we'll nev-er part.__ I of-fer what you can-not buy: de - vot-ed love un - til we

die.

Crimson and Clover

Words and Music by Tommy James and Peter Lucia

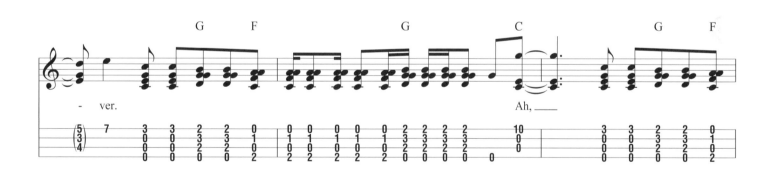

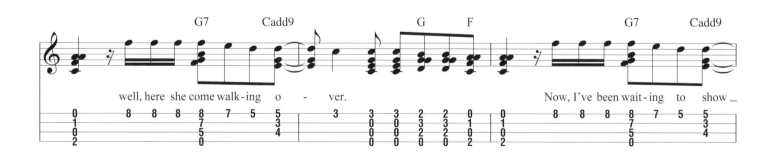

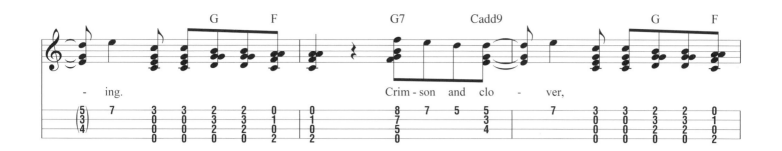

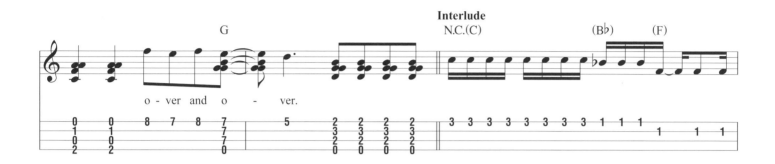

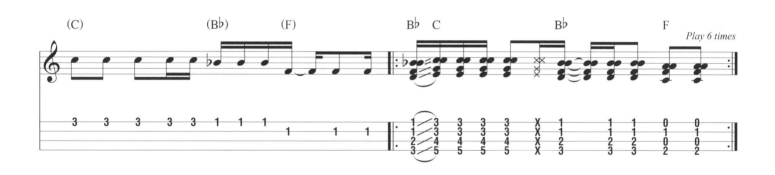

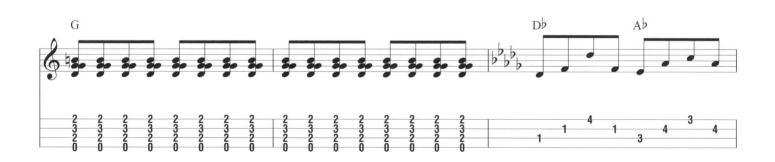

Dance with My Father

Words by Luther Vandross and Richard Marx
Music by Luther Vandross

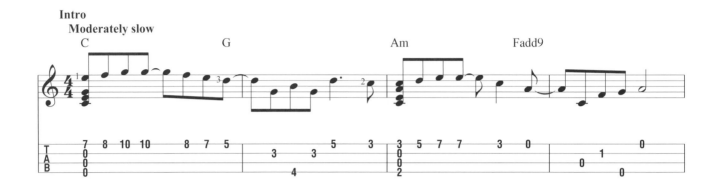

Additional Lyrics

2. When I and my mother would disagree,
   To get my way I would run from her to him.
   He'd make me laugh just to comfort me,
   Then finally make me do just what my mama said.
   Later that night when I was aleep,
   He left a dollar under my sheet.
   Never dreamed that he would be gone from me.

Chorus 2. If I could steal one final glance,
   One final step, one final dance with him,
   I'd play a song that would never end.
   'Cause I'd love, love, love to dance with my father again.

Chorus 3. I know I'm praying for much too much,
   But could You send back the only man she loved?
   I know You don't do it usually but, dear Lord,
   She's dying to dance with my father again.

Don't Know Why

Words and Music by Jesse Harris

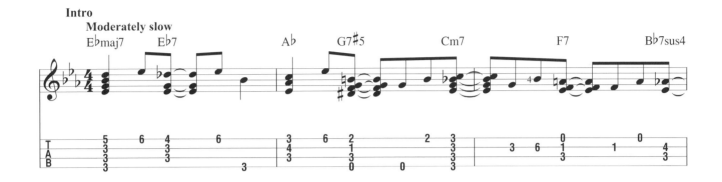

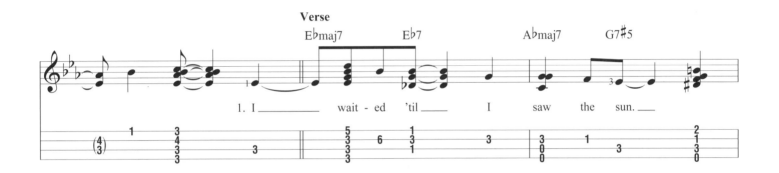

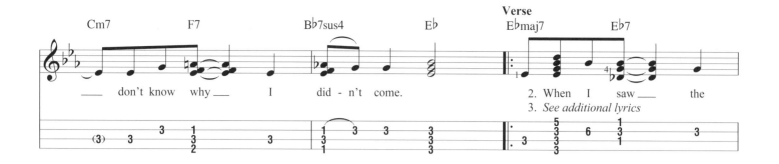

don't know why ___ I did-n't come.

2. When I saw ___ the
3. *See additional lyrics*

break of day, I wished that I ___ could fly ___ a - way

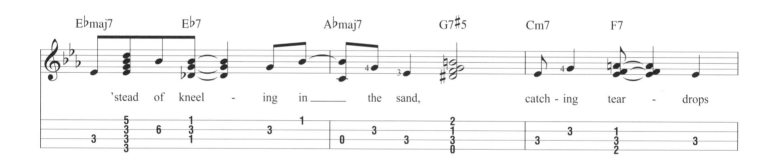

'stead of kneel - ing in ___ the sand, catch - ing tear - drops

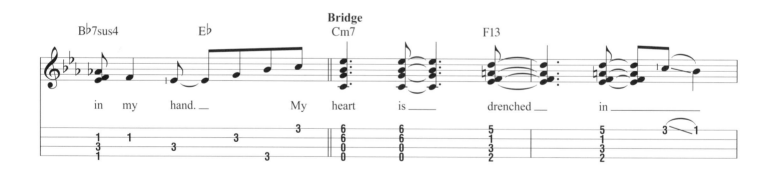

in my hand. ___ My heart is ___ drenched ___ in ___

wine, but you'll be ___ on ___

my ____ mind for - ev - er. ____

Outro-Verse

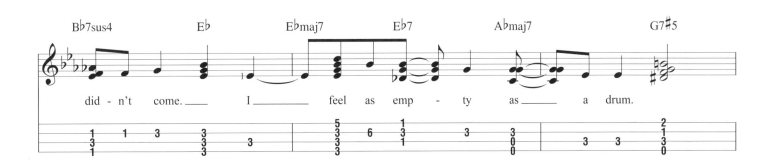

Ebmaj7   Eb7   Abmaj7   G7#5   Cm7   F7

4. Some-thing has ____ to make you run. I don't know why ____ I

Bb7sus4   Eb   Ebmaj7   Eb7   Abmaj7   G7#5

did - n't come. ____ I ____ feel as emp - ty as ____ a drum.

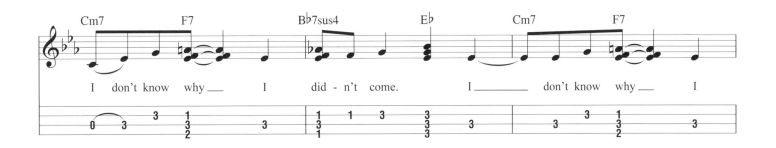

Cm7   F7   Bb7sus4   Eb   Cm7   F7

I don't know why ____ I did - n't come. I ____ don't know why ____ I

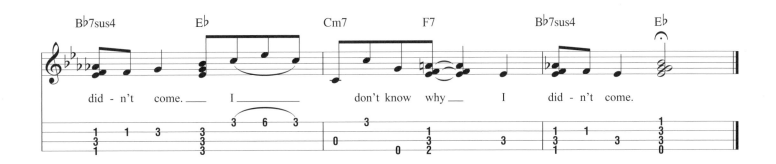

Bb7sus4   Eb   Cm7   F7   Bb7sus4   Eb

did - n't come. ____ I ____ don't know why ____ I did - n't come.

Additional Lyrics

3. Out across the endless sea,
   I would die in ecstasy.
   But I'll be a bag of bones,
   Driving down the road alone.

Don't Let the Sun Go Down on Me

Words and Music by Elton John and Bernie Taupin

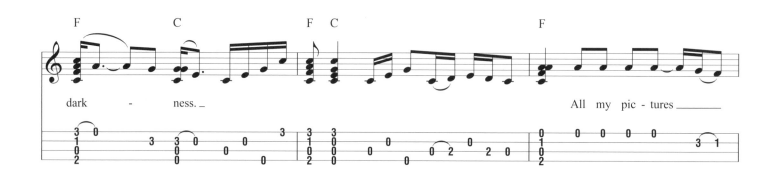

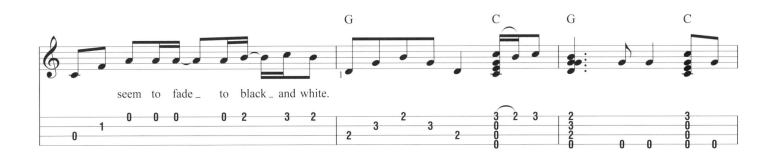

seem to fade _ to black _ and white.

I'm ___ grow-ing tired, and time stands still be - fore _____ me, _

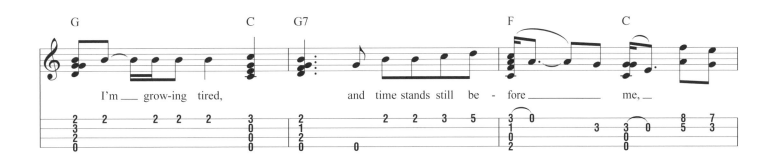

fro - zen here _ on the lad - der of ___ my ___

%**Verse**

life.

2. Too late ___ to save my - self from

3. *See additional lyrics*

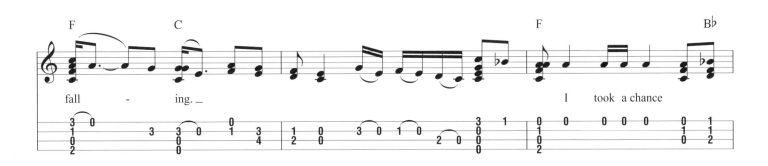

fall - ing. ___ I took a chance

59

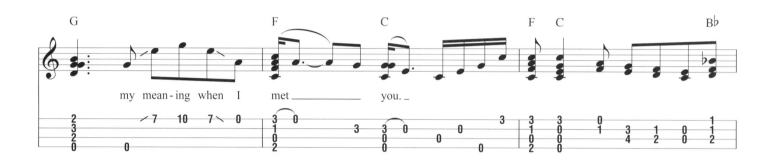

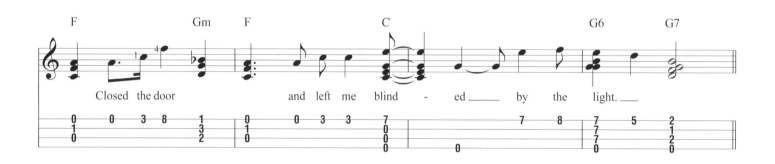

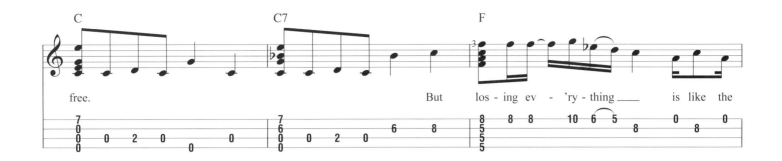

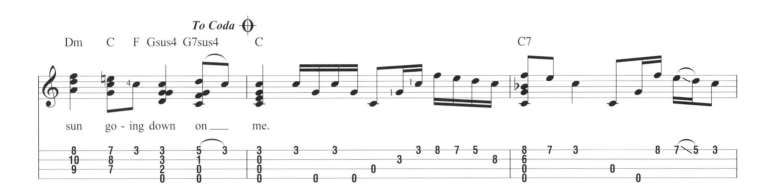

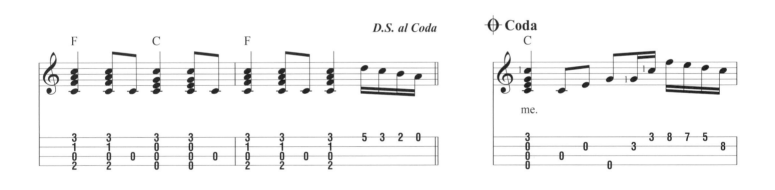

Additional Lyrics

3. I can't find, oh, the right romantic line.
But see me once and see the way I feel.
Don't discard me just because you think I mean you harm.
But these cuts I have, oh, they need love to help them heal.

(Everything I Do) I Do It for You

from the Motion Picture ROBIN HOOD: PRINCE OF THIEVES

Words and Music by Bryan Adams, R.J. Lange and Michael Kamen

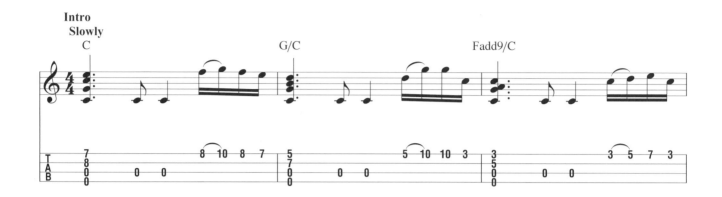

1. Look in-to my eyes, _____ you will see _____
2. Look in-to your heart, _____ you will find _____ there's

what you mean to me. Search your heart, _____ search your
noth - ing there to hide. Take me as I am, _____ take my

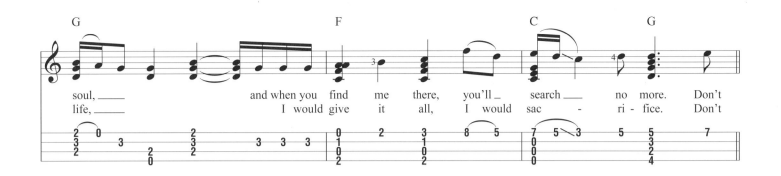

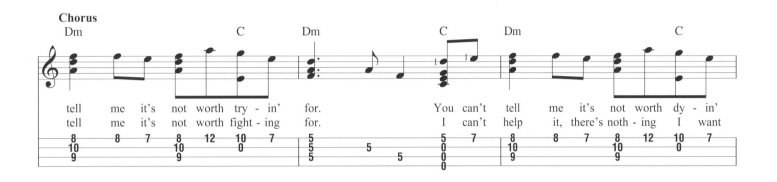

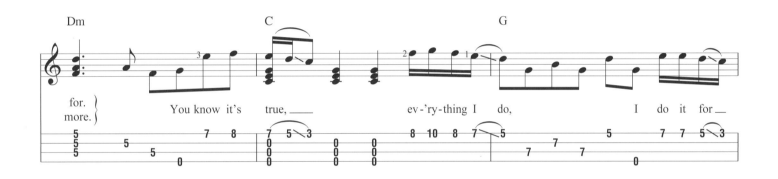

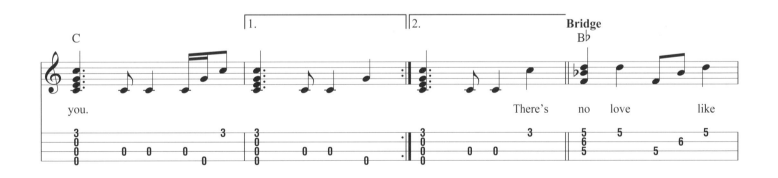

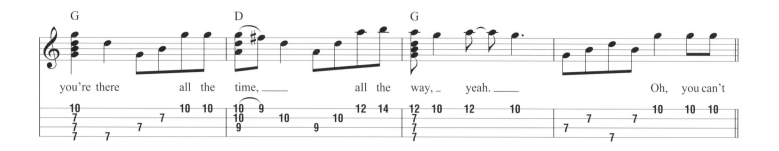

Outro-Chorus

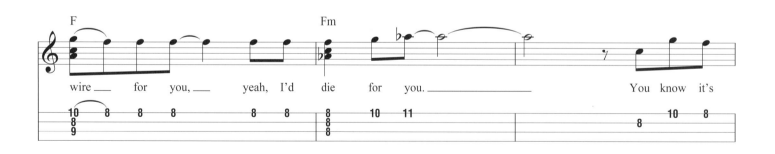

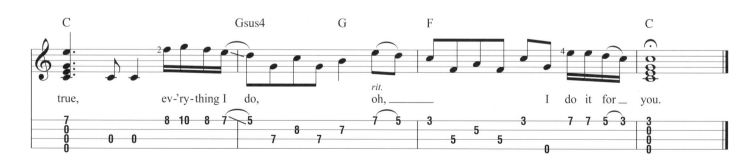

Faithfully

Words and Music by Jonathan Cain

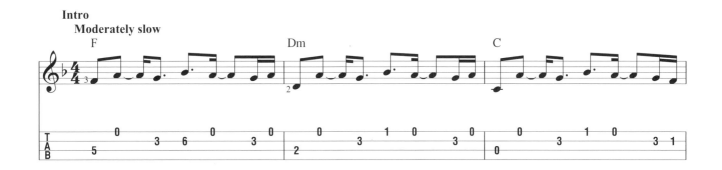

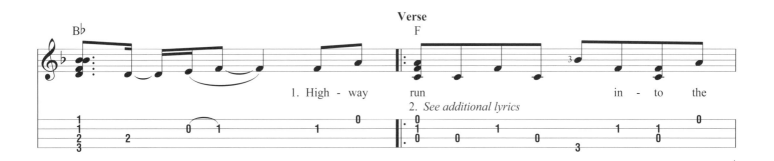

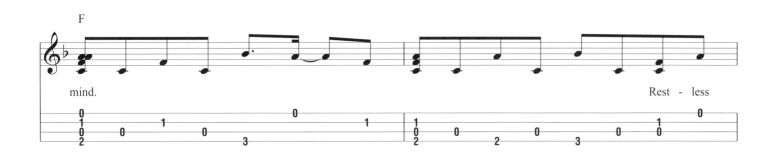

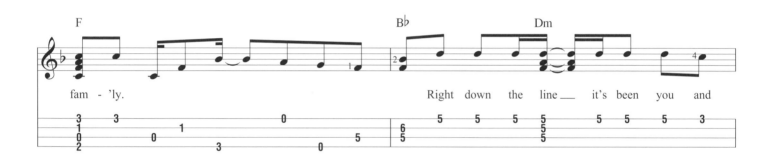

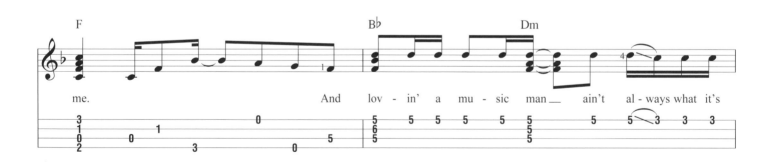

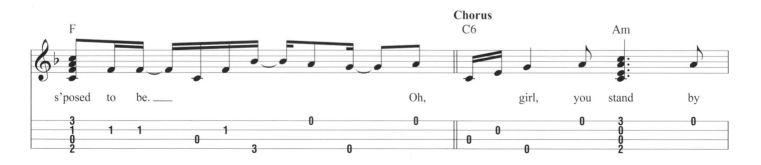

Additional Lyrics

2. Circus life under the bigtop world.
   We all need the clowns to make us smile.
   Through space and time, always another show.
   Wondering where I am, lost without you.

Pre-Chorus: And being apart ain't easy on this love affair.
   Two strangers learn to fall in love again.
   I get the joy of rediscovering you.

Falling in Love with Love

from THE BOYS FROM SYRACUSE

Words by Lorenz Hart
Music by Richard Rodgers

Verse
Moderately

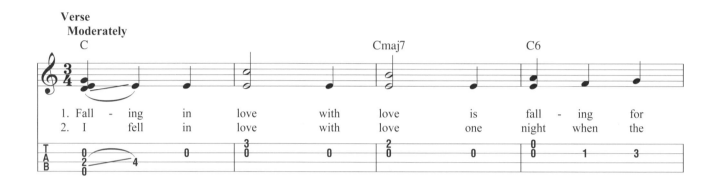

1. Fall - ing in love with love is fall - ing for
2. I fell in love with love one night when the

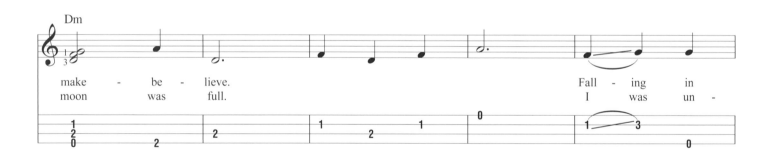

make - be - lieve. Fall - ing in
moon was full. I was un -

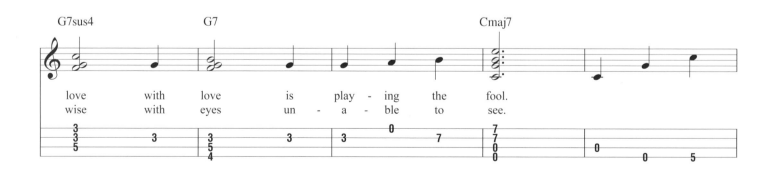

love with love is play - ing the fool.
wise with eyes un - a - ble to see.

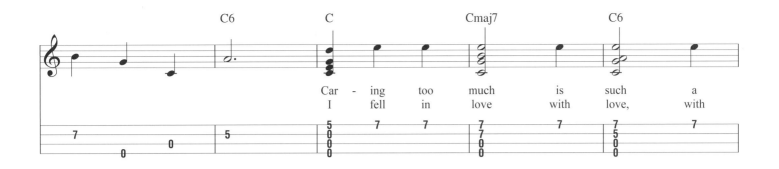

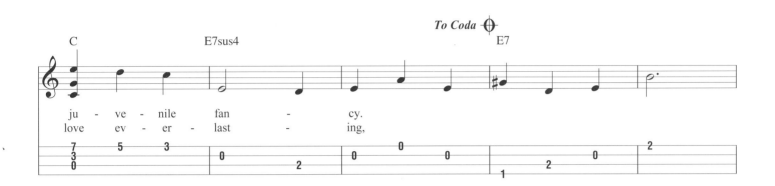

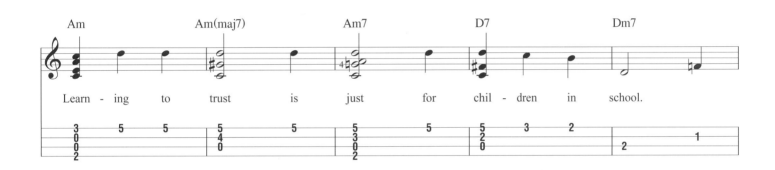

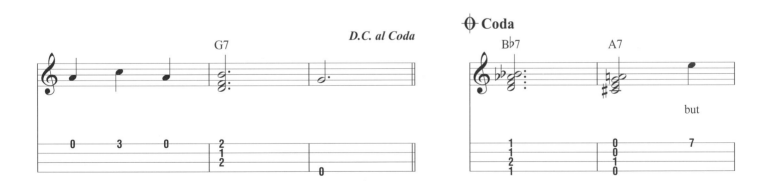

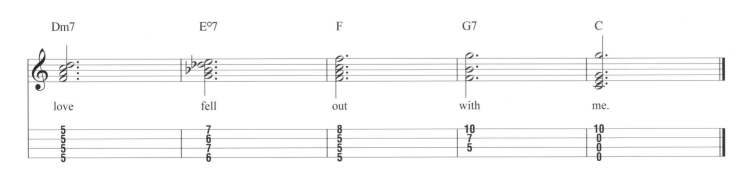

Feelings (¿Dime?)

English Words and Music by Morris Albert and Louis Gaste
Spanish Words by Thomas Fundora

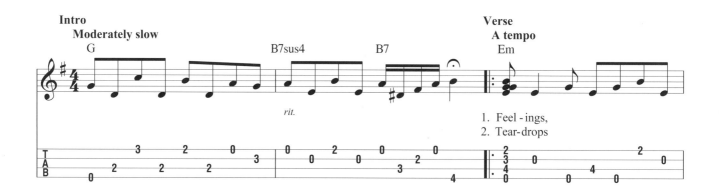

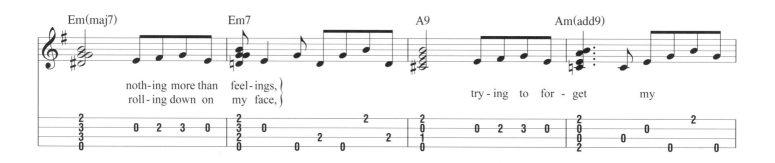

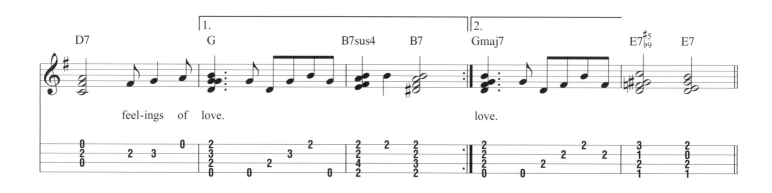

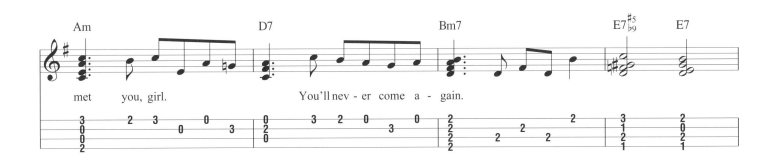

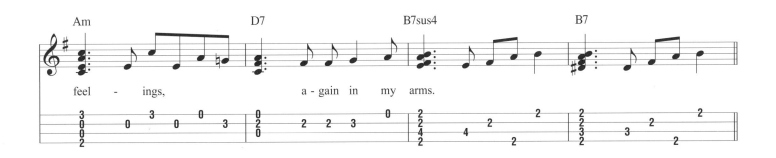

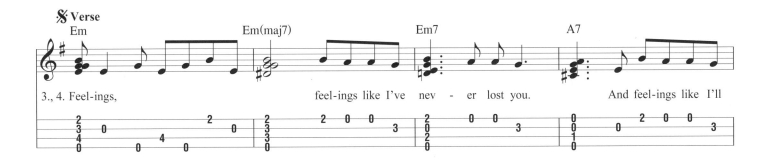

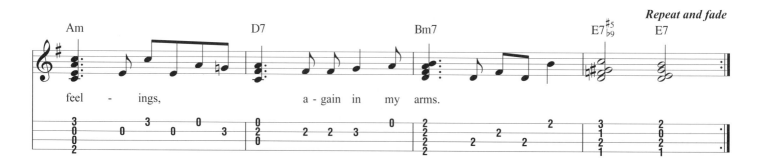

72

The First Time Ever
I Saw Your Face

Words and Music by Ewan MacColl

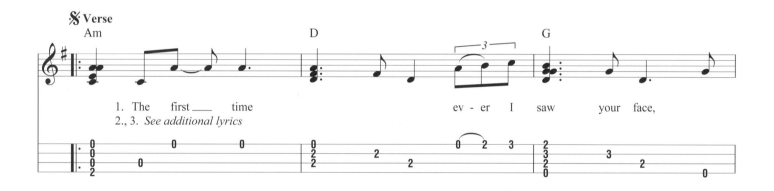

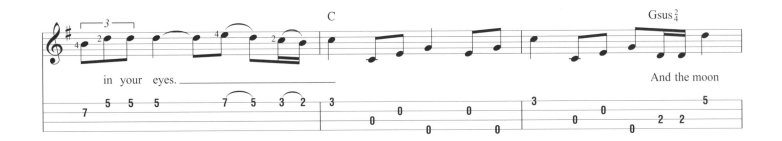

in your eyes._____ And the moon

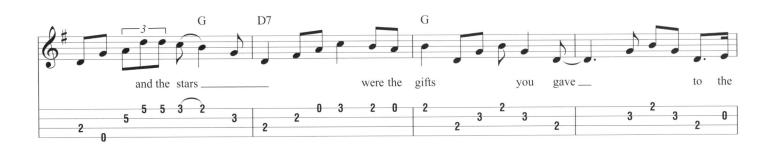

and the stars_____ were the gifts you gave___ to the

dark and the end - less skies, my

love. To the dark and the end - less

skies. mand, my love.

⊕ **Coda**

Outro

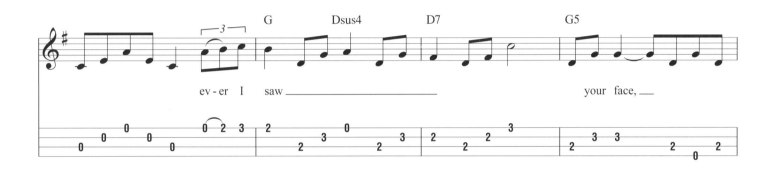

time,   my   love.   The   first ___ time

ev - er   I   saw _____   your face, ___

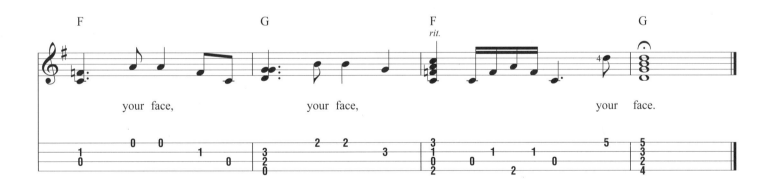

your face,   your face,   your face.

Additional Lyrics

2. And the first time ever I kissed your mouth,
   I felt the earth move in my hands
   Like the trembling heart of a captive bird
   That was there at my command, my love.
   That was there at my command, my love.

3. And the first time ever I lay with you,
   I felt your heart so close to mine.
   And I knew our joy would fill the earth
   And last 'til the end of time, my love.
   And it would last 'til the end of time, my love.

The First Cut Is the Deepest

Words and Music by Cat Stevens

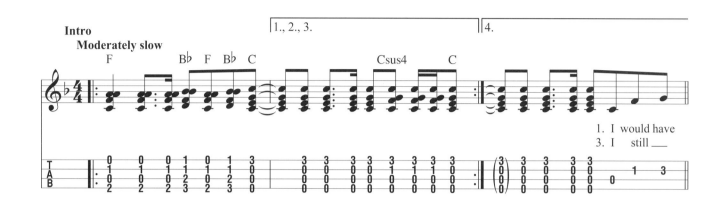

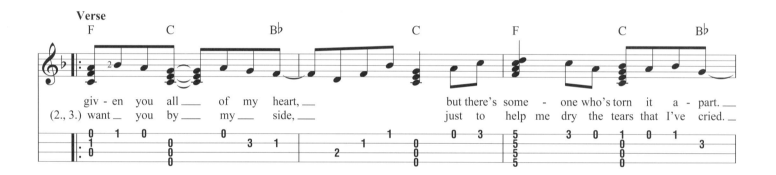

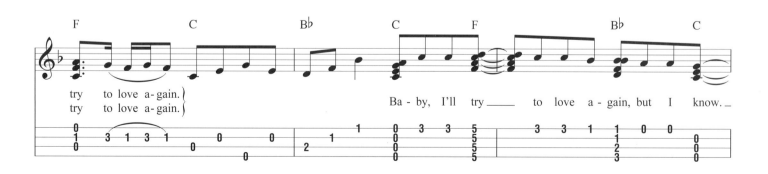

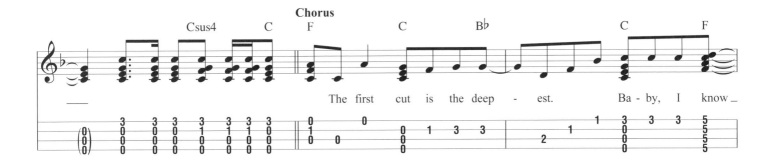

Chorus

The first cut is the deep - est. Ba - by, I know __

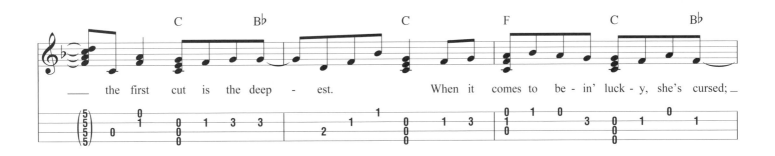

__ the first cut is the deep - est. When it comes to be - in' luck - y, she's cursed; __

To Coda ⊕

when it comes to lov - in' me, she's worst.

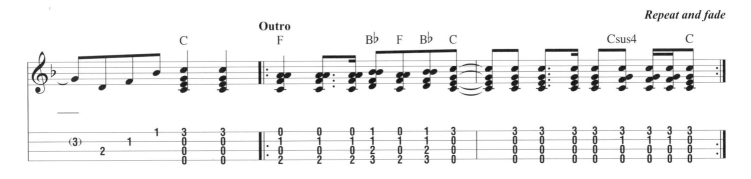

|2.

D.C. al Coda
(take repeats)

⊕ **Coda**

2. I still __

comes to lov - in' me, she's worst. __

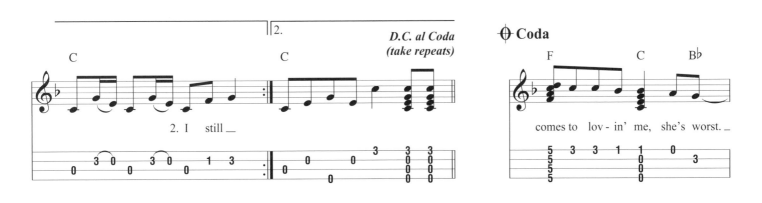

Repeat and fade

Outro

For All We Know

from the Motion Picture LOVERS AND OTHER STRANGERS

Words by Robb Wilson and Arthur James
Music by Fred Karlin

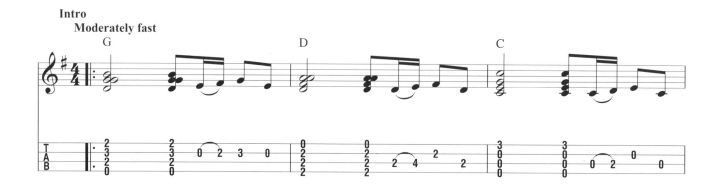

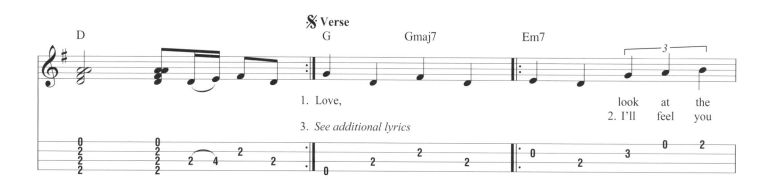

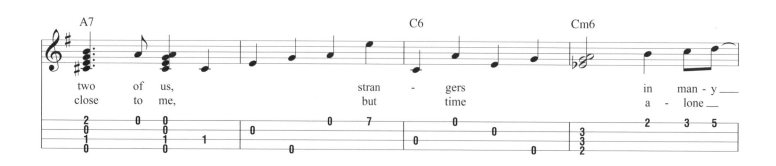

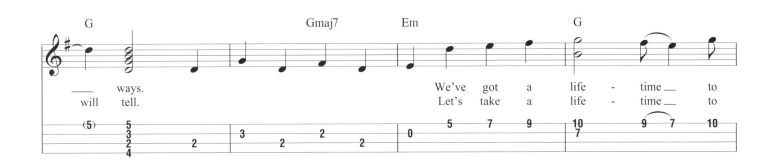

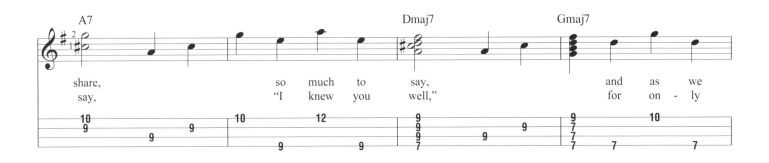

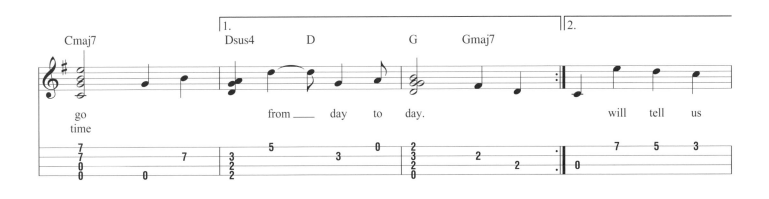

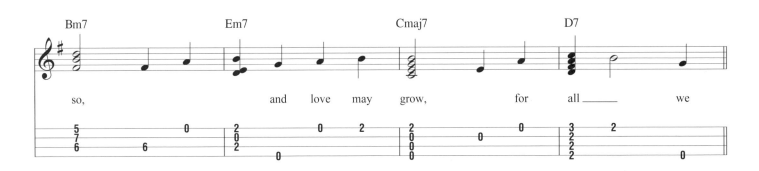

Interlude

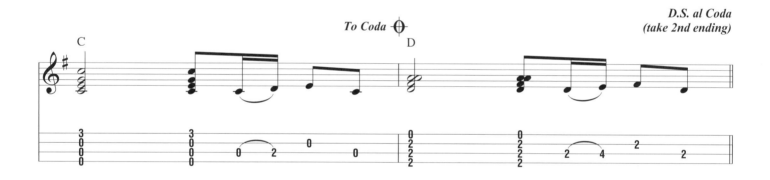

To Coda ⊕

D.S. al Coda
(take 2nd ending)

⊕ **Coda**

Additional Lyrics

3. Love, look at the two of us,
Strangers in many ways.
Let's take a lifetime to say,
"I knew you well,"
For only time will tell us so,
And love may grow, for all we know.

For Your Precious Love

Words and Music by Arthur Brooks, Richard Brooks and Jerry Butler

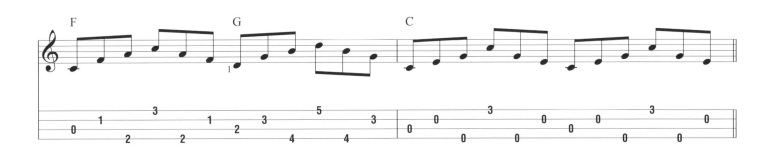

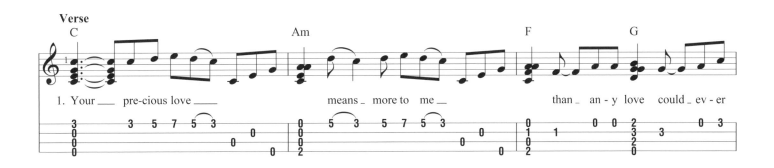

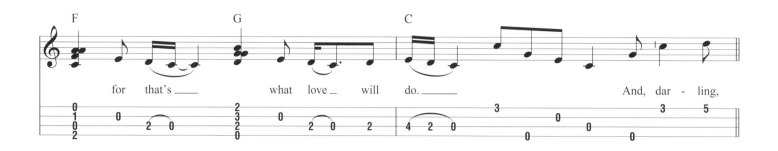

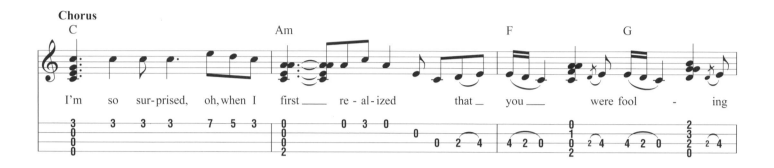

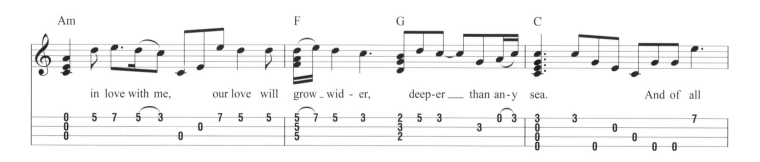

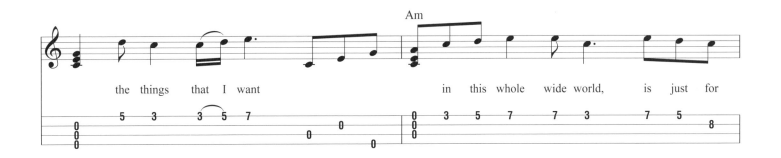

the things that I want   in this whole wide world,   is just for

you to say   that you'll be my   girl. _____   Want - ing   you,   oh, _____

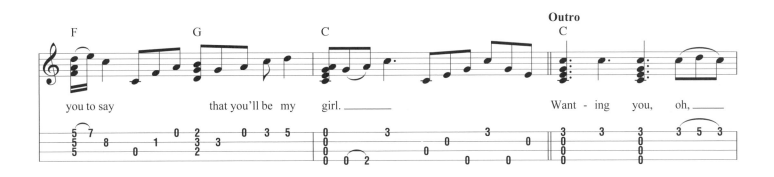

I'm   lone - ly and blue,   that's ___ what love   will   do.

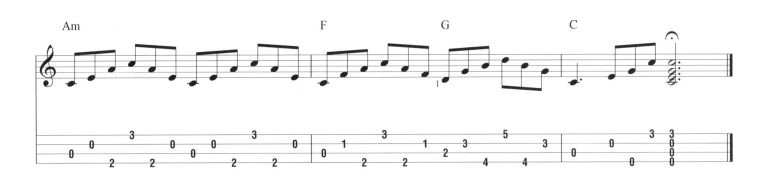

God Only Knows

Words and Music by Brian Wilson and Tony Asher

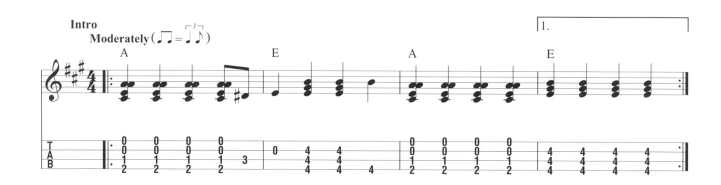

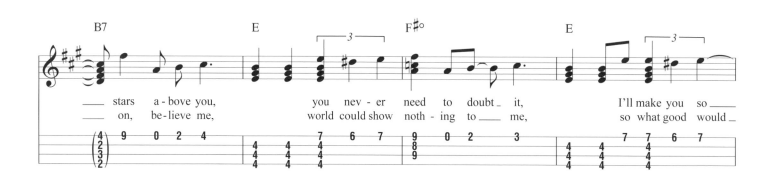

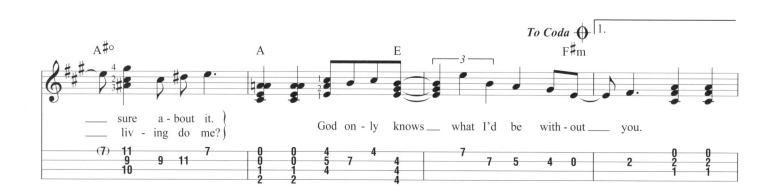

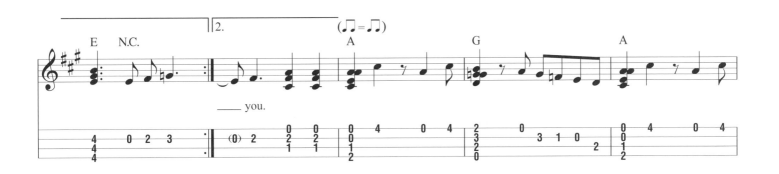

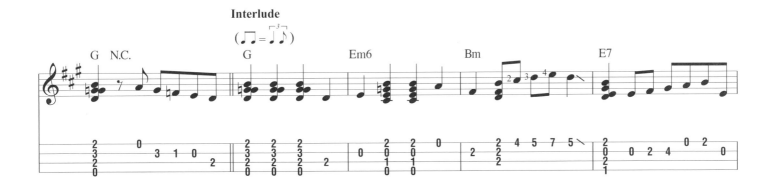

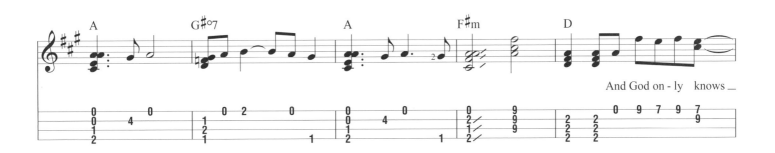

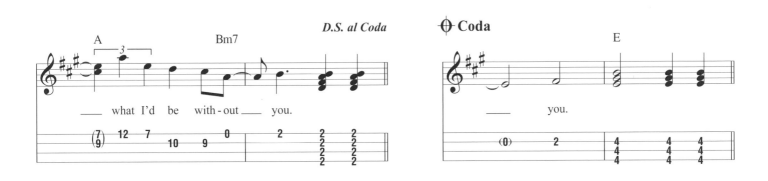

Hallelujah

Words and Music by Leonard Cohen

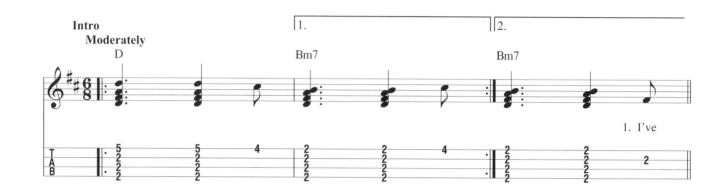

heard there was a se-cret chord ___ that Da - vid played ___ and it
2.–5. *See additional lyrics*

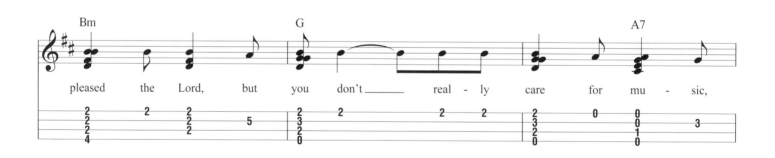

pleased the Lord, but you don't _____ real - ly care for mu - sic,

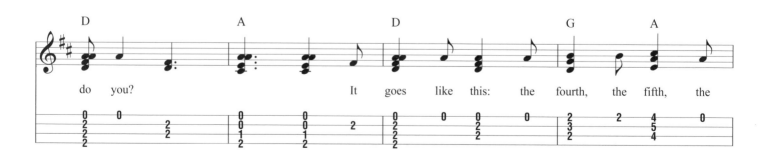

do you? It goes like this: the fourth, the fifth, the

Chorus

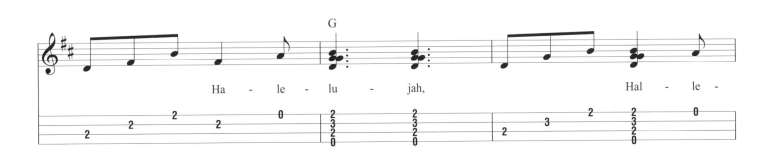

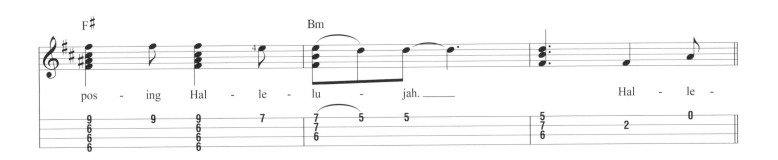

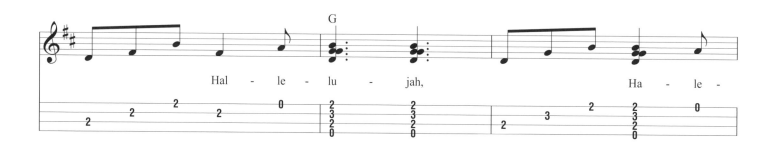

Additional Lyrics

2. Your faith was strong, but you needed proof.
   You saw her bathing on the roof.
   Her beauty and the moonlight overthrew you.
   She tied you to her kitchen chair,
   She broke your throne and she cut your hair.
   And from your lips she drew the Hallelujah.

3. Baby, I have been here before.
   I know this room; I've walked this floor.
   I used to live alone before I knew you.
   I've seen your flag on the marble arch.
   Love is not a vict'ry march,
   It's cold and it's a broken Hallelujah.

4. There was a time you let me know
   What's really going on below,
   But now you never show that to me, do you?
   Well, remember when I moved in you,
   The holy dove was moving too,
   And every breath we drew was Hallelujah.

5. Maybe there's a God above,
   But all I ever learned from love
   Was how to shoot somebody who outdrew you.
   It's not a cry that you hear at night,
   It's not somebody who's seen the light,
   It's a cold and it's a broken Hallelujah.

Have a Little Faith in Me

Words and Music by John Hiatt

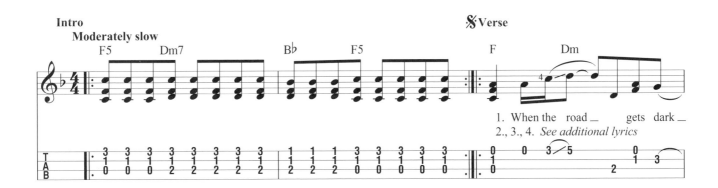

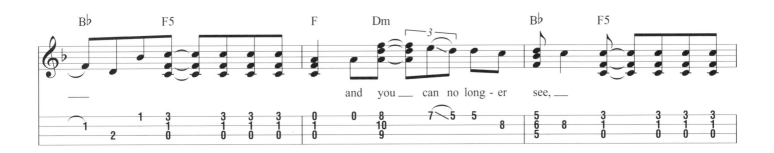

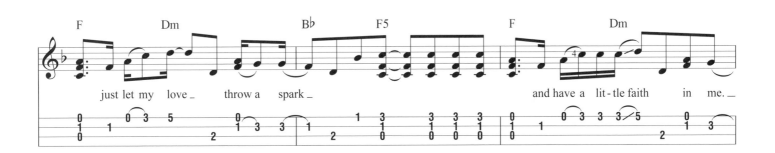

and have a lit-tle faith in ___ me. ___ And have a lit-tle

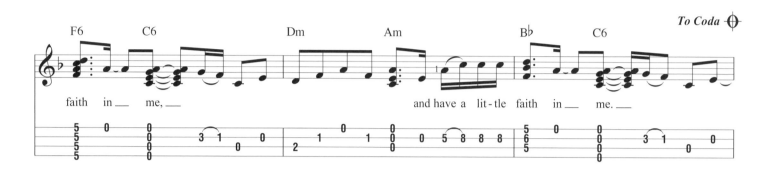

faith in ___ me, ___ and have a lit-tle faith in ___ me.

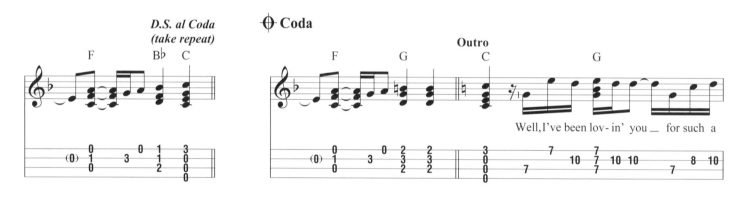

Well, I've been lov-in' you ___ for such a

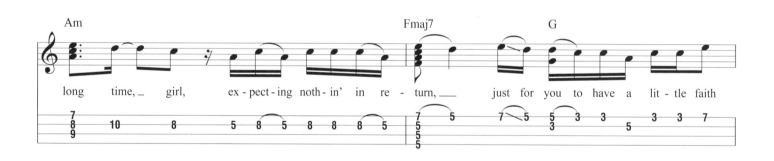

long time, ___ girl, ex-pect-ing noth-in' in re-turn, ___ just for you to have a lit-tle faith

in me. ___ You see, time, time ___ is our friend, 'cause for us there is no end, ___

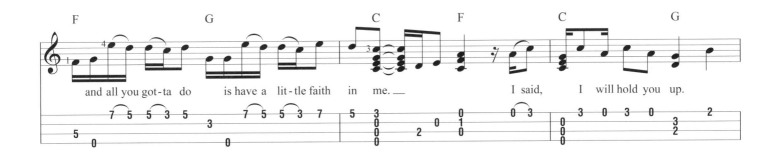

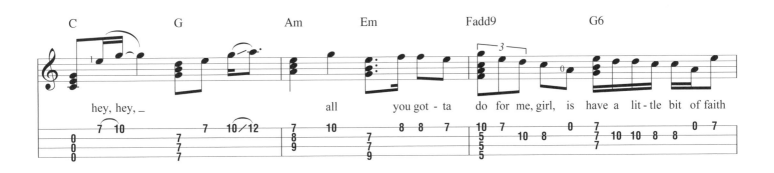

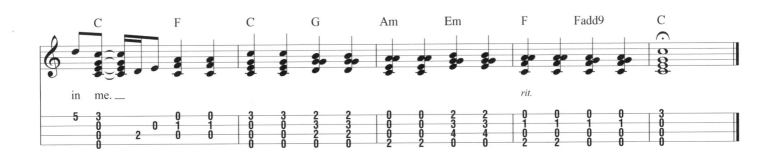

Additional Lyrics

2. And when the tears you cry are all you can believe,
   Just give these lovin' arms a try, baby, and have a little faith in me.

3. And when your secret heart cannot speak so easily,
   Come, darlin', from a whisper, start to have a little faith in me.

4. And when your back's against the wall, just turn around and you, you will see
   I will catch you, I will catch your fall, baby; just have a little faith in me.

Have I Told You Lately

Words and Music by Van Morrison

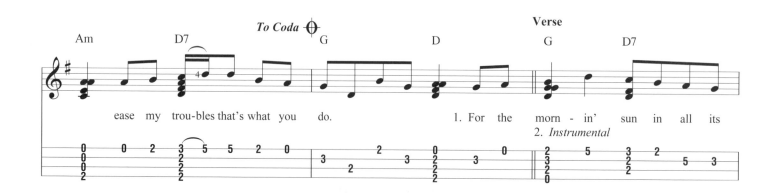

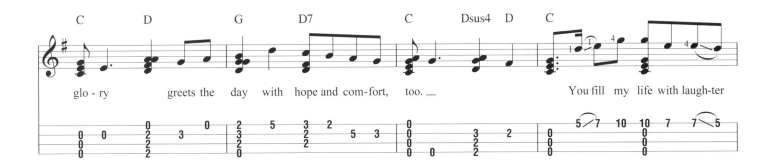

glo - ry greets the day with hope and com-fort, too. ___ You fill my life with laugh-ter

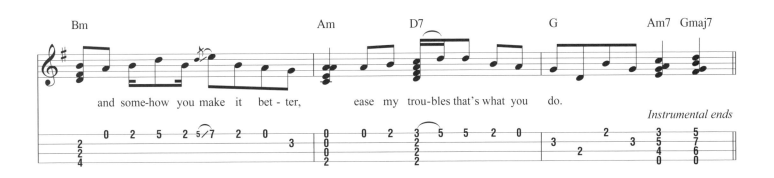

and some-how you make it bet - ter, ease my trou-bles that's what you do.

Instrumental ends

Bridge

There's a love that's di-vine and it's yours and it's mine _____ like the sun.

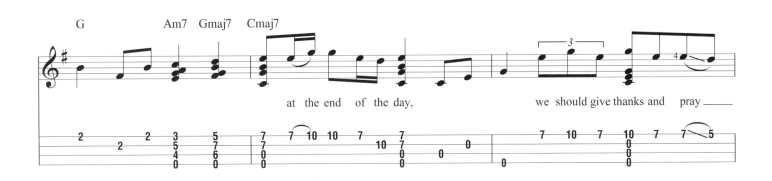

at the end of the day, we should give thanks and pray ___

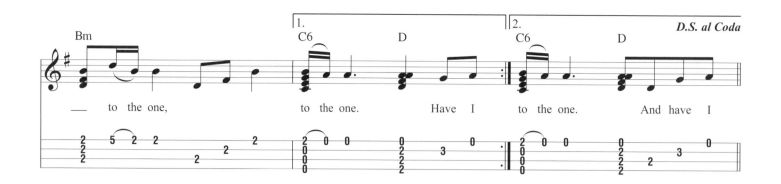

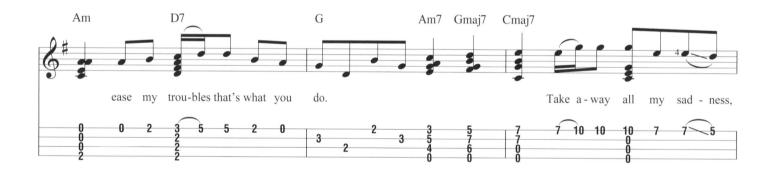

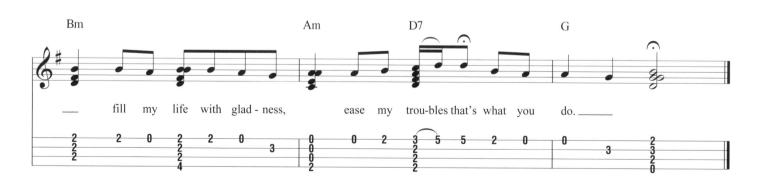

Hero

Words and Music by Mariah Carey and Walter Afanasieff

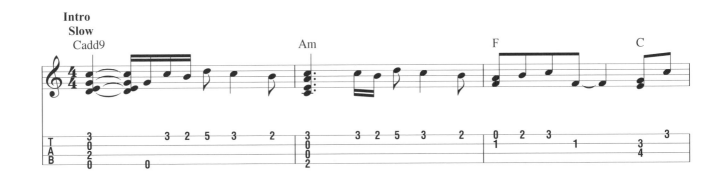

1. There's a he - ro if you look in - side __ your heart. You don't

long __ road when you face the world a - lone. No one

have to be __ a-fraid of what you are. There's an an - swer if you

reach - es out __ a hand for you to hold. You can find __ love if you

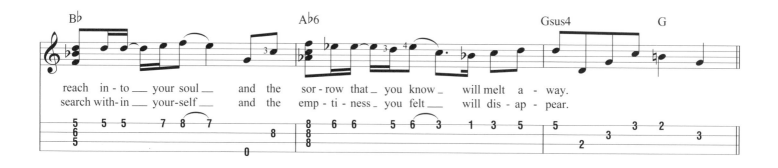

reach in-to ___ your soul ___ and the sor-row that _ you know _ will melt a - way.
search with-in ___ your-self ___ and the emp - ti - ness _ you felt ___ will dis - ap - pear.

% Chorus

And then a he - ro comes a - long with the strength to car - ry on, and you cast your fears a -

side, and you know you can sur - vive. _____ So, when you feel like hope is gone, _ look in-side you and be

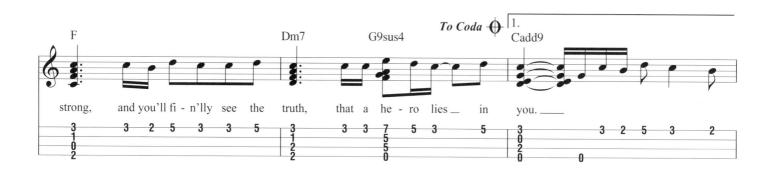

strong, and you'll fi - n'lly see the truth, that a he - ro lies _ in you. ___

To Coda ⊕ | 1.

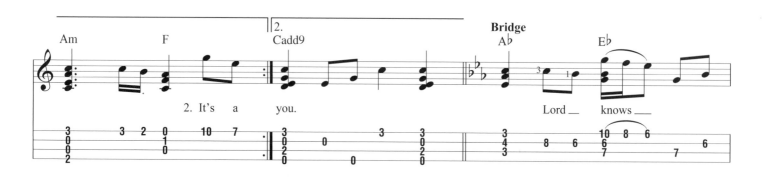

| 2.

2. It's a you.

Bridge

Lord __ knows __

dreams are hard to fol - low, but don't let an - y - one tear them a - way.

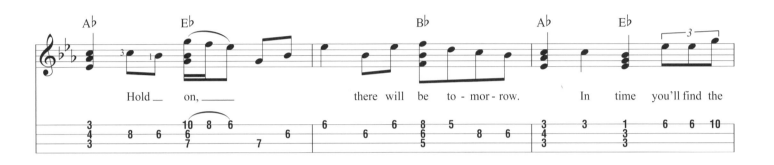

Hold — on, _____ there will be to - mor - row. In time you'll find the

D.S. al Coda

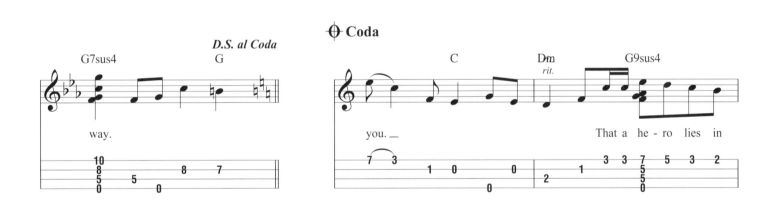

Coda

way.

you. _____ That a he - ro lies in

A Tempo

you, _____ that a he - ro lies in you.

Have You Ever Really Loved a Woman?

from the Motion Picture DON JUAN DeMARCO

Words and Music by Michael Kamen, Robert John Lange and Bryan Adams

Moderately fast

Verse

1. To real-ly love a wom-an, to un-der-stand her, you've got to

2. *See additional lyrics*

know her deep in-side. ___ Hear ev-'ry thought, see ev-'ry

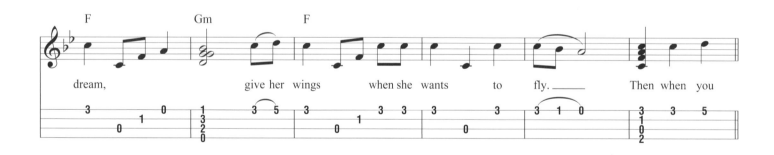

dream, give her wings when she wants to fly. ___ Then when you

Pre-Chorus

find your-self ly-ing help-less ___ in her ___ arms, ___ you

See additional lyrics

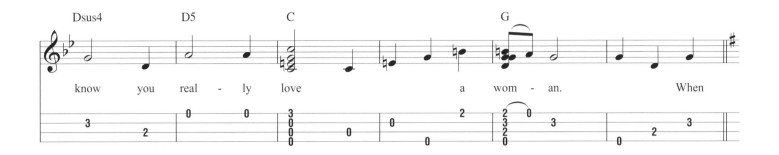

know   you   real - ly   love   a   wom - an.   When

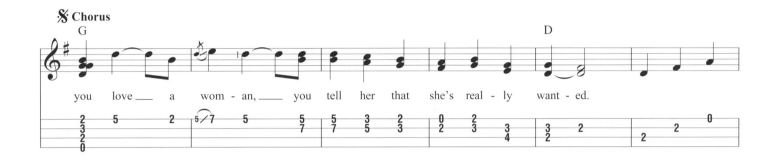

you   love ___   a   wom - an, ___   you   tell   her   that   she's   real - ly   want - ed.

When   you   love   a   wom - an, ___   you   tell   her   that   she's _____   the   one:

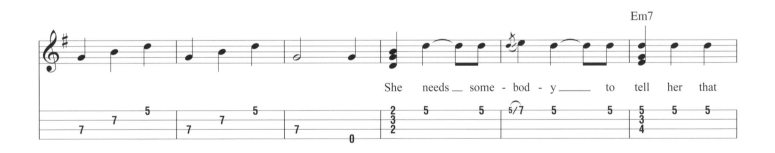

She   needs ___   some - bod - y _____   to   tell   her   that

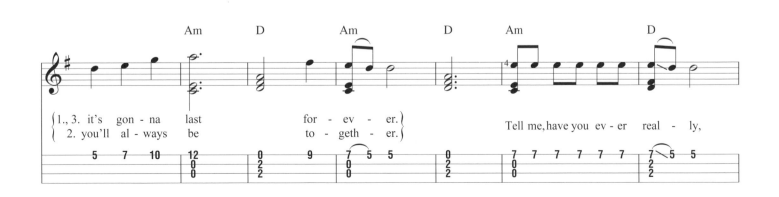

{ 1., 3. it's   gon - na   last   for - ev - er. }
{ 2.   you'll   al - ways   be   to - geth - er. }   Tell me, have   you   ev - er   real - ly,

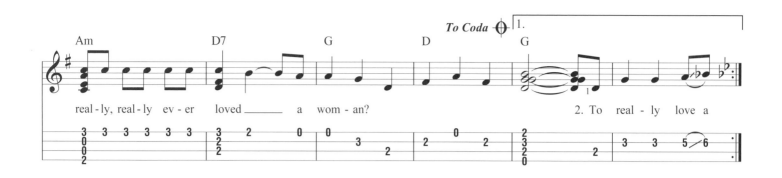

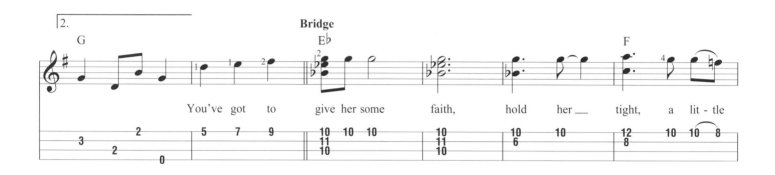

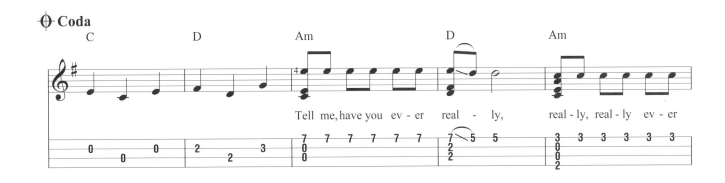

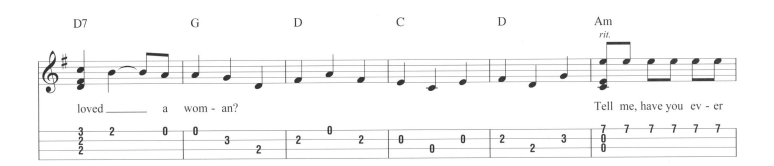

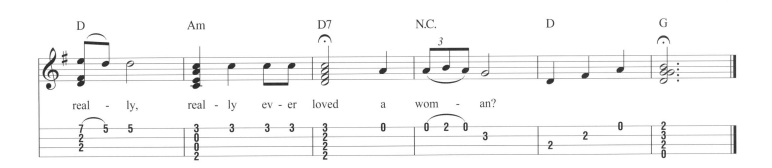

Additional Lyrics

2. To really love a woman, let her hold you
   Till you know how she needs to be touched.
   You've got to breathe her, really taste her
   Till you can feel her in your blood.

Pre-Chorus: When you see her unborn children in her eyes,
   You know you really love a woman.

Hello

Words and Music by Lionel Richie

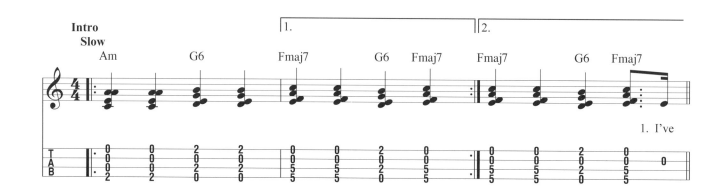

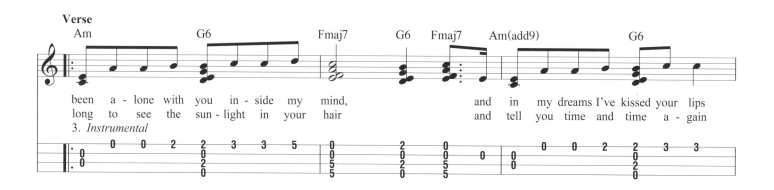

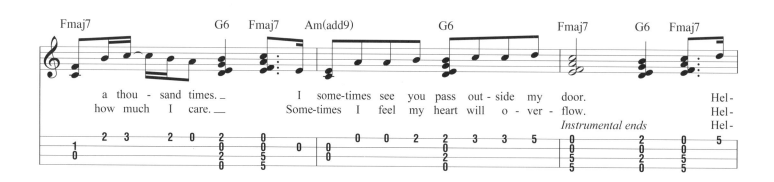

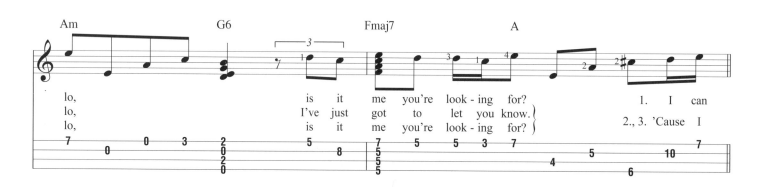

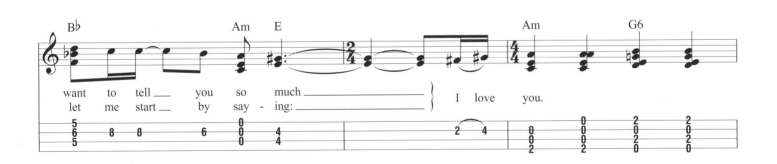

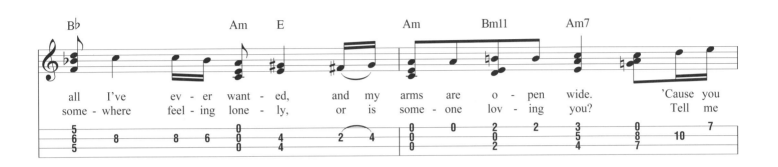

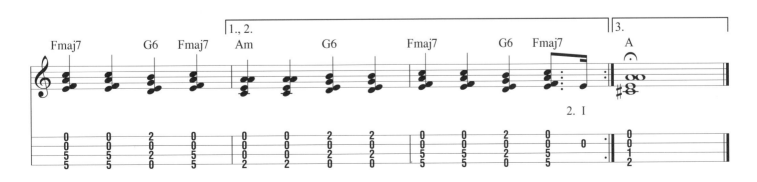

Here, There and Everywhere

Words and Music by John Lennon and Paul McCartney

Additional Lyrics

2. There, running my hands through her hair,
Both of us thinking how good it can be.
Someone is speaking,
But she doesn't know he's there.

How Deep Is Your Love

from the Motion Picture SATURDAY NIGHT FEVER

Words and Music by Barry Gibb, Robin Gibb and Maurice Gibb

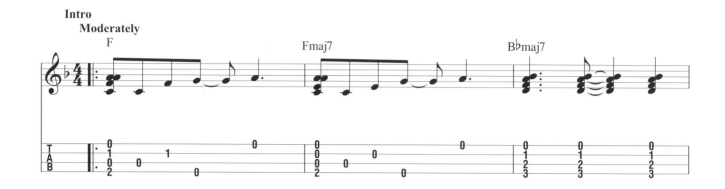

1. I know your eyes in the morn - ing sun.
I be - lieve in you.
Na, na, na, na, na, —

I feel you touch _____ me in the pour - ing rain.
You know the door _____ to my ver - y soul.
na, na, na, na, na, na, na, na, na.

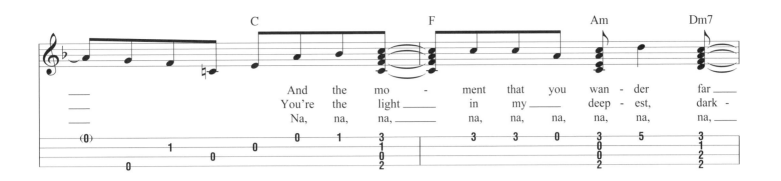

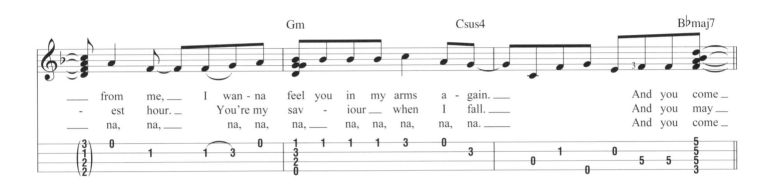

Pre-Chorus

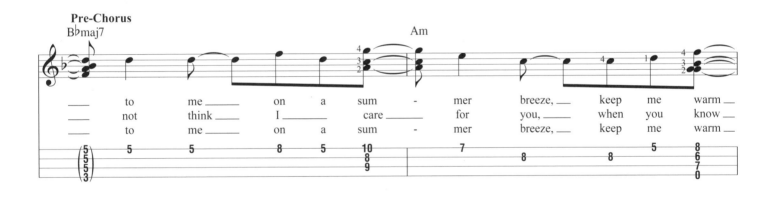

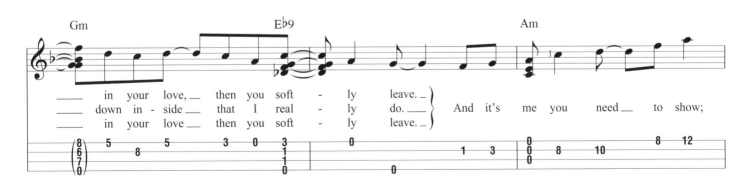

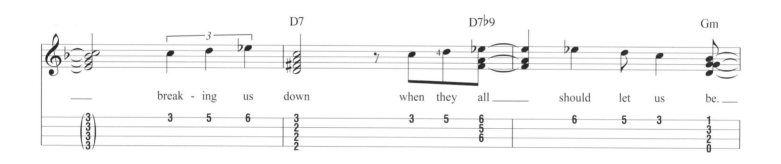

I Believe I Can Fly

from SPACE JAM

Words and Music by Robert Kelly

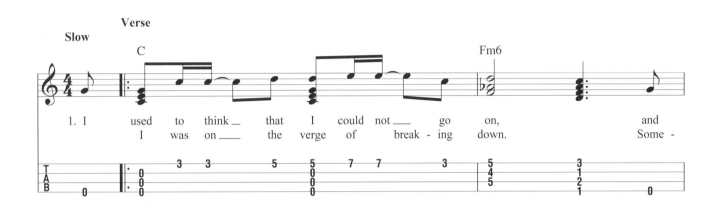

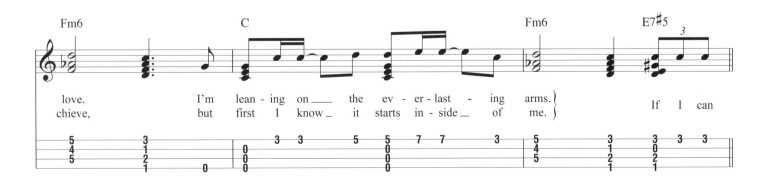

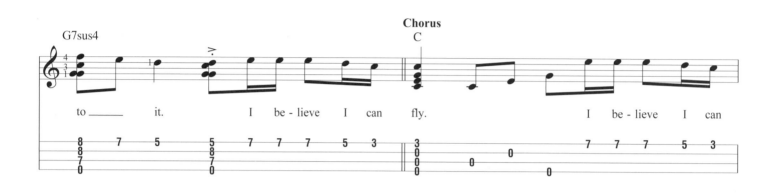

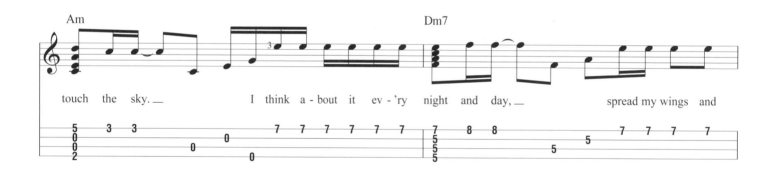

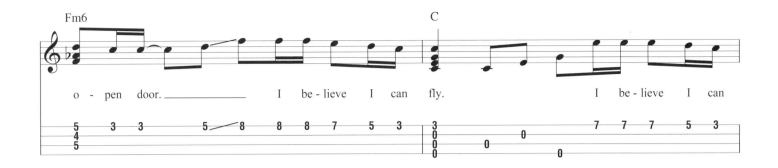

o - pen door._____ I be-lieve I can fly. I be-lieve I can

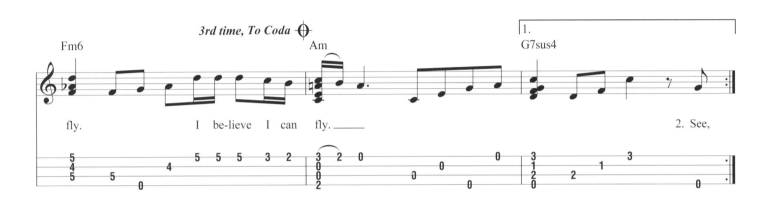

fly. I be-lieve I can fly._____ 2. See,

Hey, 'cause I be-lieve___ in me,_____ oh._____ If I can

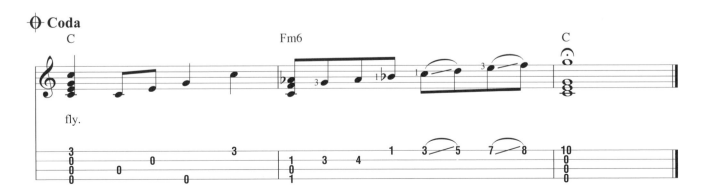

fly.

I Hope You Dance

Words and Music by Tia Sillers and Mark D. Sanders

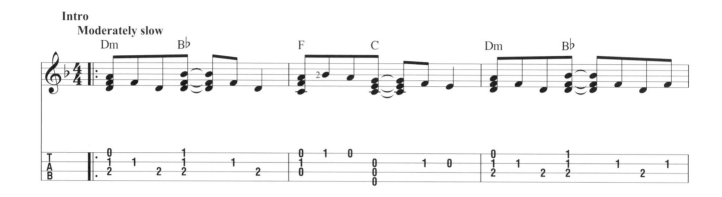

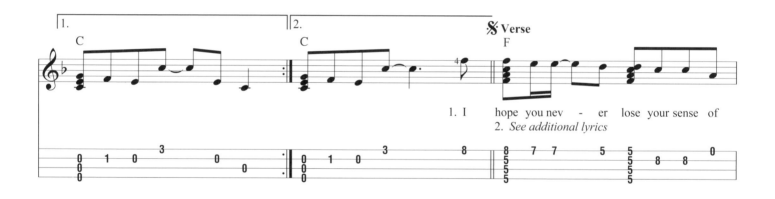

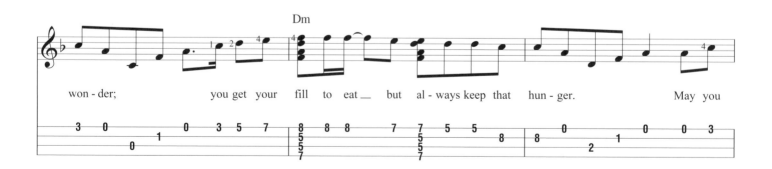

Bᵇadd9   C

nev - er take one sin - gle breath __ for grant - ed.   God for - bid love ev - er leave you emp - ty

𝄋 𝄋 **Pre-Chorus**

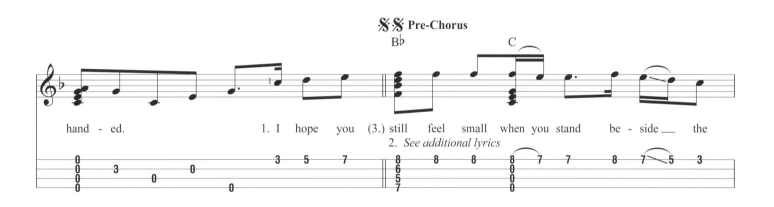

Bᵇ   C

hand - ed.   1. I hope you (3.) still feel small when you stand be - side __ the
              2. *See additional lyrics*

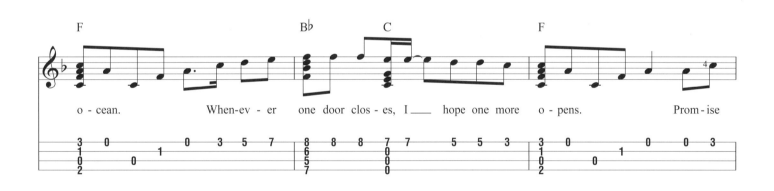

F   Bᵇ   C   F

o - cean.   When-ev - er one door clos - es, I __ hope one more o - pens.   Prom - ise

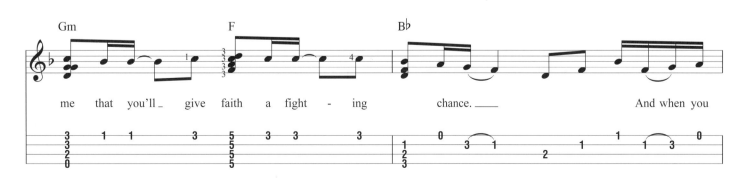

Gm   F   Bᵇ

me that you'll __ give faith a fight - ing chance. ____   And when you

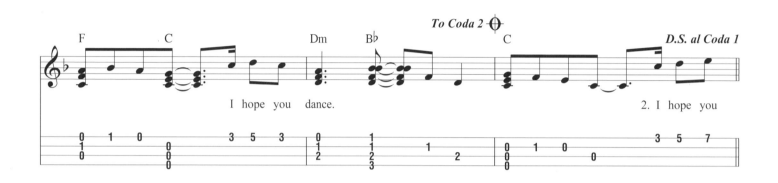

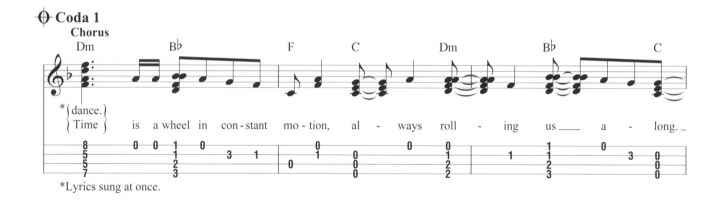

*Lyrics sung at once.

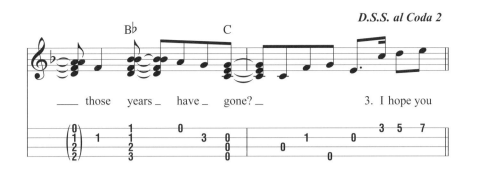

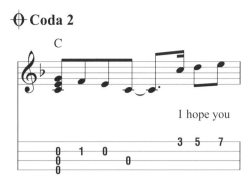

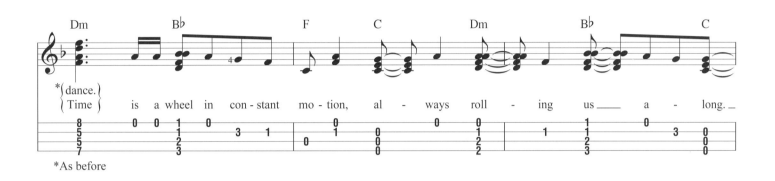

Additional Lyrics

2. I hope you never fear those mountains in the distance.
Never settle for the path of least resistance.
Livin' might mean takin' chances, but they're worth takin'.
Lovin' might be a mistake, but it's worth makin'.

Pre-Chorus 2. Don't let some hell-bent heart leave you bitter.
When you come close to sellin' out, reconsider.
Give the heavens above more than just a passing glance.
And when you get the choice to sit it out or dance,
I hope you…

I Say a Little Prayer

Lyric by Hal David
Music by Burt Bacharach

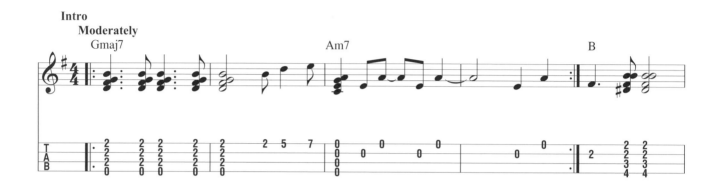

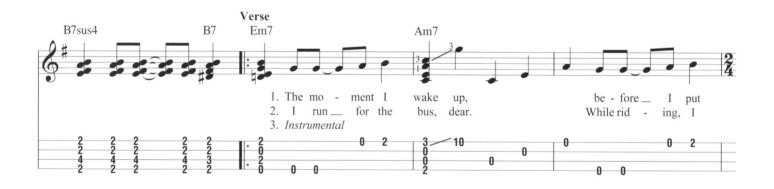

1. The mo - ment I wake up, be - fore __ I put
2. I run __ for the bus, dear. While rid - ing, I
3. *Instrumental*

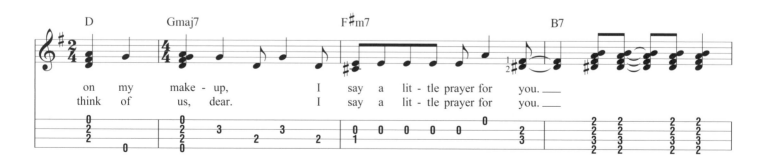

on my make - up, I say a lit - tle prayer for you. __
think of us, dear. I say a lit - tle prayer for you. __

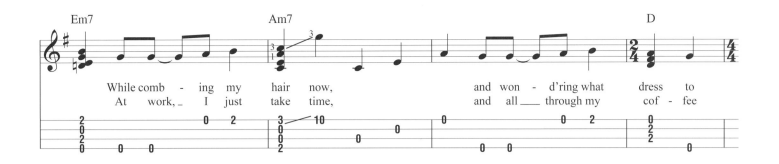

While comb - ing my hair now, and won - d'ring what dress to
At work, I just hair take time, and all through my cof - fee

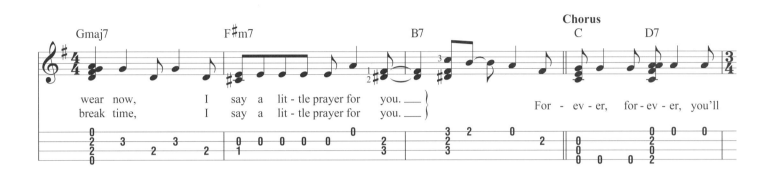

wear now, I say a lit - tle prayer for you.
break time, I say a lit - tle prayer for you.

Chorus

For - ev - er, for - ev - er, you'll

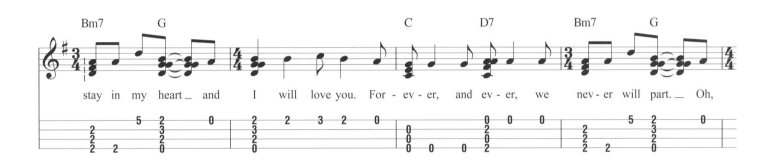

stay in my heart and I will love you. For - ev - er, and ev - er, we nev - er will part. Oh,

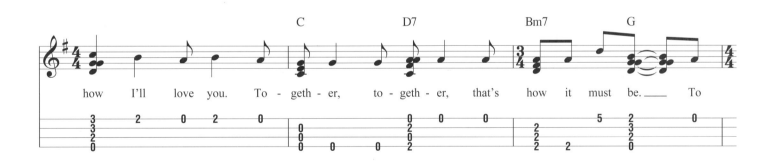

how I'll love you. To - geth - er, to - geth - er, that's how it must be. To

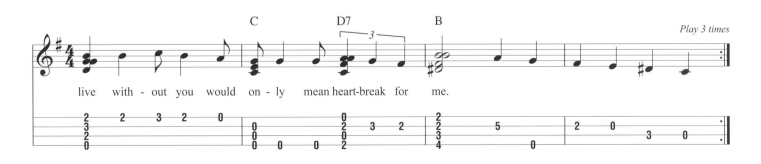

Play 3 times

live with - out you would on - ly mean heart-break for me.

Outro-Verse

My dar - ling be - lieve me, for me — there is no one but _____

you. Please love me too. I'm — in love with

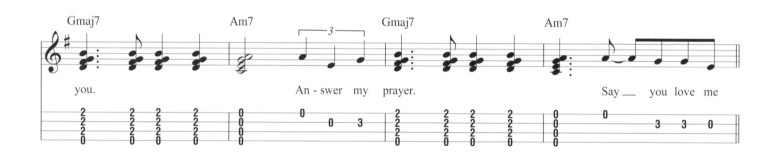

you. An - swer my prayer. Say — you love me

Outro

too. Why don't you an - swer my

Repeat and fade

prayer? You know I say a lit - tle

I'll Be There

Words and Music by Berry Gordy Jr.,
Hal Davis, Willie Hutch and Bob West

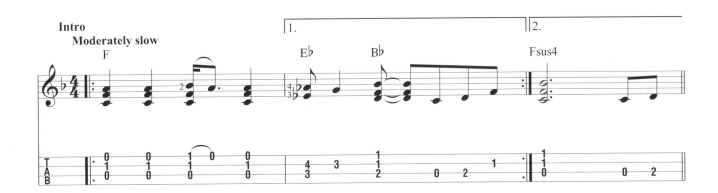

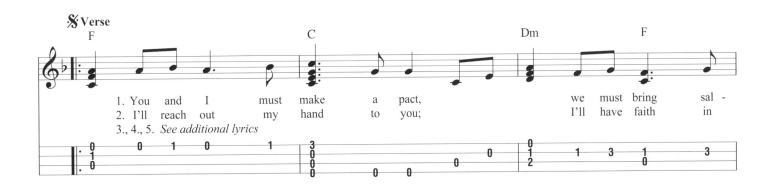

1. You and I must make a pact, we must bring sal-
2. I'll reach out my hand to you; I'll have faith in
3., 4., 5. *See additional lyrics*

va- tion back.
all you do.

Where there is love, I'll _____
Just call my name and I'll

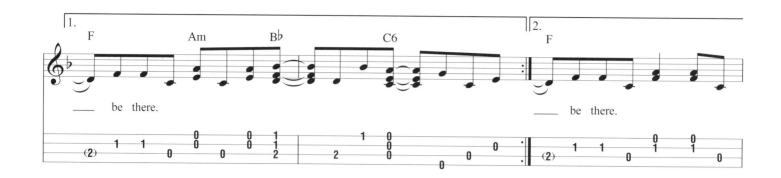

be there.

be there.

Bridge

I'll be there to com - fort you, build my world

of dreams a - round you, I'm so glad that I found you. I'll be there with a love

1st time, D.S. (take repeat)
2nd time, D.S. al Coda

that's strong. I'll be your strength. I'll keep hold - in' on.

⊕ Coda

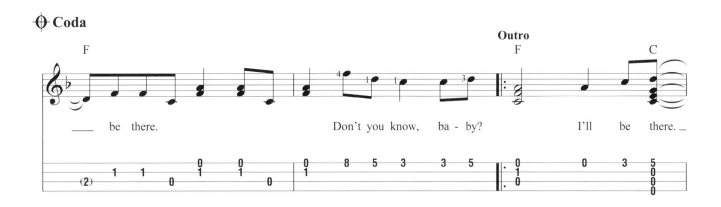

be there.   Don't you know,   ba - by?   I'll   be   there.

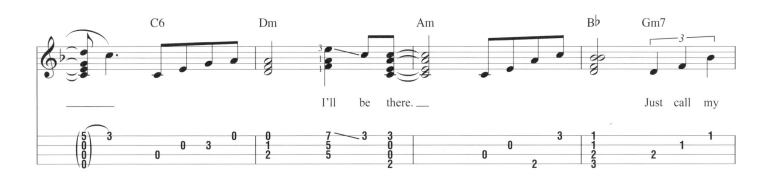

                         I'll   be   there.   Just call my

Repeat and fade

name,   I'll   be   there.

Additional Lyrics

3. Let me fill your heart with joy and laughter.
   Togetherness, girl, is all I'm after.
   Whenever you need me, I'll be there.

4. I'll be there to protect you,
   With an unselfish love, I'll respect you.
   Just call my name, and I'll be there.

5. If you should ever find someone new,
   I know he better be good to you.
   'Cause if he doesn't, I'll be there.

I Will Always Love You

Words and Music by Dolly Parton

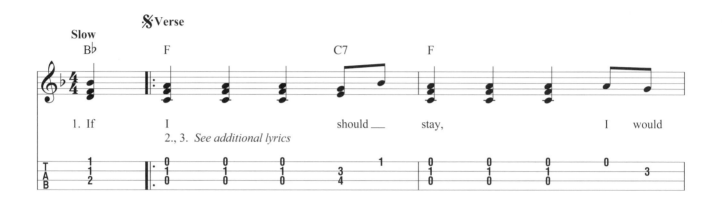

1. If I should stay, I would

2., 3. *See additional lyrics*

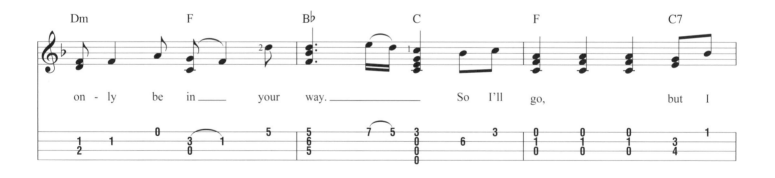

on - ly be in your way. So I'll go, but I

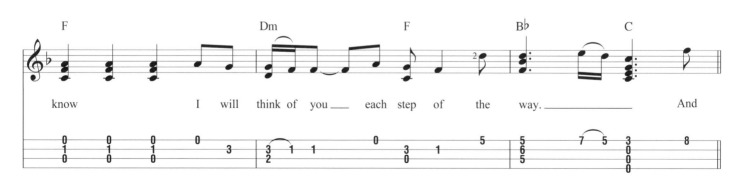

know I will think of you each step of the way. And

Chorus

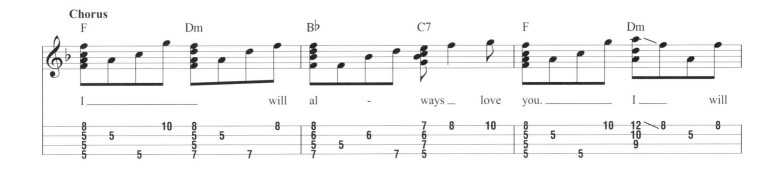

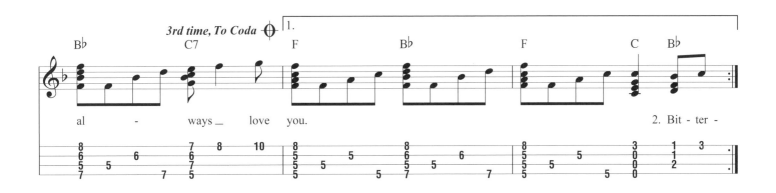

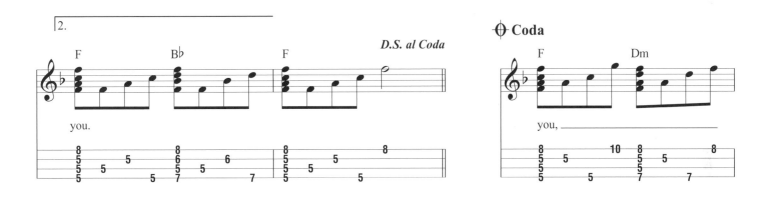

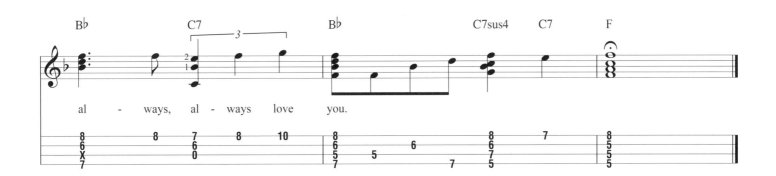

Additional Lyrics

2. Bittersweet memories,
   That's all I am taking with me.
   Goodbye. Please don't cry.
   We both know that I'm not what you need.
   But…

3. *Spoken:* I hope life treats you kind.
   And I hope that you have all that you ever dreamed of.
   And I wish you joy and happiness.
   Sung: But, above all of this, I wish you love.
   And…

I Will Remember You

Theme from THE BROTHERS McMULLEN

Words and Music by Sarah McLachlan, Seamus Egan and Dave Merenda

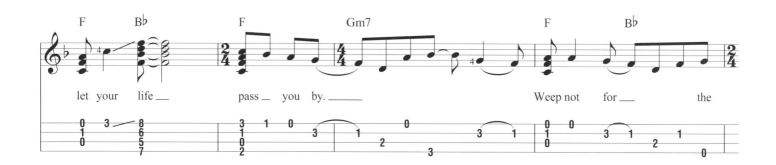

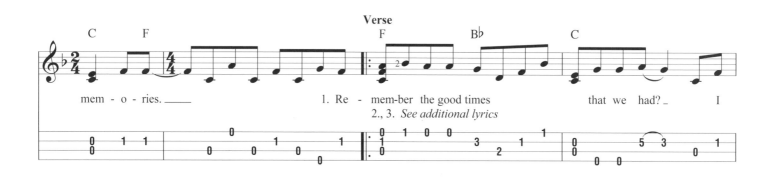

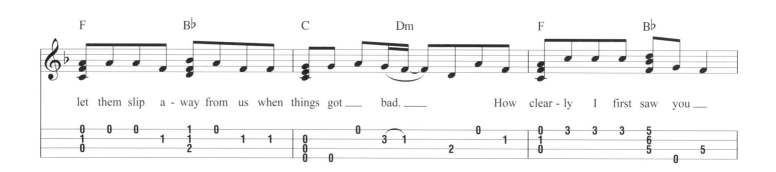

Additional Lyrics

2. I'm so tired, but I can't sleep.
   Standin' on the edge of something much too deep.
   It's funny how I feel so much but cannot say a word.
   We are screaming inside, oh, we can't be heard.

3. I'm so afraid to love you, but more afraid to lose,
   Clinging to a past that doesn't let me choose.
   Once there was a darkness, a deep and endless night.
   You gave me everything you had. Oh, you gave me light.

I Will Wait for You

from THE UMBRELLAS OF CHERBOURG

Music by Michel Legrand
Original French Text by Jacques Demy
English Words by Norman Gimbel

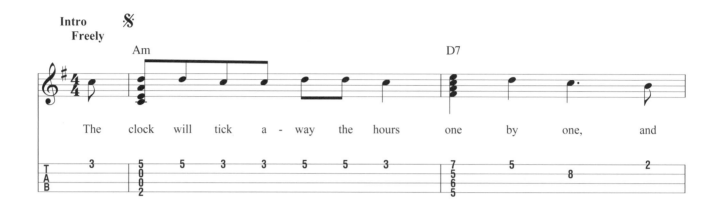

The clock will tick a-way the hours one by one, and

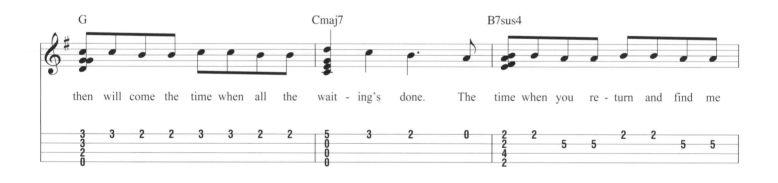

then will come the time when all the wait-ing's done. The time when you re-turn and find me

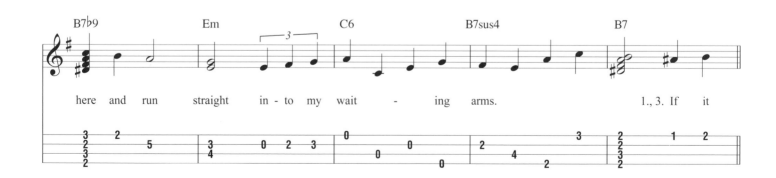

here and run straight in-to my wait - ing arms. 1., 3. If it

Verse
Moderately

takes for - ev - er, I will wait for you; for a thou - sand
2. *See additional lyrics*

sum - mers I will wait for you. 'Til you're back be - side me, 'til I'm

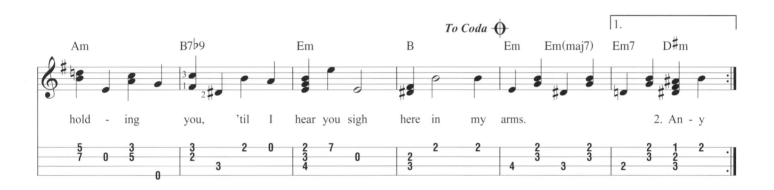

To Coda ⊕

hold - ing you, 'til I hear you sigh here in my arms. 2. An - y

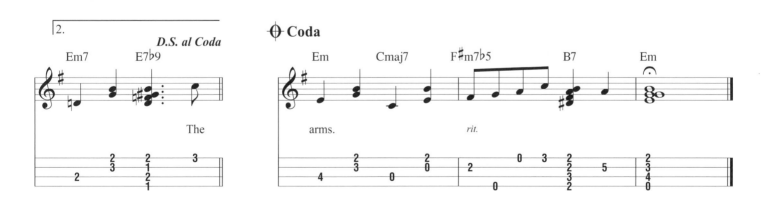

D.S. al Coda

⊕ **Coda**

The

arms. *rit.*

Additional Lyrics

2. Anywhere you wander, anywhere you go,
   Everyday, remember how I love you so.
   In your heart believe what in my heart I know,
   That forevermore I'll wait for you.

I'll Follow the Sun

Words and Music by John Lennon and Paul McCartney

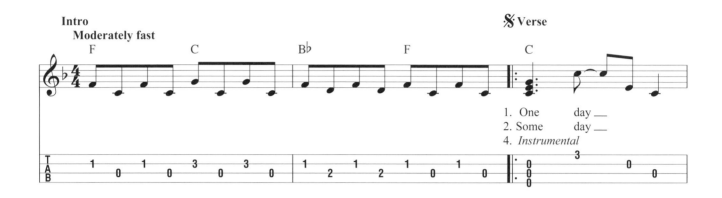

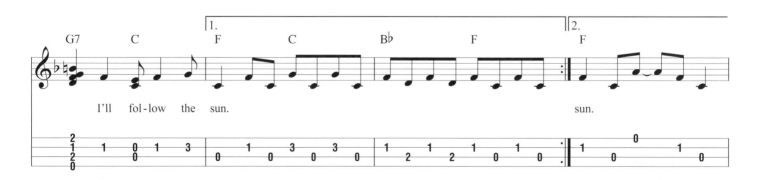

Chorus

And now the time has come,_ and so, my love,_ I must go.

And though I lose a friend, _ in the end, _ you will know.

Verse

Oh. _____ 3., 5. One day _ you'll find _ that I have gone.

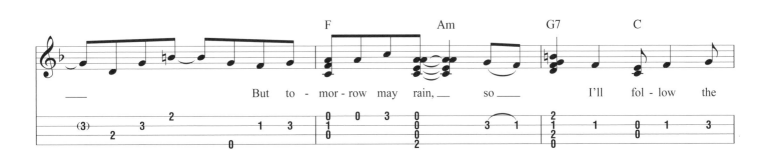

But to - mor - row may rain, _ so ___ I'll fol - low the

To Coda ⊕   *D.S. al Coda*
(take 2nd ending)   ⊕ **Coda**

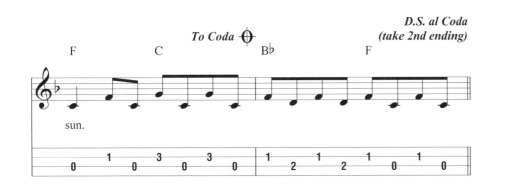

sun.

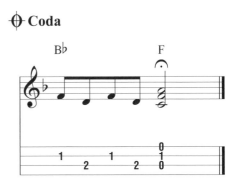

I'll Have to Say I Love You in a Song

Words and Music by Jim Croce

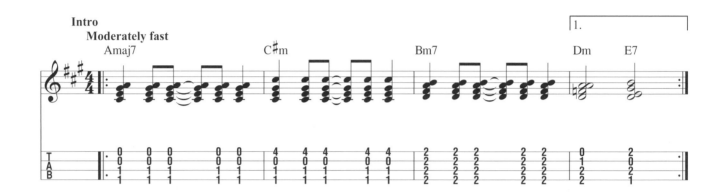

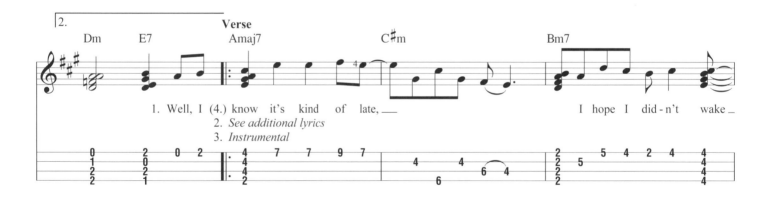

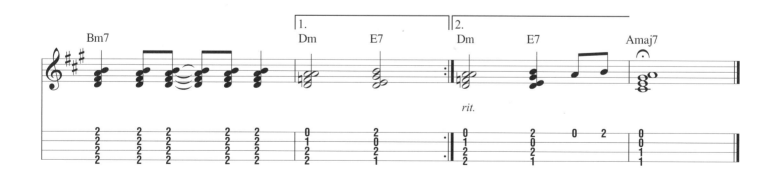

Additional Lyrics

2. Yeah, I know it's kind of strange.
   But ev'rytime I'm near you
   I just run out of things to say.
   I know you'd understand.

If

Words and Music by David Gates

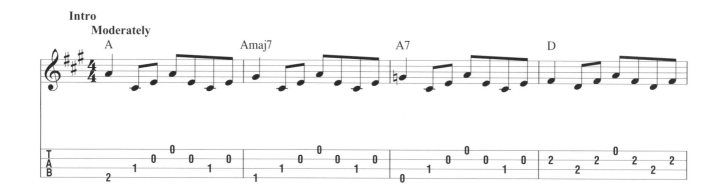

1. If a

pic - ture paints a thou - sand words, __ then why __ can't I paint
man could be two plac - es at __ one time, __ I'd be with

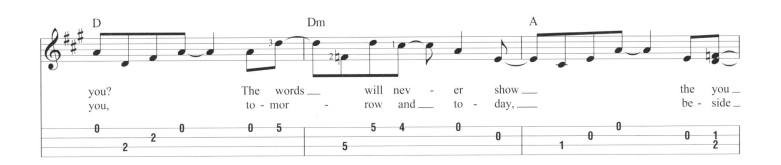

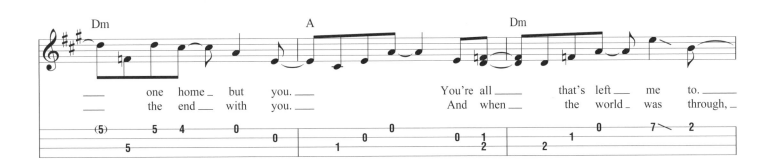

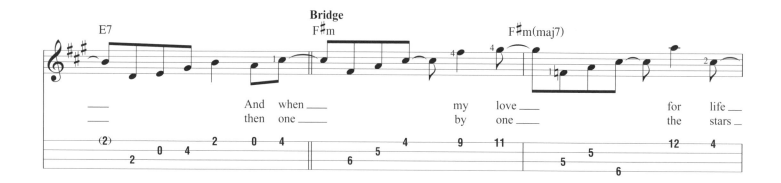

And when ____ my love ____ for life ____
then one ____ by one ____ the stars ___

___ is run-ning dry, ___ you come and pour ___ your-
___ would all go out. ___ Then you and I _____ would

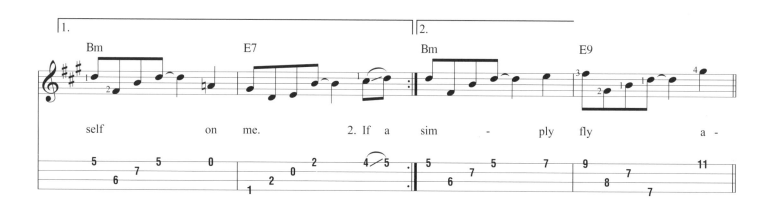

self on me. 2. If a sim - ply fly a -

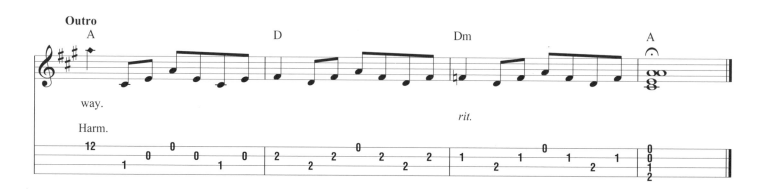

way.
Harm.

If You Leave Me Now

Words and Music by Peter Cetera

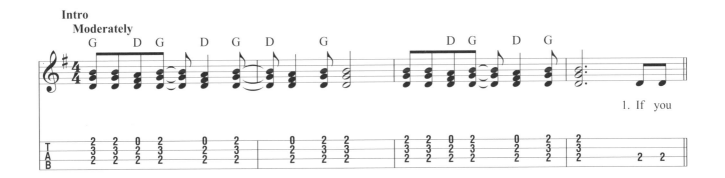

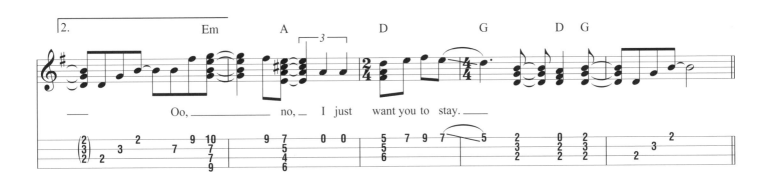

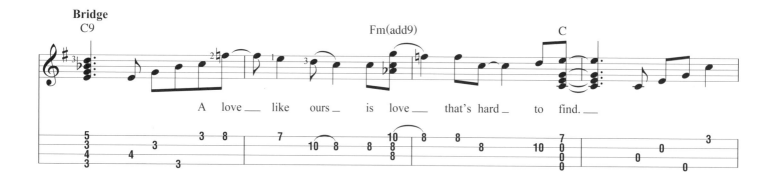

A love ___ like ours ___ is love ___ that's hard ___ to find. ___

How could we let ___ it slip ___ a - way? ___

We've come ___ too far ___ to leave ___ it all ___ be - hind. ___

How could we end ___ it all ___ this way? When to - mor - row comes, then we'll both ___

To Coda ⊕

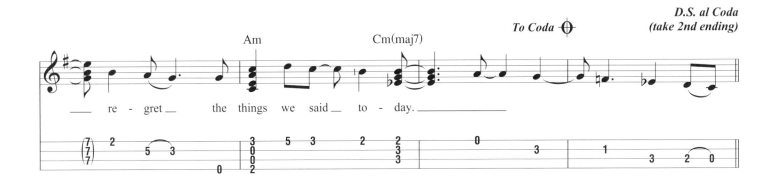

_____ re - gret _____ the things we said _____ to - day. _____

⊕ **Coda**

Outro-Verse

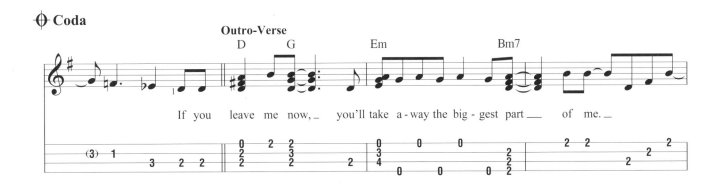

If you leave me now, _____ you'll take a - way the big - gest part _____ of me. _____

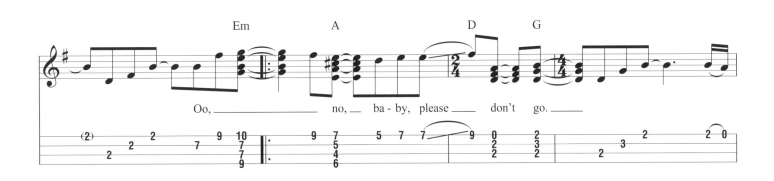

Oo, _____ no, _____ ba - by, please _____ don't go. _____

Repeat and fade

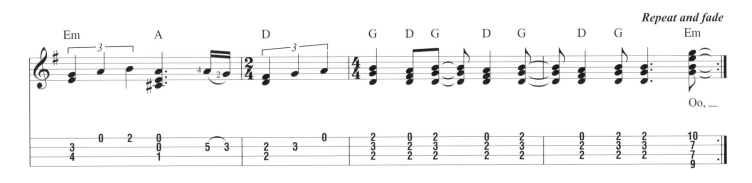

Oo, _____

It Must Have Been Love

Words and Music by Per Gessle

1. Lay a whis-per on my pil-low, leave the win-ter on the
2. *See additional lyrics*

ground. I wake up lone-ly, a stare of si-lence in the

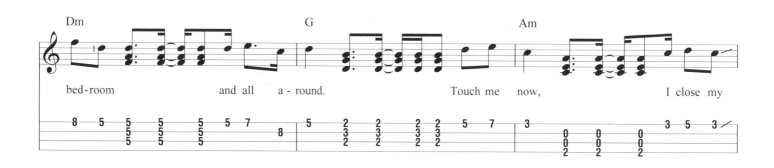

bed-room and all a-round. Touch me now, I close my

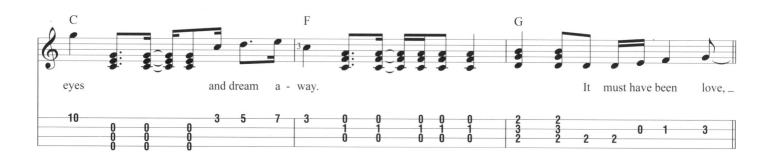

eyes and dream a-way. It must have been love, _

Chorus

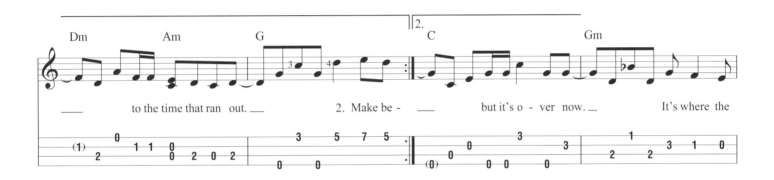

Chorus

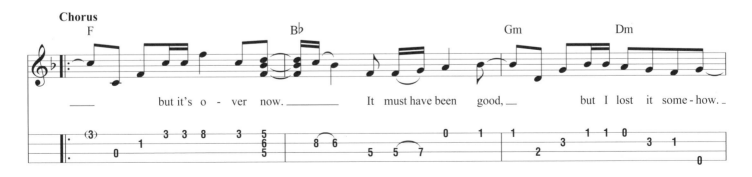

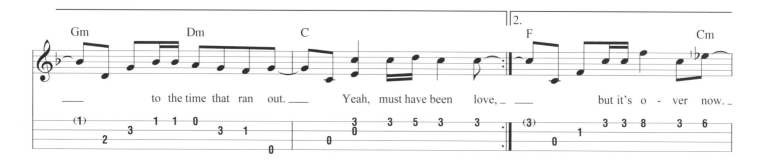

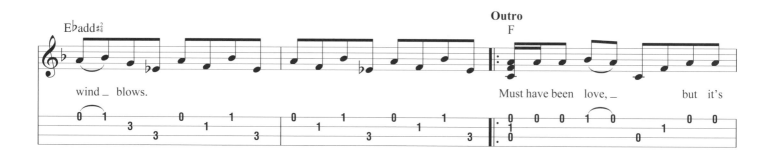

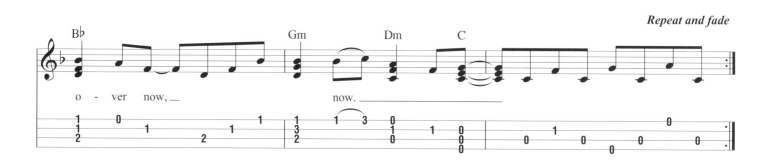

Additional Lyrics

2. Make believing we're together,
   That I'm sheltered by your arms.
   But in and outside I turn to water
   Like a teardrop in your heart.
   And it's a hard winter's day I dream away.

Killing Me Softly with His Song

Words by Norman Gimbel
Music by Charles Fox

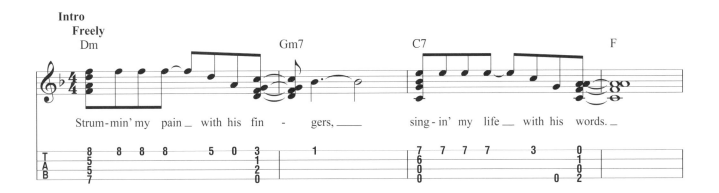

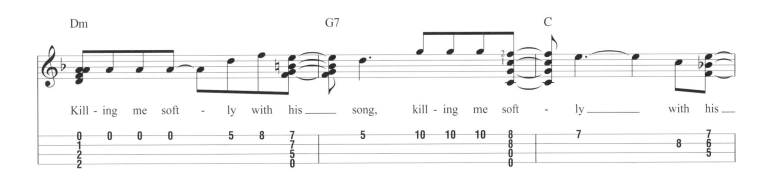

Verse

1. I heard he sang ___ a good ___ song. I ___ heard he had a style. ___
2., 3. *See additional lyrics*

And so I came ___ to see ___ him to lis - ten for a - while.

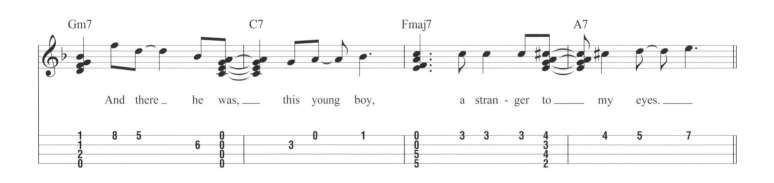

And there ___ he was, ___ this young boy, a stran - ger to ___ my eyes. ___

𝄋 Chorus

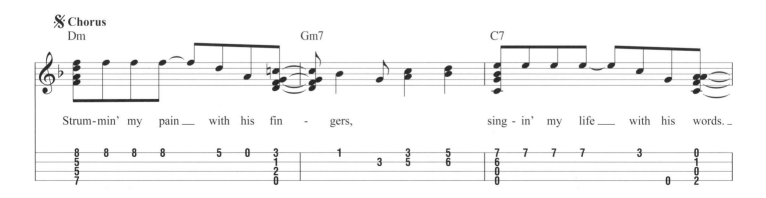

Strum - min' my pain ___ with his fin - gers, sing - in' my life ___ with his words. ___

142

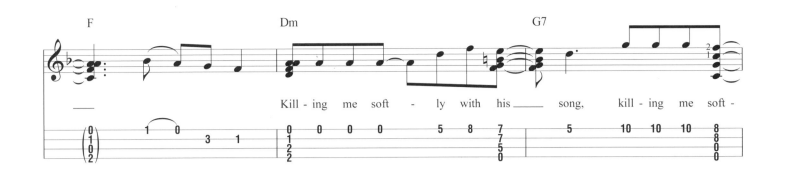

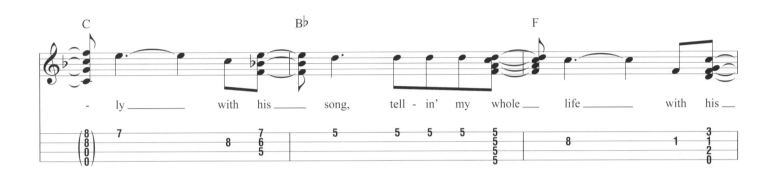

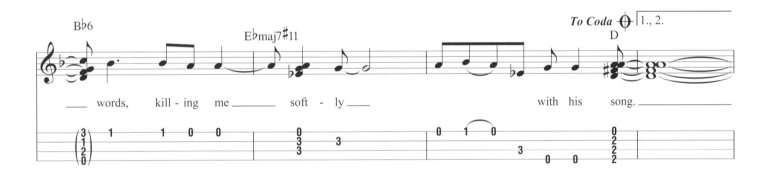

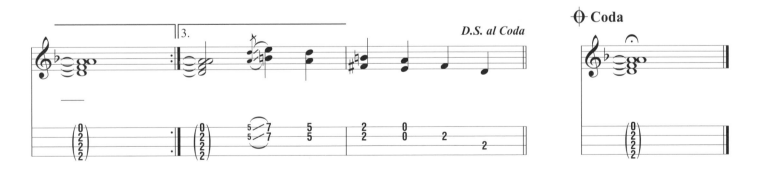

Additional Lyrics

2. I felt all flushed with fever, embarrassed by the crowd,
I felt he found my letters and read each one out loud.
I prayed that he would finish, but he just kept right on.

3. He sang as if he knew me, in all my dark despair,
And then he looked right through me, as if I wasn't there.
But he was there, this stranger, singing clear and strong.

Just Once

Words by Cynthia Weil
Music by Barry Mann

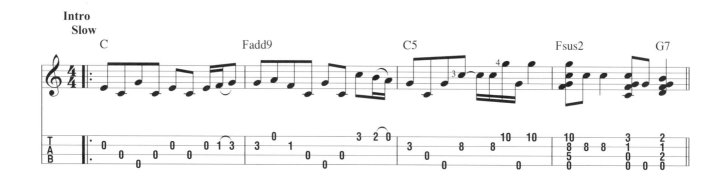

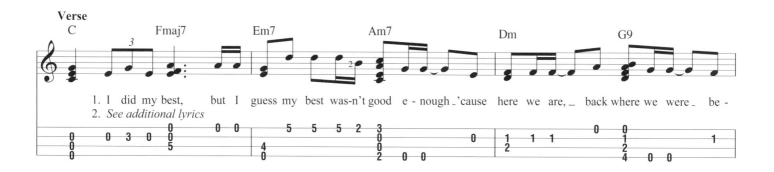

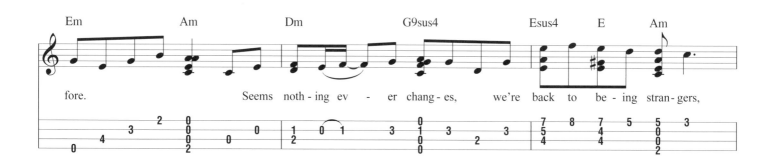

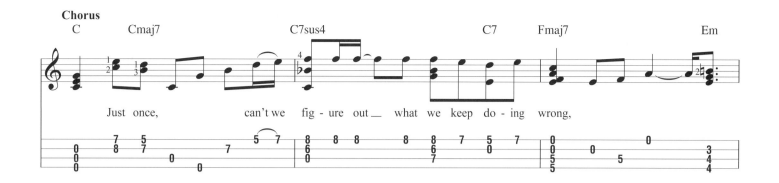

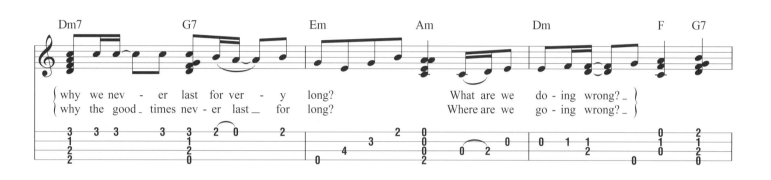

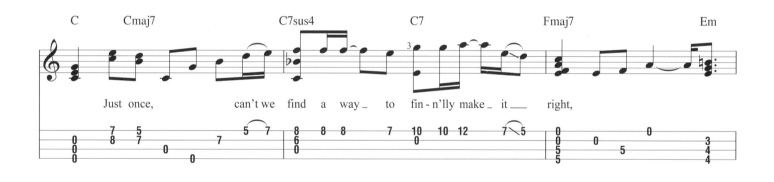

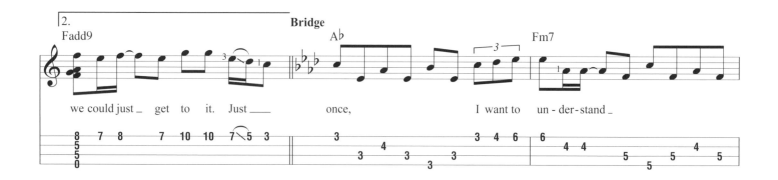

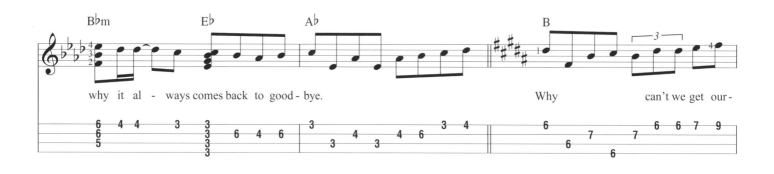

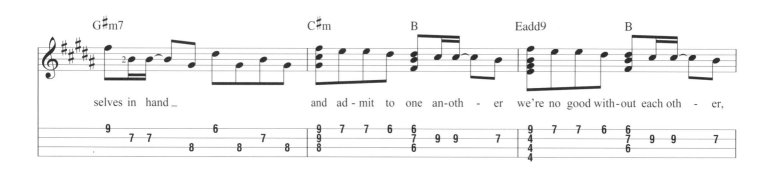

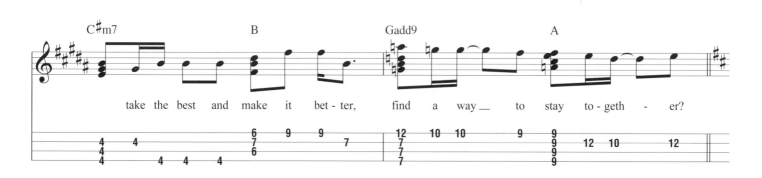

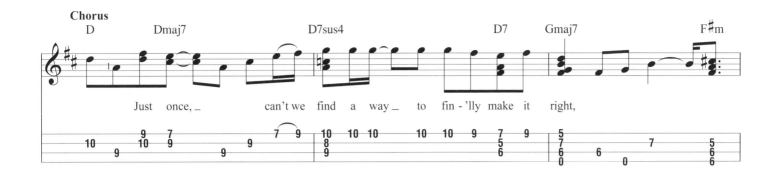

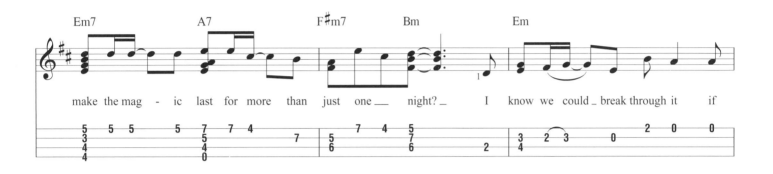

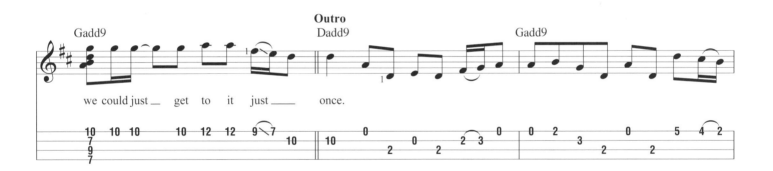

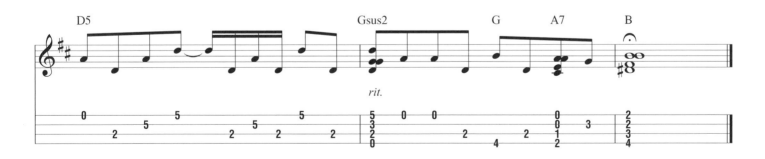

Additional Lyrics

2. I gave my all, but I think my all may have been too much
'Cause, Lord knows, we're not getting anywhere.
It seems we're always blowin' whatever we've got goin',
And it seems, at times, with all we've got, we haven't got a prayer.

Keep on Loving You

Words and Music by Kevin Cronin

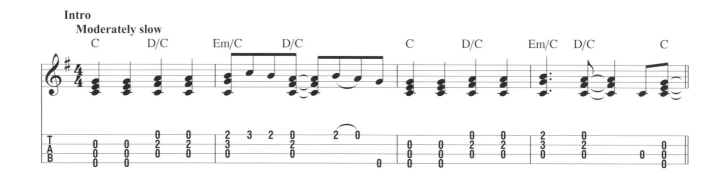

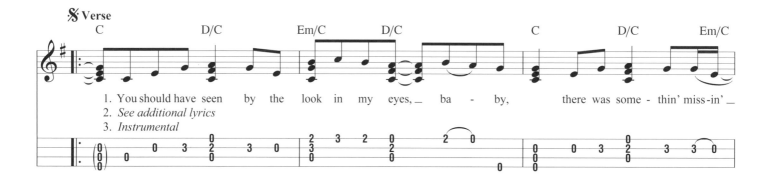

1. You should have seen by the look in my eyes, __ ba - by, there was some - thin' miss-in' __
2. *See additional lyrics*
3. *Instrumental*

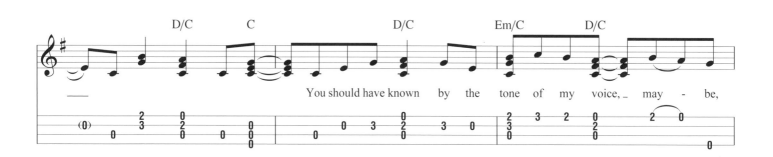

You should have known by the tone of my voice, __ may - be,

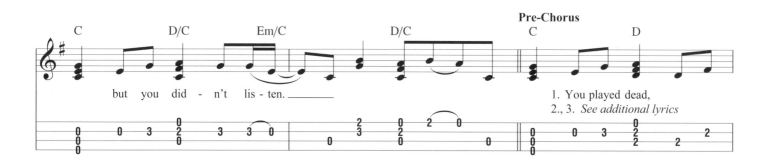

but you did - n't lis - ten. _____

1. You played dead,
2., 3. *See additional lyrics*

Additional Lyrics

2. And though I know all about those men, still I don't remember.
   'Cause it was us, baby, way before them, and we're still together.

Pre-Chorus 2., 3. And I meant ev'ry word I said.
   When I said that I love you, I meant that I'll love you forever.

Lady in Red

Words and Music by Chris DeBurgh

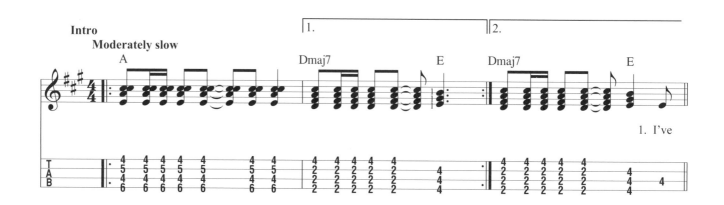

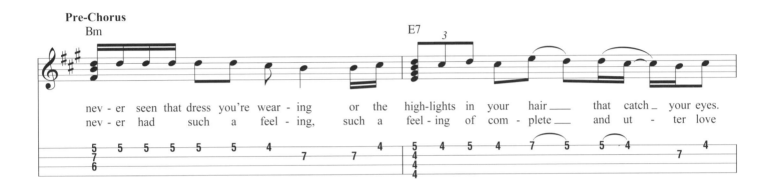

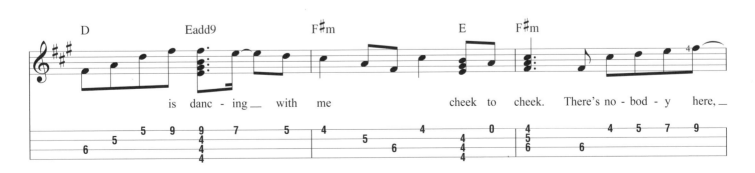

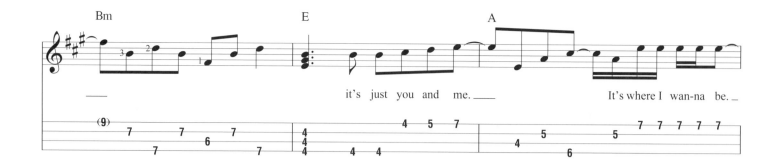

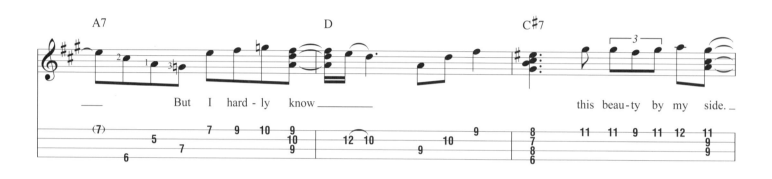

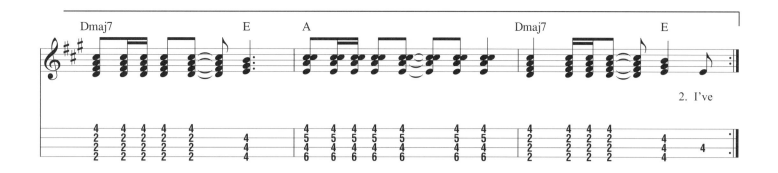

2. I've

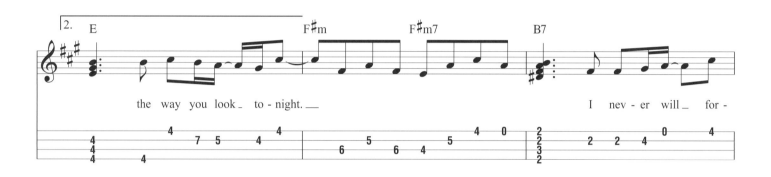

the way you look __ to-night. __   I nev-er will __ for-

Outro

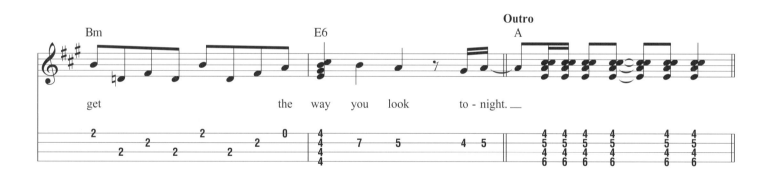

get   the   way   you   look   to - night. __

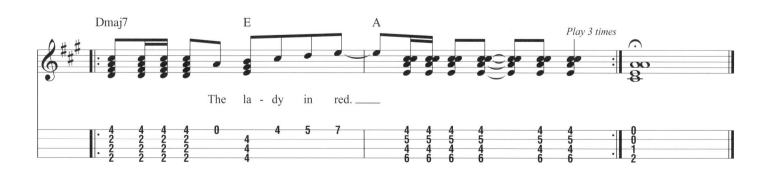

The la - dy in red. __

Let It Be Me
(Je T'appartiens)

English Words by Mann Curtis
French Words by Pierre Delanoë
Music by Gilbert Becaud

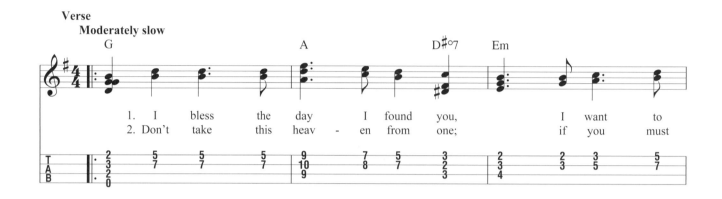

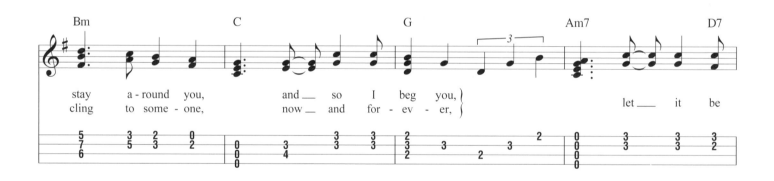

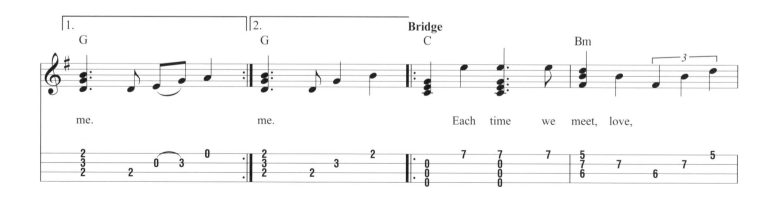

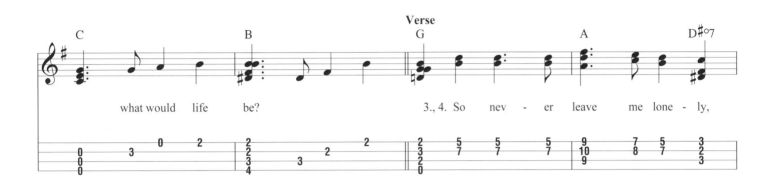

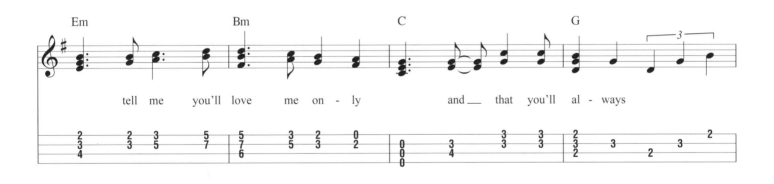

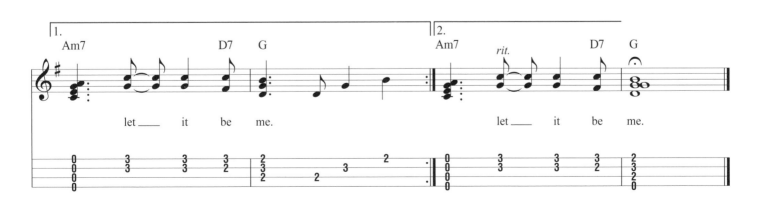

The Long and Winding Road

Words and Music by John Lennon and Paul McCartney

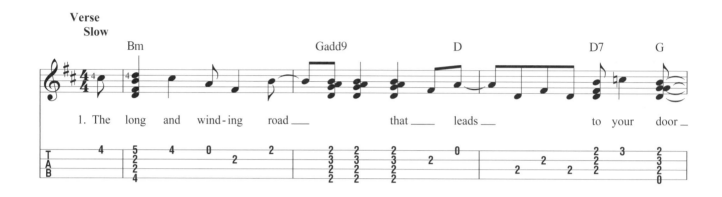

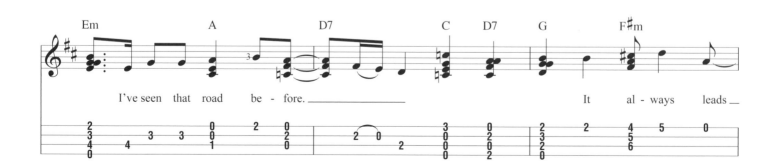

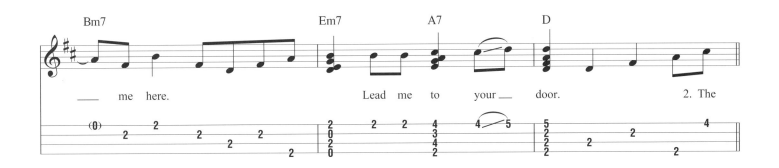

me here.   Lead me to your ___ door.   2. The

％ Verse

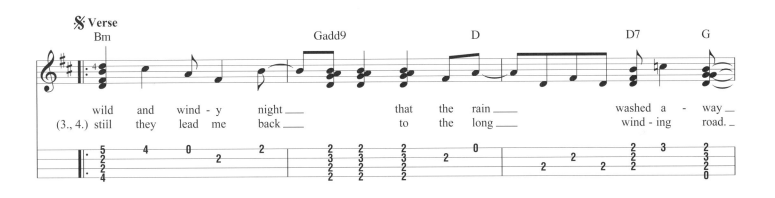

wild   and   wind-y   night ___   that   the   rain ___   washed a -   way ___
(3., 4.) still   they   lead   me   back ___   to   the   long ___   wind - ing   road. _

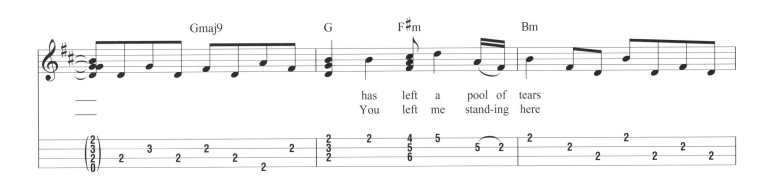

___   has   left   a   pool of   tears
___   You   left   me   stand-ing   here

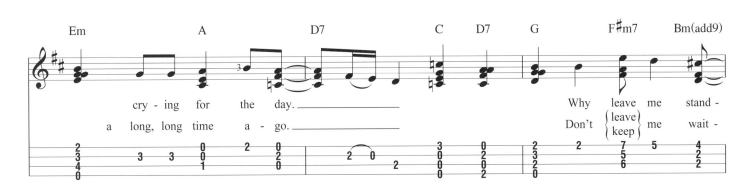

cry - ing   for   the   day. ___   Why   leave   me   stand -
a   long, long time   a - go. ___   Don't {leave} me   wait -
                                                                                        {keep}

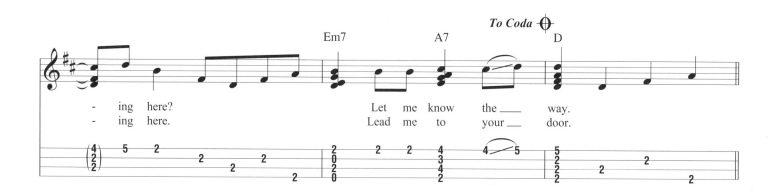

-ing here?
-ing here.

Let me know the ___ way.
Lead me to your ___ door.

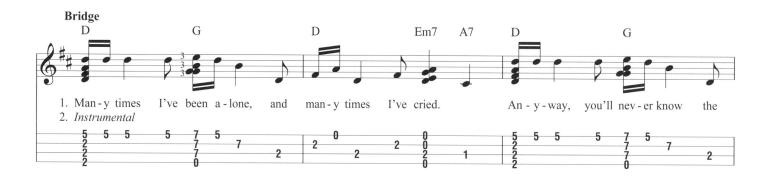

Bridge

1. Man-y times I've been a-lone, and man-y times I've cried. An-y-way, you'll nev-er know the
2. *Instrumental*

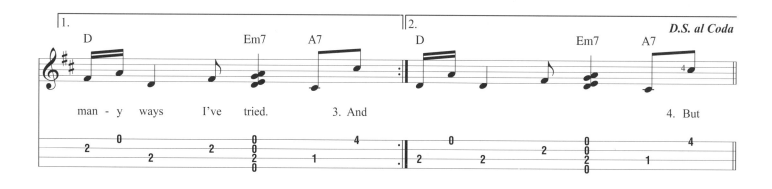

1.

man-y ways I've tried. 3. And

2.

D.S. al Coda

4. But

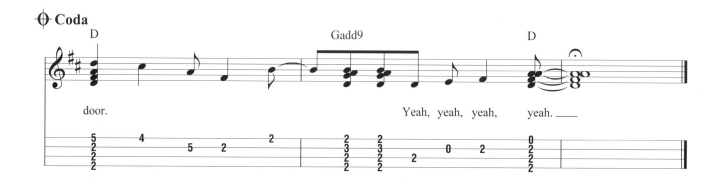

Coda

door.

Yeah, yeah, yeah, yeah. ___

Morning Has Broken

Words by Eleanor Farjeon
Music by Cat Stevens

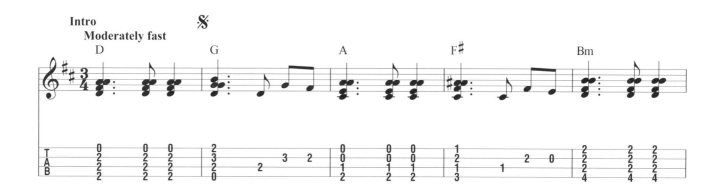

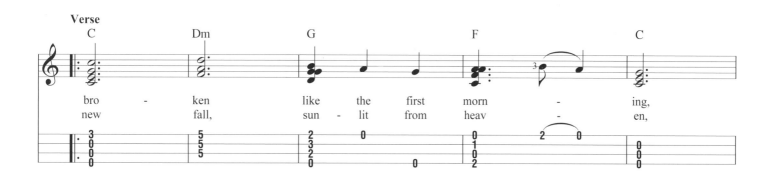

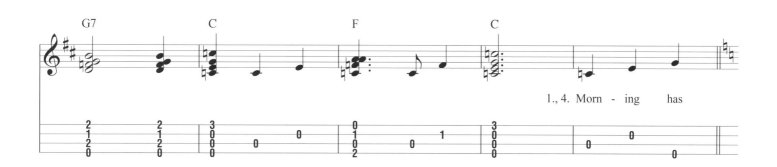

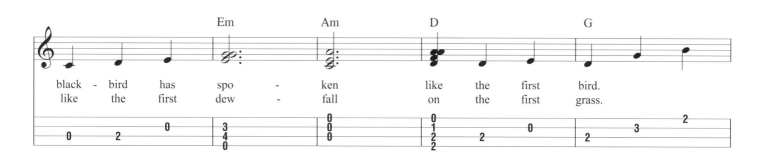

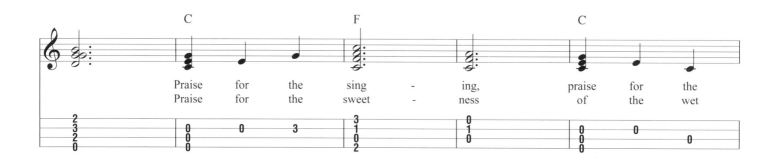

Praise for the sing - ing, praise for the
Praise for the sweet - ness of for the wet

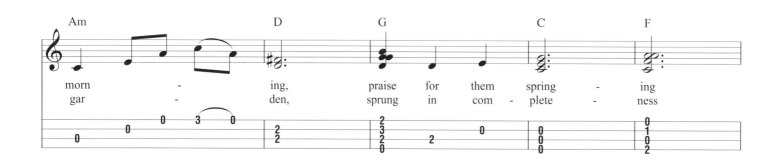

morn - ing, praise for them spring - ing
gar - den, sprung in com - plete - ness

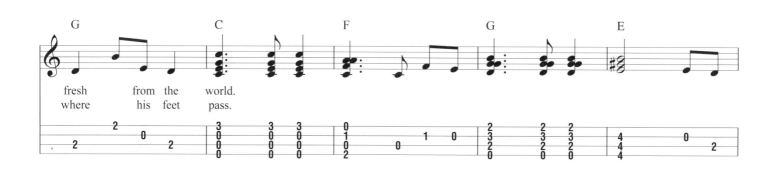

fresh from the world.
where his feet pass.

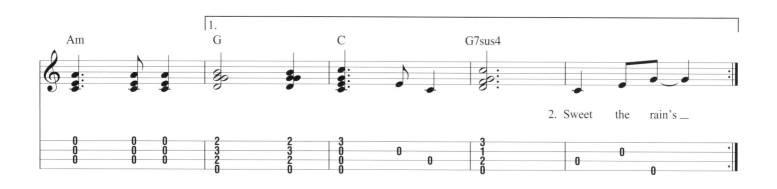

2. Sweet the rain's

160

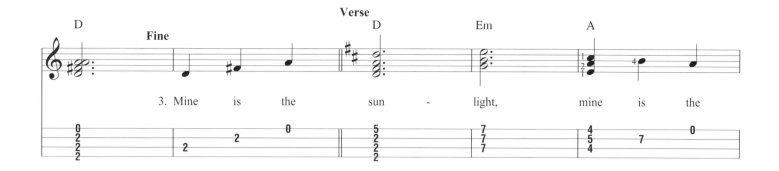

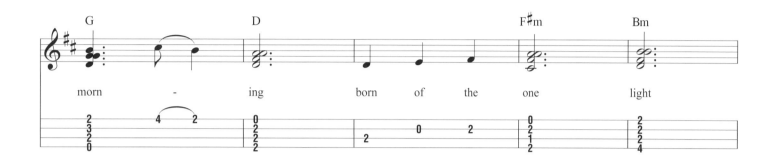

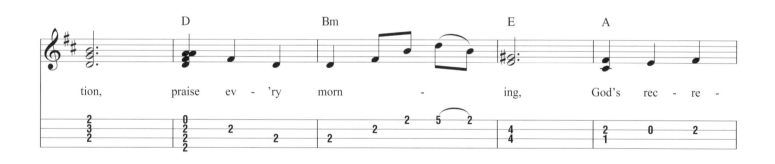

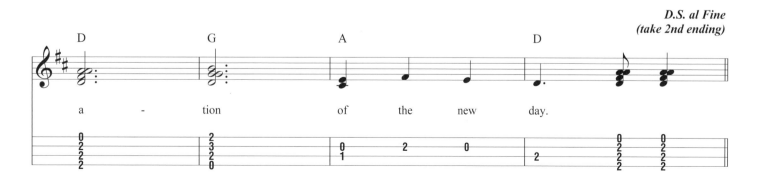

Lover, You Should've Come Over

Words and Music by Jeff Buckley

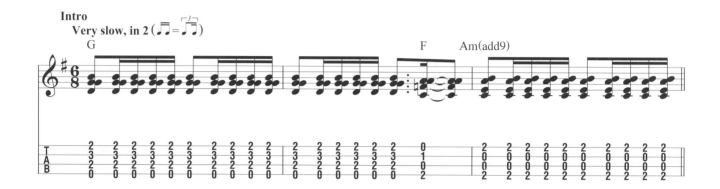

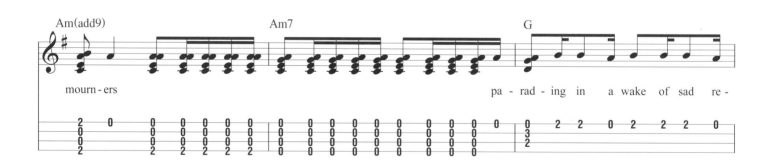

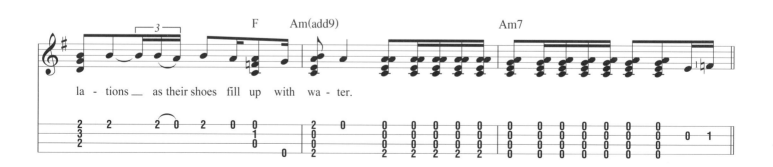

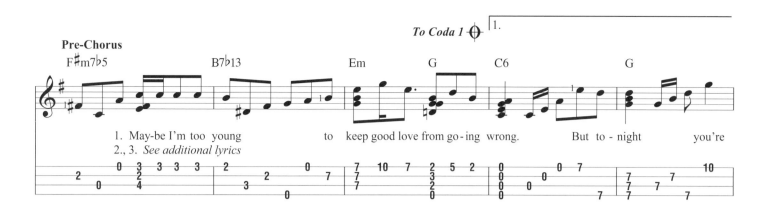

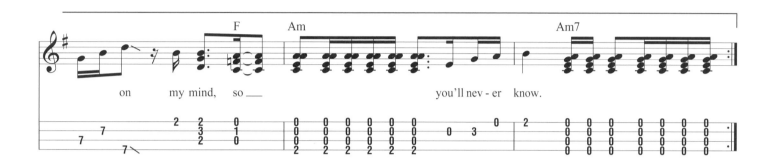

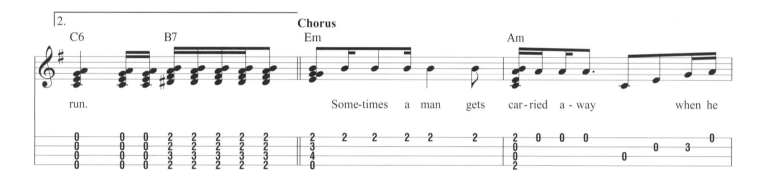

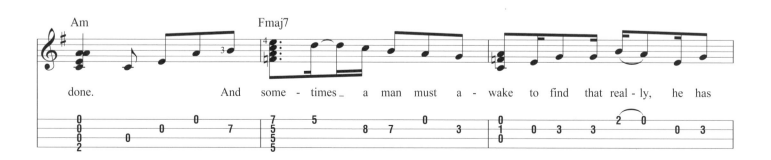

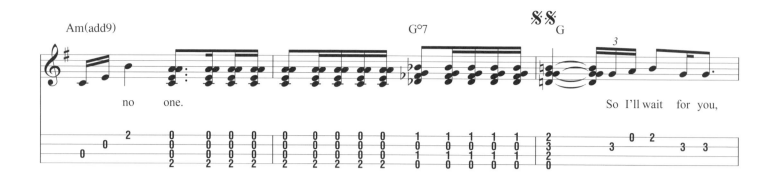

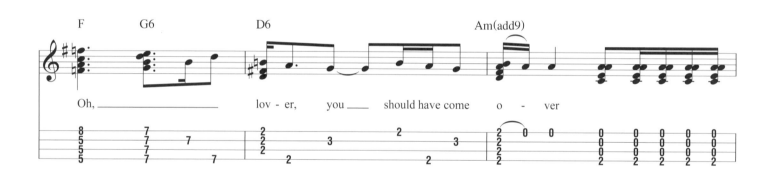

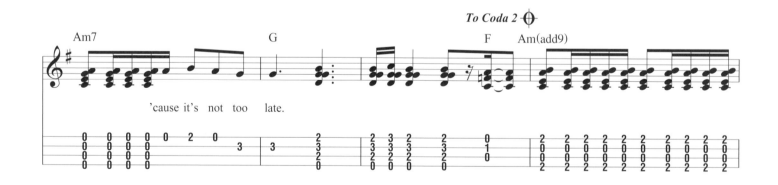

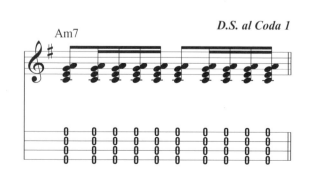

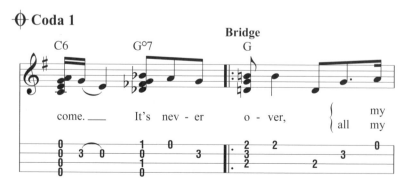

king - dom for a kiss up - on her shoul - der.
blood for the sweet - ness of her laugh - ter.

It's nev - er

o - ver, all my rich - es for her smiles when I slept so soft a - gainst her.
she's a tear that hangs in - side my soul for - ev - er.

It's nev - er

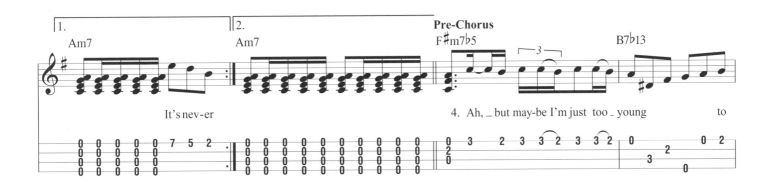

It's nev-er

4. Ah, but may-be I'm just too young to

Coda 2

D.S.S. al Coda 2

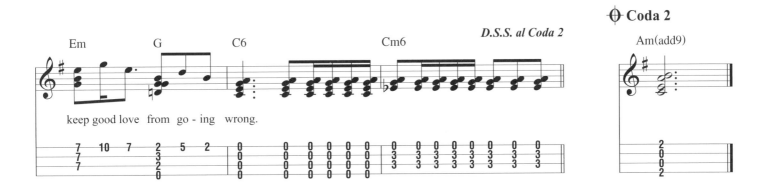

keep good love from go - ing wrong.

Additional Lyrics

2. Broken down and hungry for your love, with no way to feed it.
Where are you tonight? Child, you know how much I need it.

Pre-Chorus 2. Too young to hold on and too old to just break free and run.

3. Lonely is the room, the bed is made, the open window lets the rain in.
Burning in the corner is the only one, he dreams he had you with him.

Pre-Chorus 3. My body turns and yearns for a sleep that won't ever come.

Man in the Mirror

Words and Music by Glen Ballard and Siedah Garrett

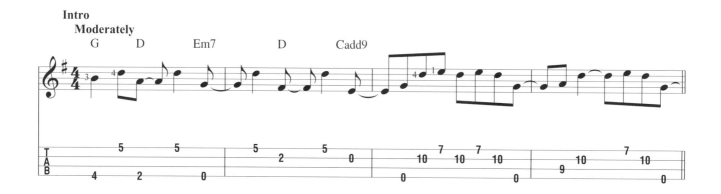

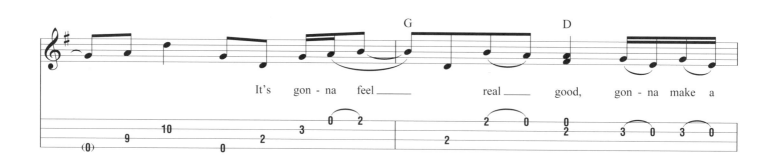

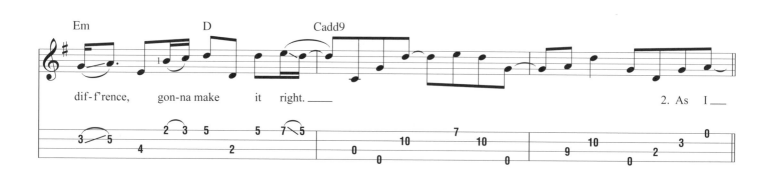

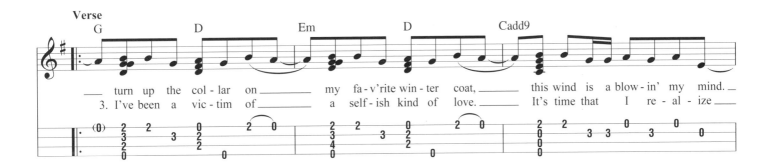

Verse

___ turn up the col - lar on ___ my fa - v'rite win - ter coat, ___ this wind is a blow - in' my mind. ___
3. I've been a vic - tim of ___ a self - ish kind of love. ___ It's time that I re - al - ize ___

___ I see the kids ___ in the street ___ with not e -
___ that there are some ___ with no home, ___ not a nick -

nough to eat. Who am I to be blind, pre - tend - ing not to see their ___ needs? ___
el to loan. Could it be real - ly me, pre - tend - ing that they're not a - lone? ___

Pre-Chorus

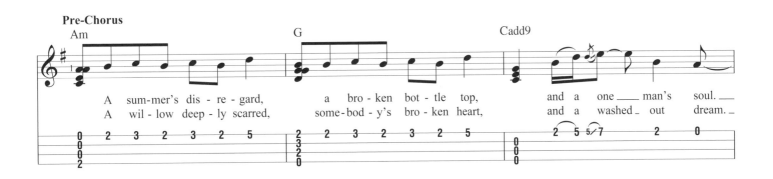

A sum - mer's dis - re - gard, a bro - ken bot - tle top, and a one ___ man's soul. ___
A wil - low deep - ly scarred, some - bod - y's bro - ken heart, and a washed ___ out dream. ___

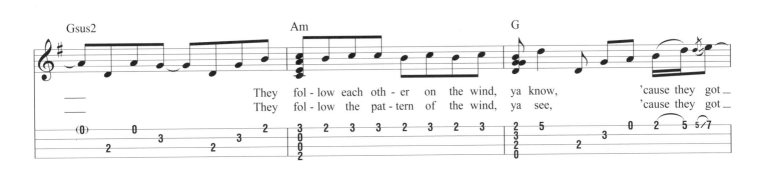

___ They fol - low each oth - er on the wind, ya know, 'cause they got ___
They fol - low the pat - tern of the wind, ya see, 'cause they got ___

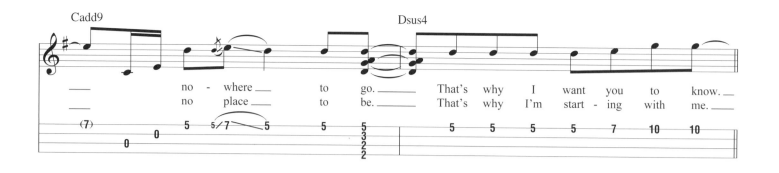

no-where ___ to go. ___ That's why I want you to know. ___
no place ___ to be. ___ That's why I'm start-ing with me. ___

Chorus

I'm start-ing with the man ___ in the mir-ror. I'm ask-ing him to

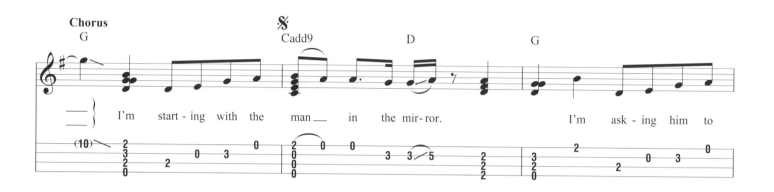

change ___ his ways. ___ And no ___ mes-sage could have been an-y clear-er: if you

To Coda

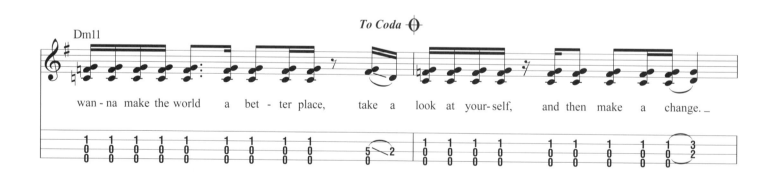

wan-na make the world a bet-ter place, take a look at your-self, and then make a change. ___

1.

Na, na, na, na, na, na, na, na, ___ na, na.

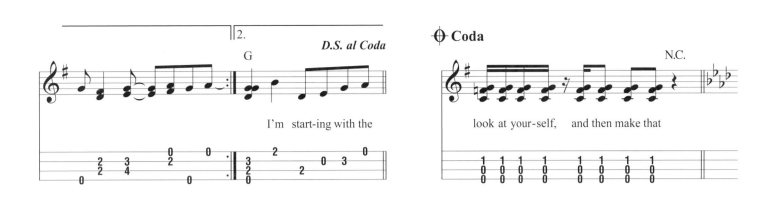

D.S. al Coda

✛ **Coda**

I'm start-ing with the

look at your-self, and then make that

Outro-Chorus

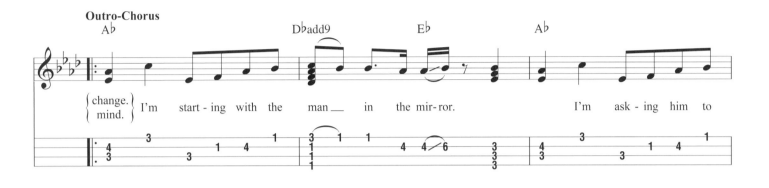

A♭   D♭add9   E♭   A♭

change.
mind. } I'm start-ing with the man ___ in the mir-ror. I'm ask-ing him to

D♭add9   E♭   A♭   A♭7   D♭   B♭7

change ___ his ways. ___ And no ___ mes-sage could have been an - y clear-er: if you

D♭m11

wan-na make the world a bet-ter place, ___ take a look at your-self, and then make the change. ___You got-ta

Repeat and fade

get it right ___ while you got the time, ___ 'cause when you close your heart ___ then you close your

Memory

from CATS

Music by Andrew Lloyd Webber
Text by Trevor Nunn after T.S. Eliot

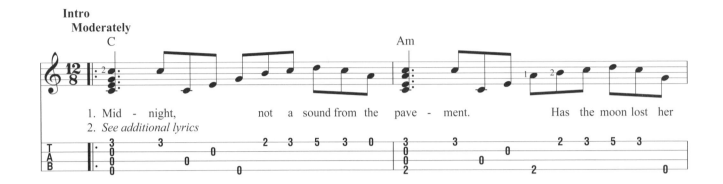

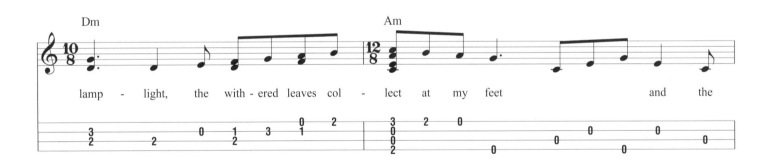

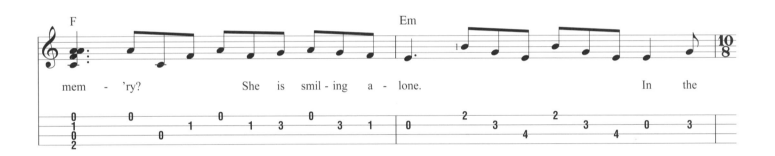

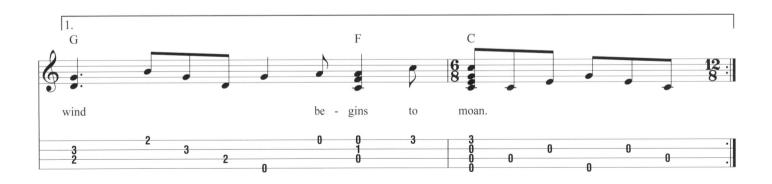

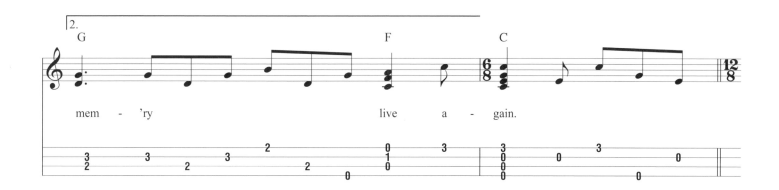

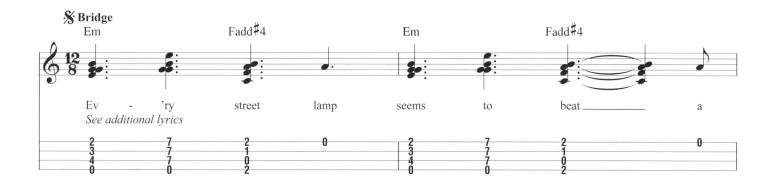

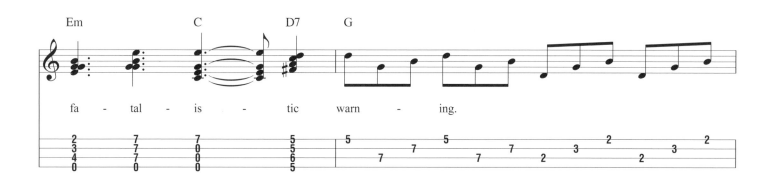

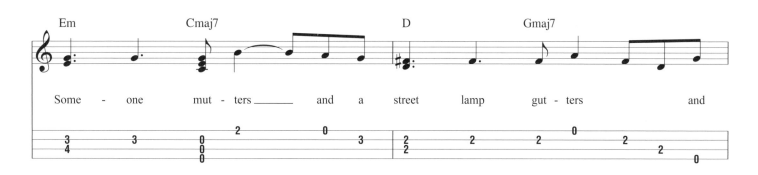

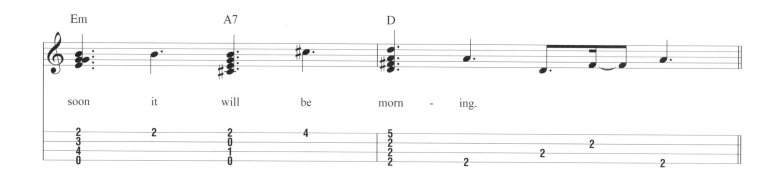

soon   it   will   be   morn - ing.

Verse

3. Day - light,   I   must wait for   the   sun - rise.   I   must think of a
4. *See additional lyrics*

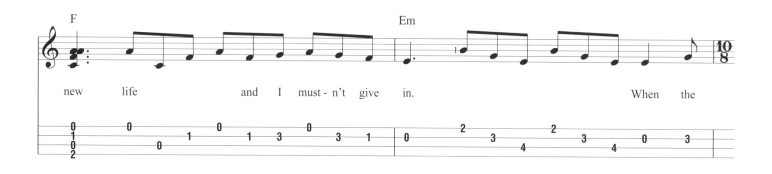

new   life   and   I   must - n't give   in.   When   the

To Coda

dawn   comes,   to - night will   be   a   mem - o - ry too,   and   the

new   day   will   be - gin.

Interlude

D.S. al Coda

Coda

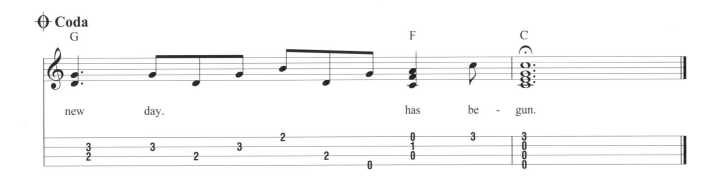

new   day.   has   be - gun.

Additional Lyrics

2. Mem'ry, all alone in the moonlight.
   I can smile at the old days.
   I was beautiful then.
   I remember the time I knew what happiness was.
   Let the mem'ry live again.

Bridge: Burnt-out ends of smoky days,
   The stale cold smell of morning.
   The street lamp dies, another night is over,
   Another day is dawning.

4. Touch me, it's so easy to leave me
   All alone with the mem'ry of my days in the sun.
   If you touch me, you'll understand what happiness is.
   Look, a new day has begun.

Moon River

from the Paramount Picture BREAKFAST AT TIFFANY'S

Words by Johnny Mercer
Music by Henry Mancini

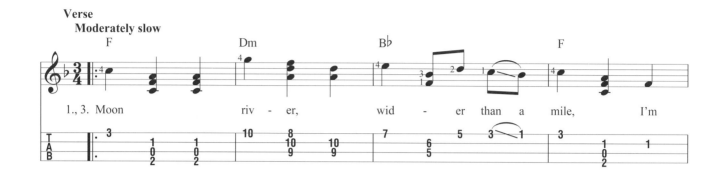

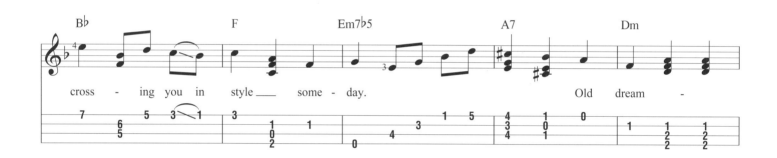

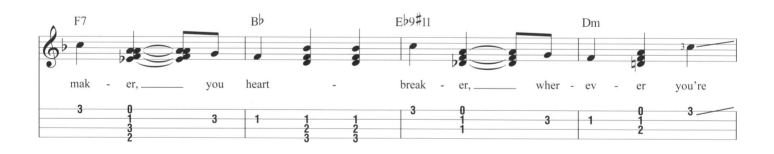

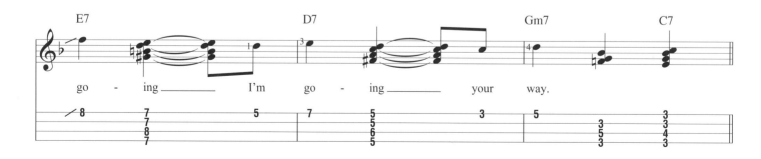

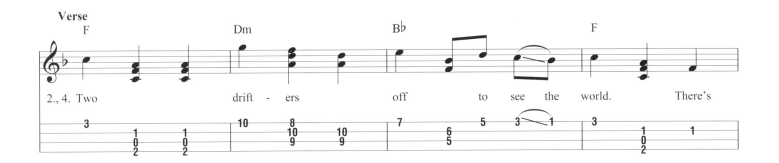

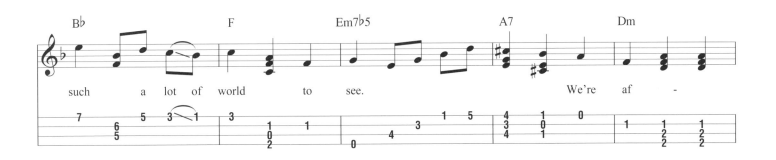

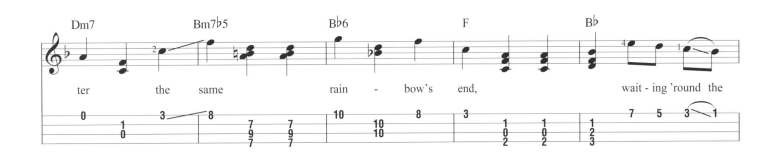

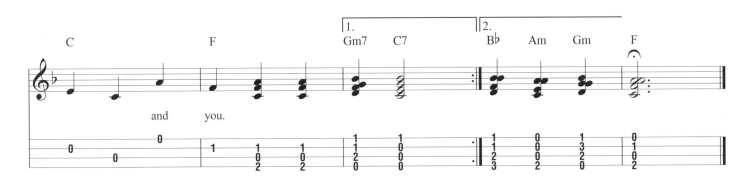

More
(Ti Guarderò Nel Cuore)

from the film MONDO CANE

Music by Nino Oliviero and Riz Ortolani
Italian Lyrics by Marcello Ciorciolini
English Lyrics by Norman Newell

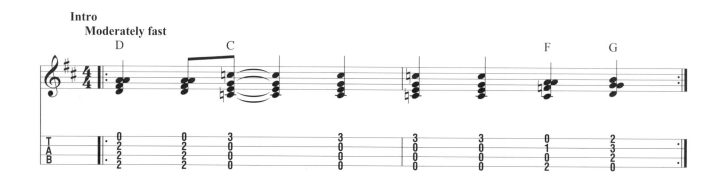

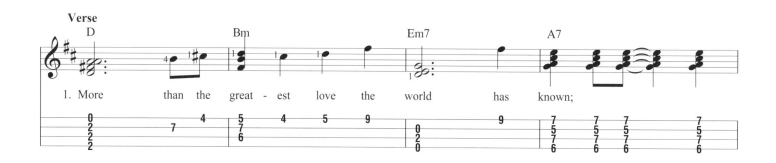

1. More than the great-est love the world has known;

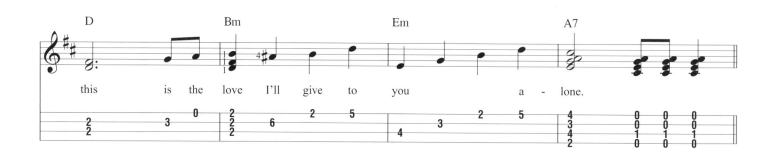

this is the love I'll give to you a - lone.

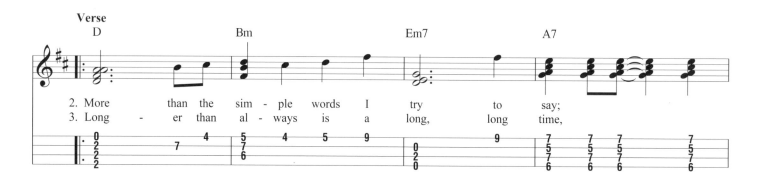

2. More than the sim-ple words I try to say;
3. Long - er than al - ways is a long, long time,

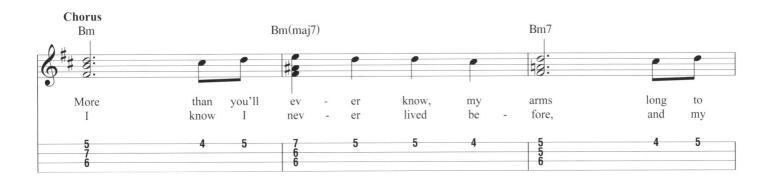

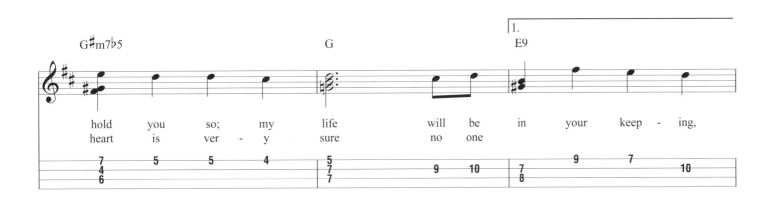

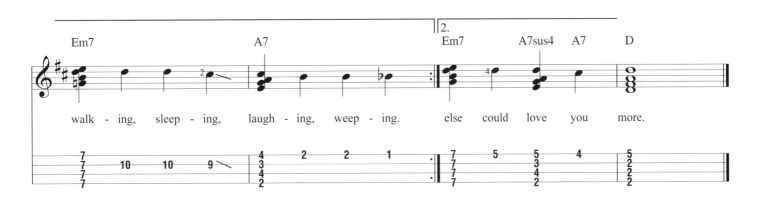

My Funny Valentine

from BABES IN ARMS
Words by Lorenz Hart
Music by Richard Rodgers

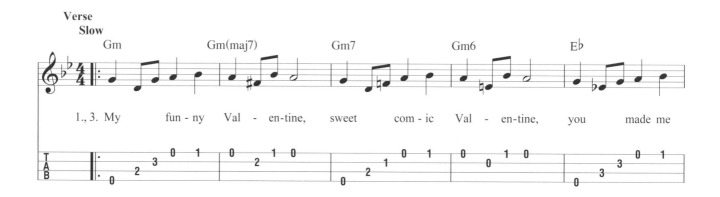

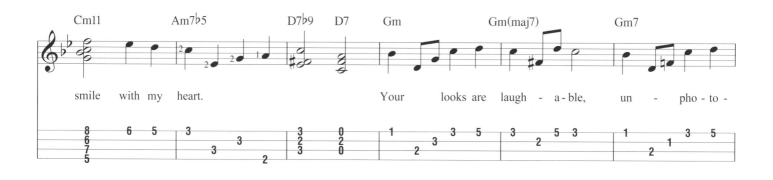

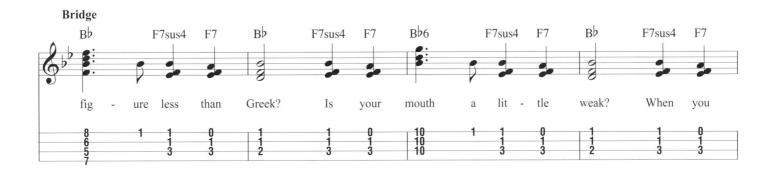

Bridge

fig - ure less than Greek? Is your mouth a lit - tle weak? When you

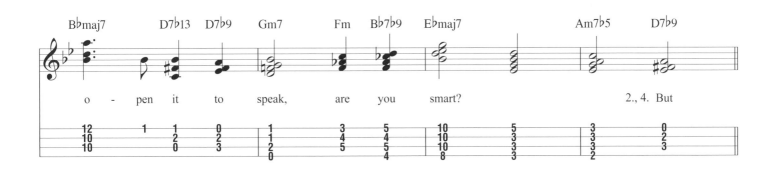

o - pen it to speak, are you smart? 2., 4. But

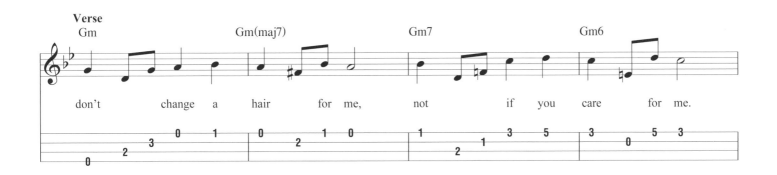

Verse

don't change a hair for me, not if you care for me.

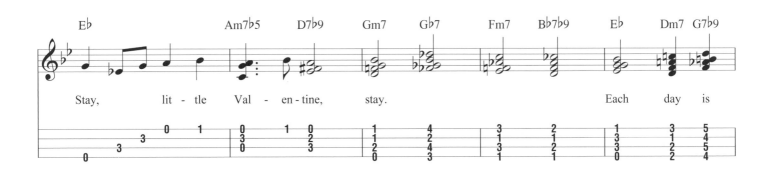

Stay, lit - tle Val - en - tine, stay. Each day is

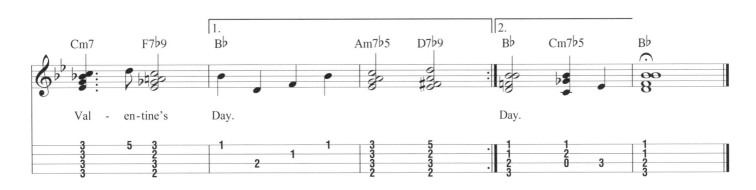

Val - en - tine's Day. Day.

Nuages

By Django Reinhardt

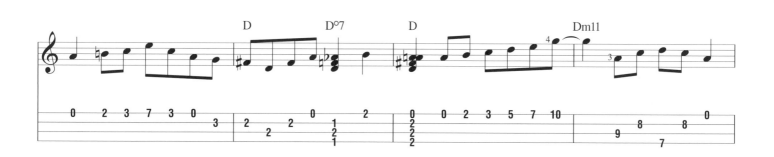

B

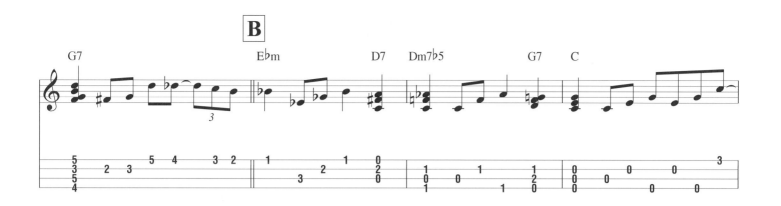

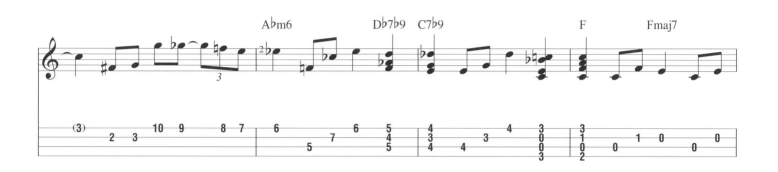

On the Wings of Love

Words and Music by Jeffrey Osborne and Peter Schless

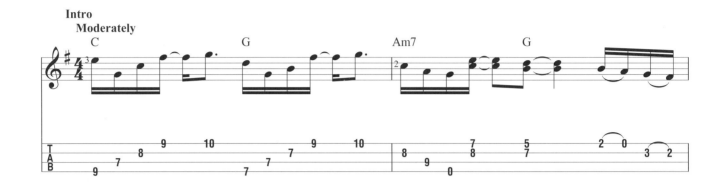

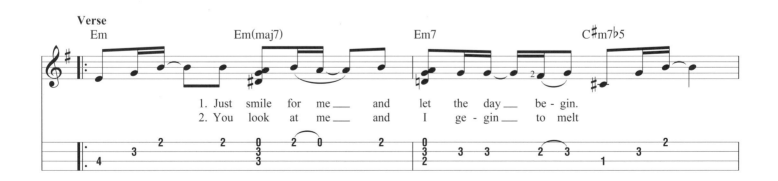

1. Just smile for me ___ and let the day ___ be - gin.
2. You look at me ___ and I ge - gin ___ to melt

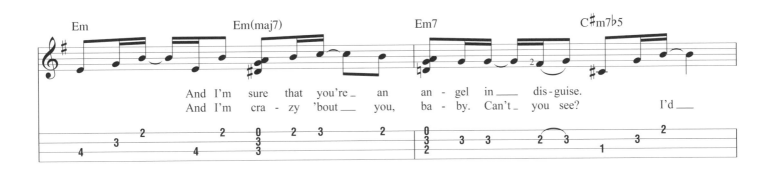

Chorus

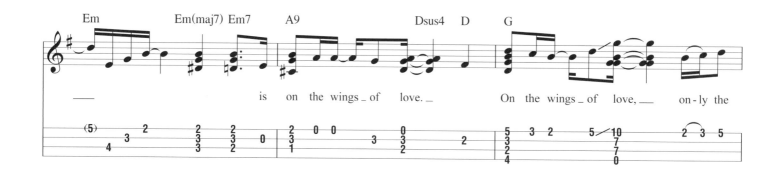

breathe each oth - er. In - sep - 'ra - ble, _ it seems we're flow - ing like _ a

D.S. al Coda

stream run - ning free, trav'l - ing on the wings _ of love. ____

$\oplus$ **Coda**

fly - ing high _ up - on _ the wings of love, ___

of love. _____ *rit.*

Only You (And You Alone)

Words and Music by Buck Ram and Ande Rand

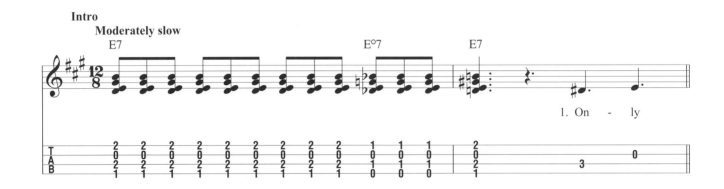

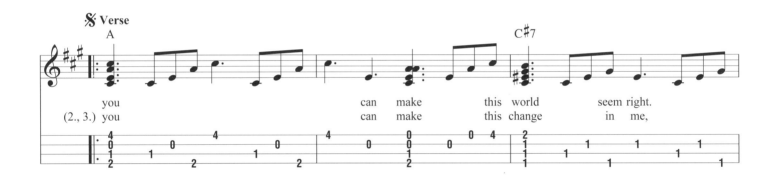

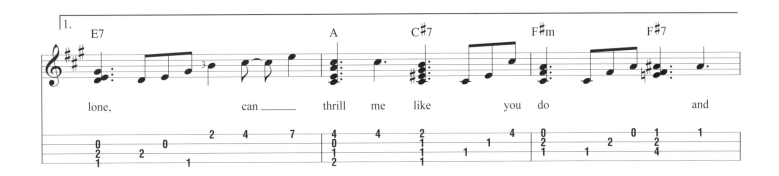

lone,   can _____ thrill   me   like   you   do   and

fill   my heart   with love   for on - ly   you. _____   2. Oh, on - ly

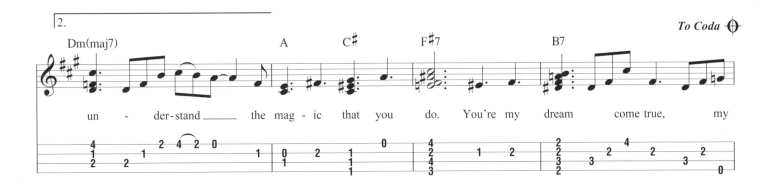

To Coda ⊕

un   -   der-stand _____ the mag - ic   that   you   do.   You're my   dream   come true,   my

D.S. al Coda
(take 2nd ending)

one   and on - ly   you. _____   3. Oh, oh,   on - ly

⊕ **Coda**

Freely

one   and on - ly   you.   One and _ on - ly _____ you.

Over the Rainbow

from THE WIZARD OF OZ

Music by Harold Arlen
Lyric by E.Y. "Yip" Harburg

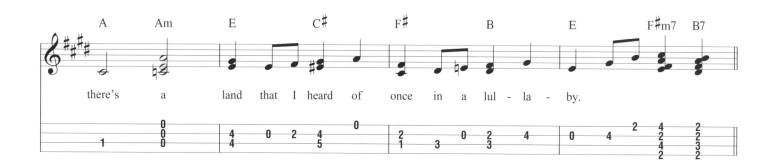

Bridge

day I'll wish up-on a star and wake up where the clouds are far be-hind me. Where

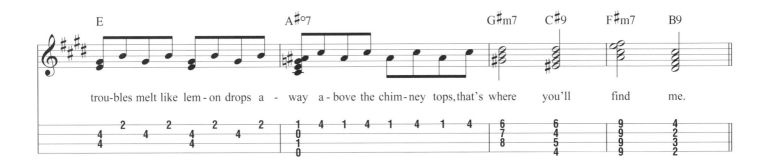

trou-bles melt like lem-on drops a - way a-bove the chim-ney tops, that's where you'll find me.

Verse

3. Some - where o - ver the rain - bow blue - birds fly.

Birds fly o - ver the rain - bow, why then, oh why can't I? If

Outro

hap-py lit-tle blue-birds fly be-yond the rain-bow why, oh why can't I?

The Power of Love

Words by Mary Susan Applegate and Jennifer Rush
Music by Candy Derouge and Gunther Mende

1. The whis-pers in the morn-ing of lov-ers sleep-ing tight
2. *See additional lyrics*

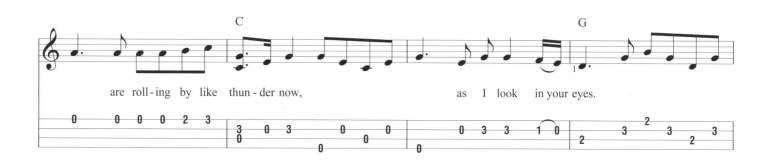

are roll-ing by like thun-der now, as I look in your eyes.

I hold on to your bod-y ___ and feel each move you make.

Your voice is warm and ten-der, a love that I could not for-sake.

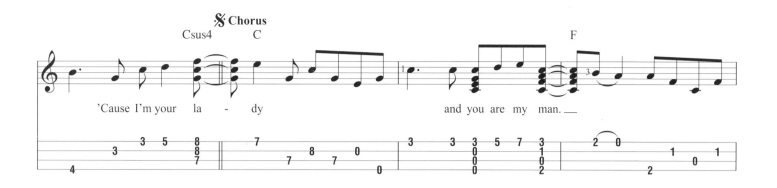

§ **Chorus**

'Cause I'm your la - dy and you are my man.

When-ev - er you reach __ for me, I'll do all that I can. ___

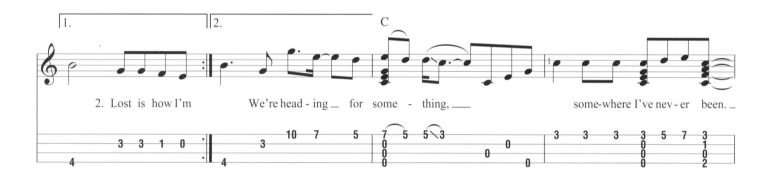

1. 2.

2. Lost is how I'm We're head - ing __ for some - thing, ___ some-where I've nev - er been. __

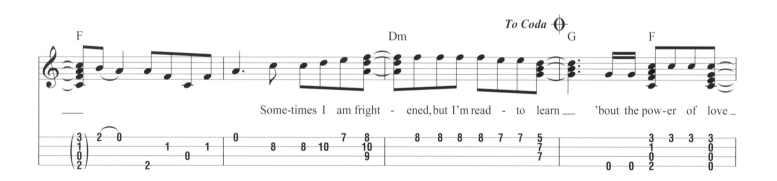

To Coda

Some-times I am fright - ened, but I'm read - to learn __ 'bout the pow-er of love __

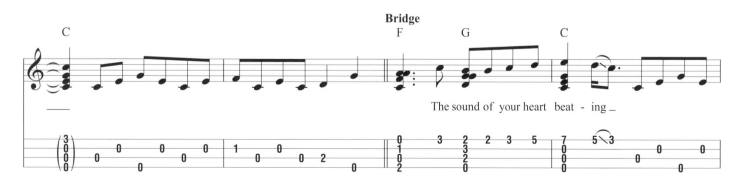

Bridge

The sound of your heart beat - ing __

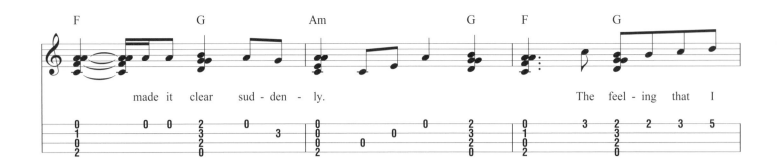

Coda

D.S. al Coda
(take 2nd ending)

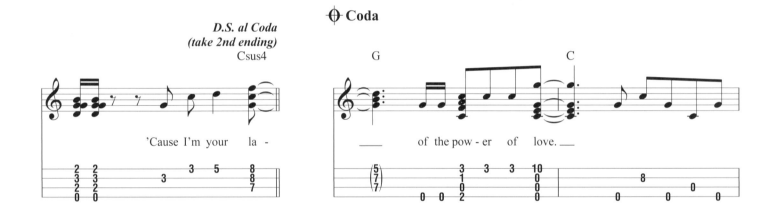

Outro

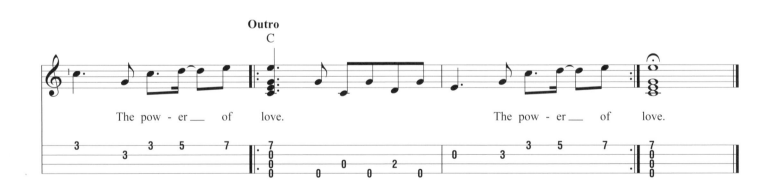

Additional Lyrics

2. Lost is how I'm feeling, lying in your arms.
   When the world that sends too much to take,
   That all ends when I'm with you.
   Even though there may be times
   It seems I'm far away,
   Never wonder where I am
   'Cause I am always by your side.

Ribbon in the Sky

Words and Music by Stevie Wonder

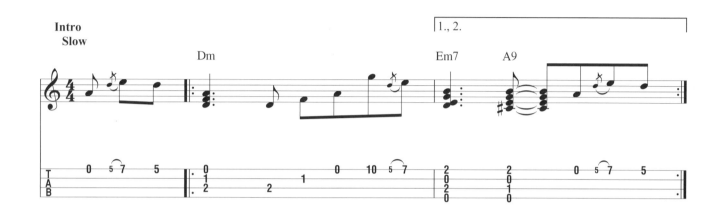

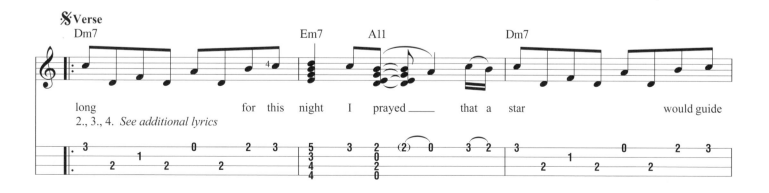

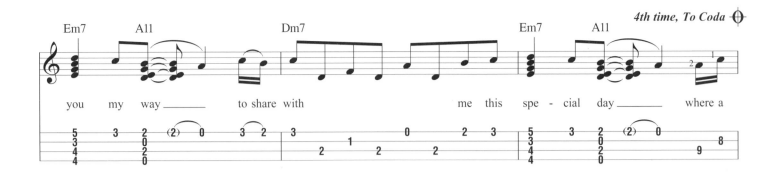

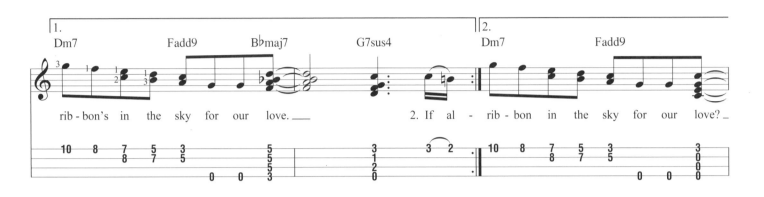

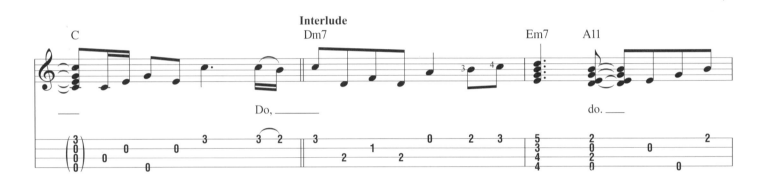

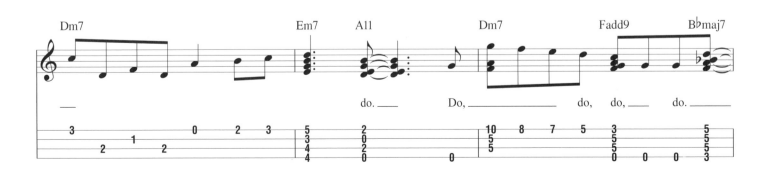

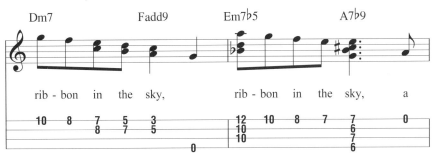

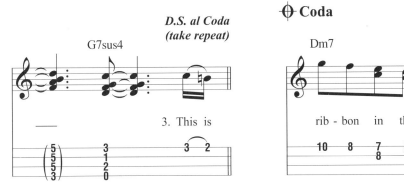

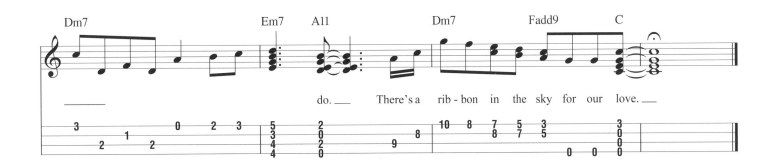

Additional Lyrics

2. If allowed, may I touch your hand;
And if pleased, may I once gain,
So that you too will understand
There's a ribbon in the sky for our love?

3. This is not a coincidence,
And far more than a lucky chance,
But what is that was always meant
Is our ribbon in the sky for our love.

4. Love, we can't lose with God on our side.
We'll find strength in each tear we cry.
From now on it will be you and I
And our...

Reason to Believe

Words and Music by Tim Hardin

Verse
Moderately, in 2

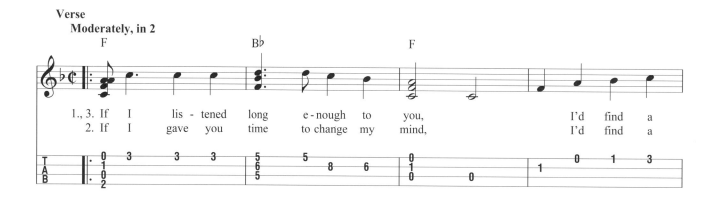

1., 3. If I lis - tened long e - nough to you, I'd find a
2. If I gave you time to change my mind, I'd find a

way to be - lieve that it's all true,
way just to leave the past be - hind,

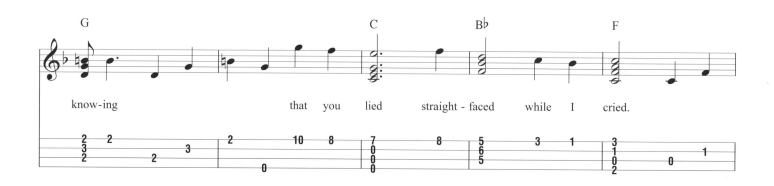

know-ing that you lied straight - faced while I cried.

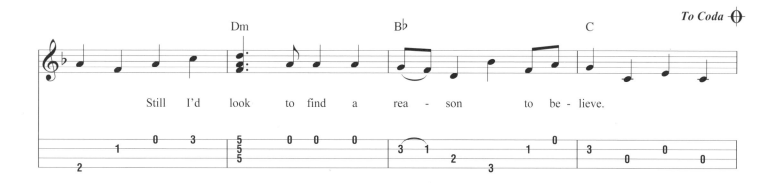

Still I'd look to find a rea - son to be - lieve.

Chorus

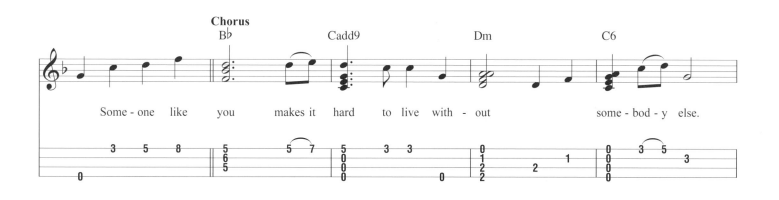

Some - one like you makes it hard to live with - out some - bod - y else.

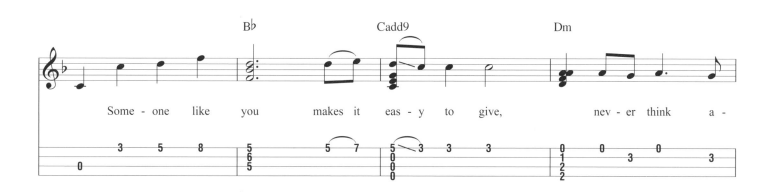

Some - one like you makes it eas - y to give, nev - er think a -

2nd time, D.C. al Coda

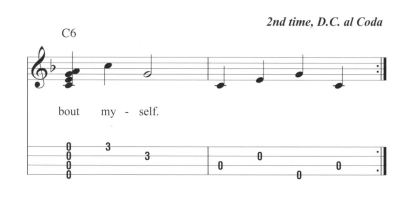

bout my - self.

⊕ Coda

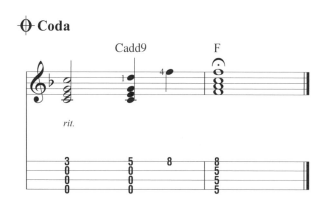

rit.

Sailing

Words and Music by Christopher Cross

Intro
Moderately slow, in 2

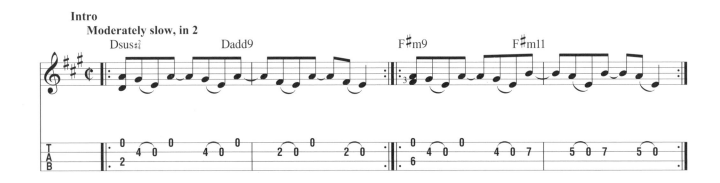

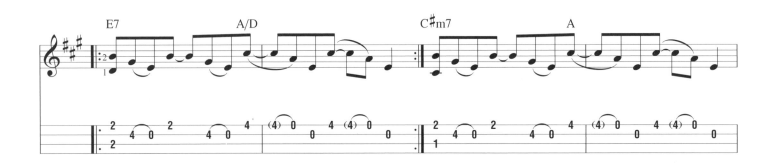

1. Well, it's not ___ far down ___ to par - a - dise, at
2., 3. *See additional lyrics*

least it's not ___ for me, ___ and if the wind ___ is right ___ you can sail ___ a - way ___ and

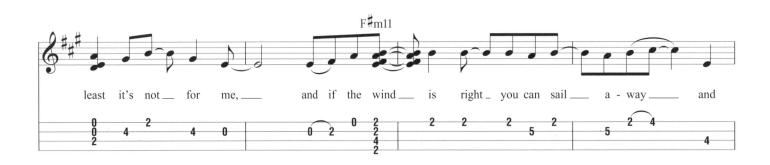

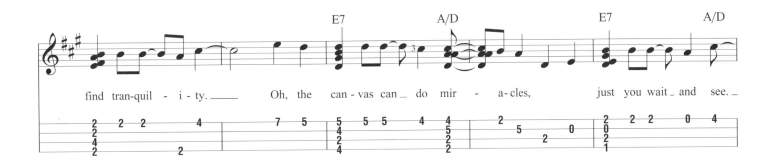

find tran-quil - i - ty.___ Oh, the can-vas can_ do mir - a-cles, just you wait_ and see.___

___ Be - lieve___ me.___

2. It's_ not far___

Sail - ing___ takes me a - way___ to where___ I've al - ways

heard it___ could be.___ Just a dream_

___ and the wind_ to car - ry me,_ and soon I will_ be free.___

Bridge

To Coda 1 ⊕

To Coda 2 ⊕

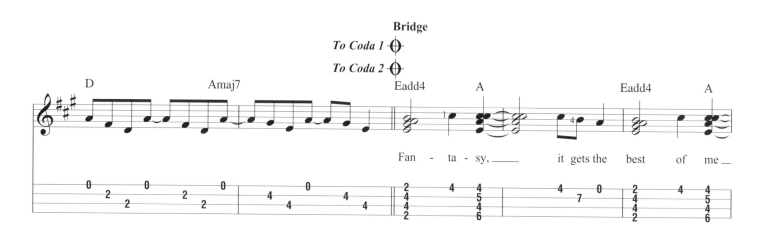

Fan - ta - sy, _____ it gets the best of me _____

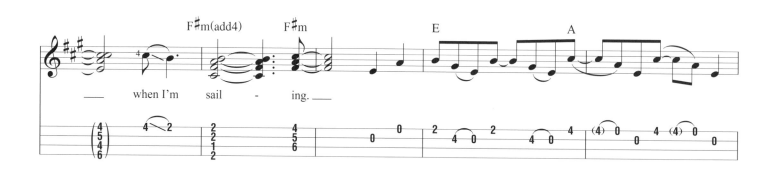

_____ when I'm sail - ing. _____

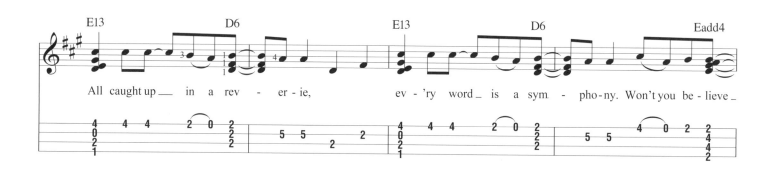

All caught up _____ in a rev - er - ie, ev - 'ry word _ is a sym - pho - ny. Won't you be - lieve

D.S. al Coda 1

_____ me?

⊕ **Coda 1**

Interlude

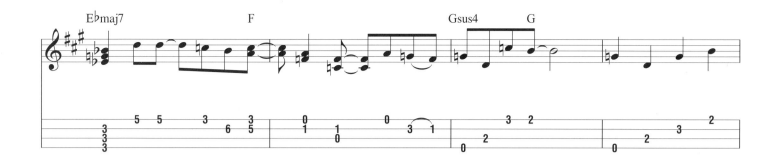

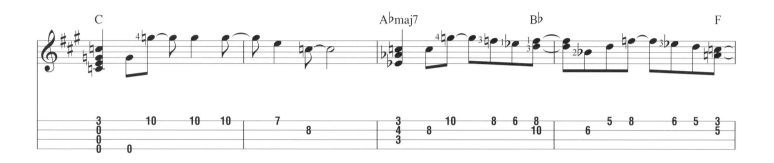

3. Well, it's   not ___

⊕ Coda 2
Outro

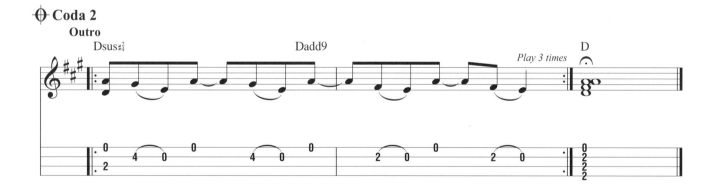

Additional Lyrics

2. It's not far to never-neverland, no reason to pretend,
   And if the wind is right you can find the joy of innocence again.
   Oh, the canvas can do miracles, just you wait and see.
   Believe me.

3. Well, it's not far back to sanity, at least it's not for me.
   And if the wind is right you can sail away and find serenity.
   Oh, the canvas can do miracles, just you wait and see.
   Believe me.

Save the Best for Last

Words and Music by Wendy Waldman, Phil Galdston and Jon Lind

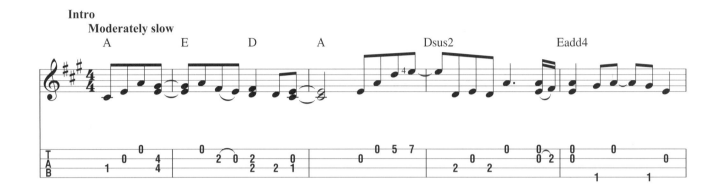

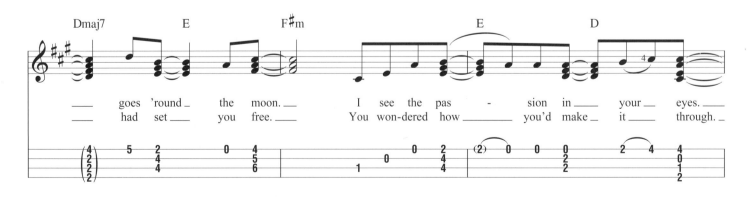

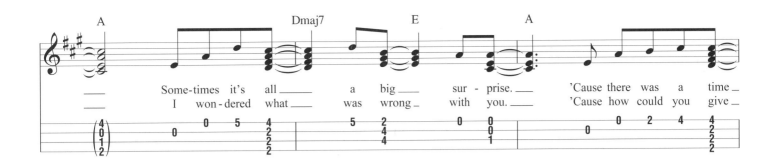

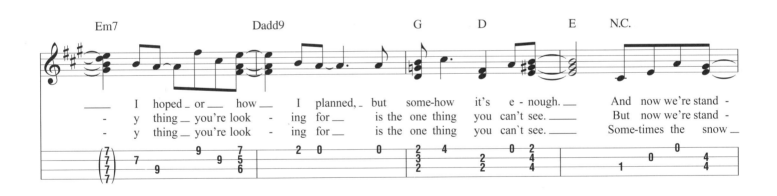

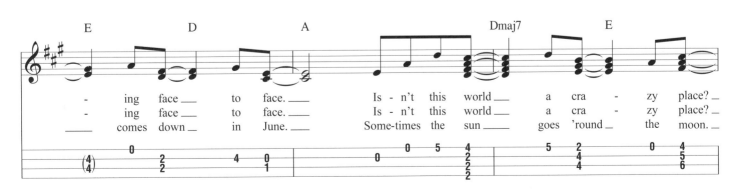

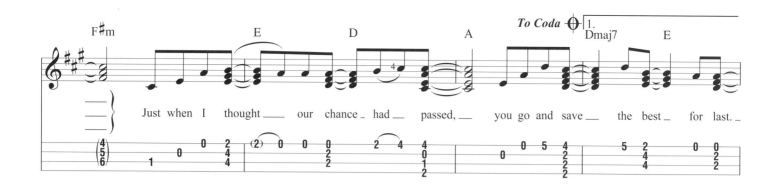

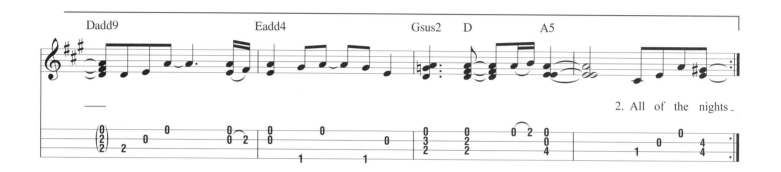

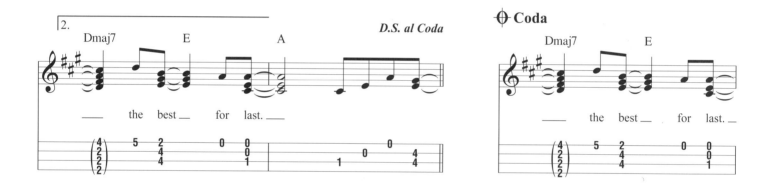

The Song Is You

from MUSIC IN THE AIR

Lyrics by Oscar Hammerstein II
Music by Jerome Kern

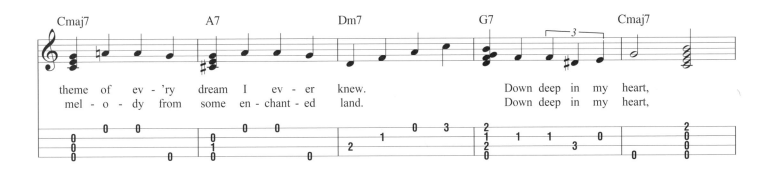

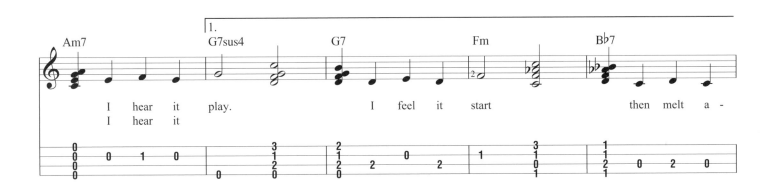

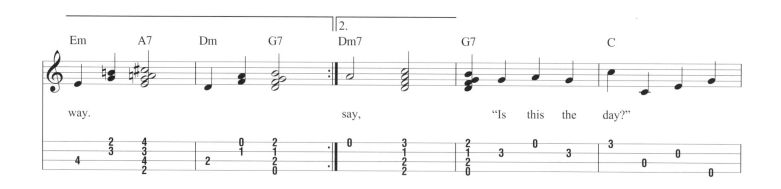

way.   say,   "Is this the day?"

Bridge

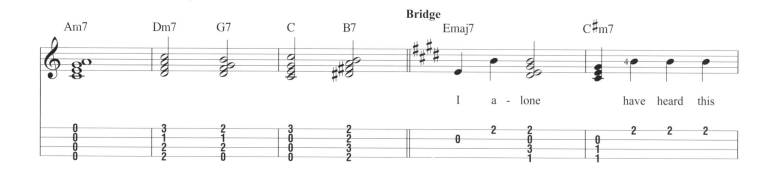

I a - lone   have heard this

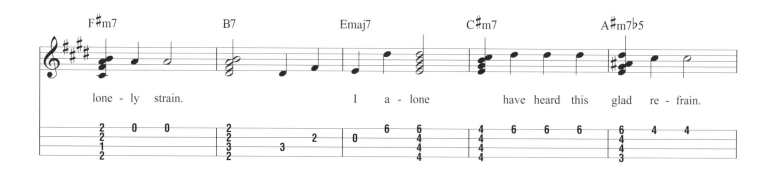

lone - ly strain.   I a - lone   have heard this glad re - frain.

Must it be   for ev - er in - side of me?   Why can't I

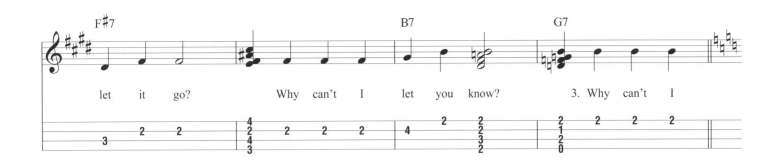

let it go? Why can't I let you know? 3. Why can't I

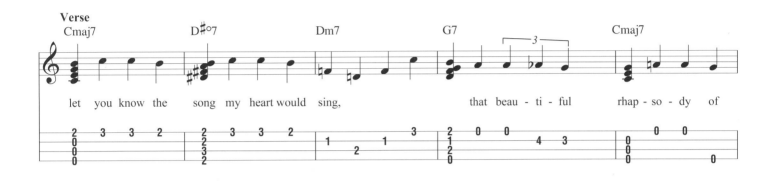

Verse

let you know the song my heart would sing, that beau - ti - ful rhap - so - dy of

love and youth and spring? The mu - sic is sweet,

the words are true, the song is you.

Smoke Gets in Your Eyes

from ROBERTA

Words by Otto Harbach
Music by Jerome Kern

1. They asked me how I knew my true love was true.
2. They said some-day you'll find all who love are blind.

I of course re-plied,
When your heart's on fire,

"Some-thing here in-side,
you must re-al-ize,

can-not be de-
smoke gets in your

nied."

eyes.

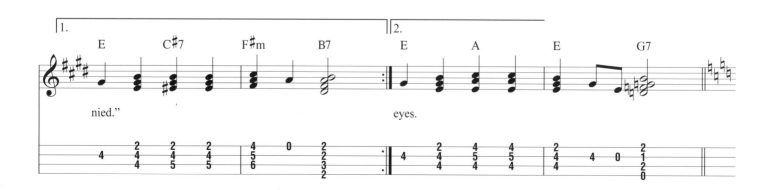

Bridge

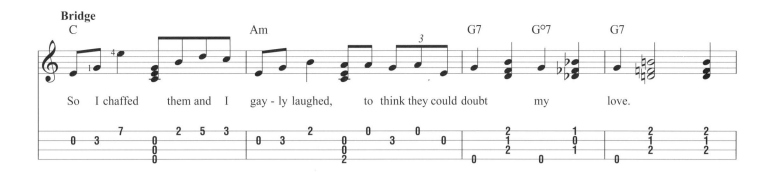

So I chaffed them and I gay - ly laughed, to think they could doubt my love.

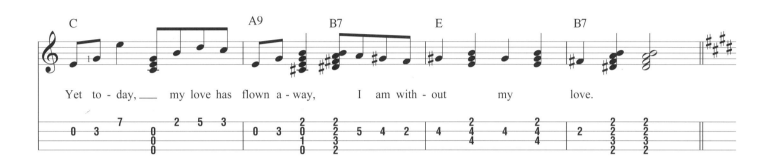

Yet to - day, ___ my love has flown a - way, I am with - out my love.

Verse

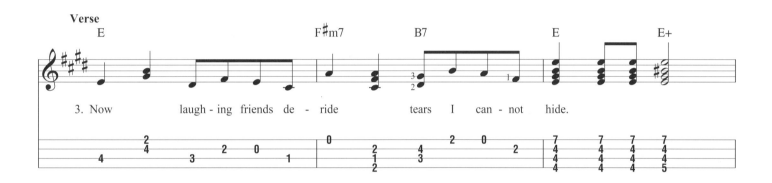

3. Now laugh - ing friends de - ride tears I can - not hide.

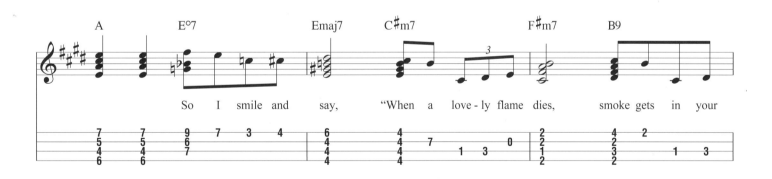

So I smile and say, "When a love - ly flame dies, smoke gets in your

Very slow

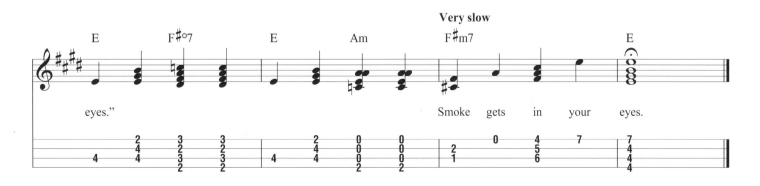

eyes." Smoke gets in your eyes.

Someone Like You

Words and Music by Van Morrison

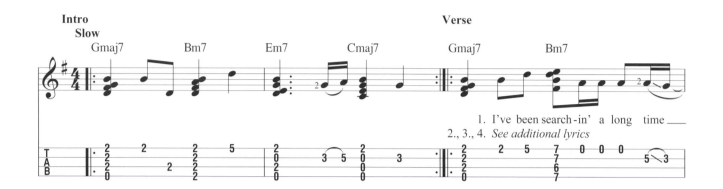

1. I've been search-in' a long time ___
2., 3., 4. *See additional lyrics*

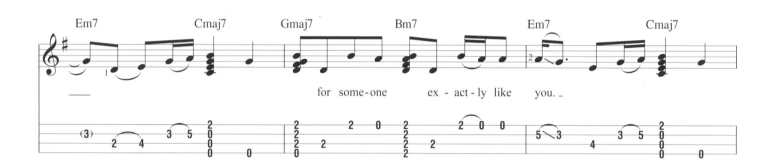

for some-one ex - act - ly like you. _

I've been trav -'lin' all ___ a - round the world _   wait-in' for you _____ to come through. _

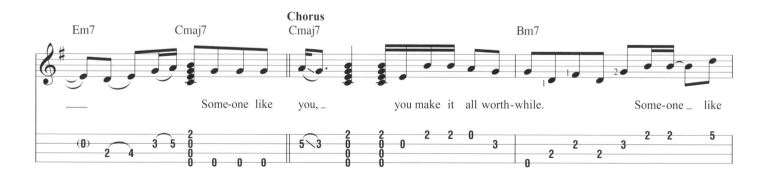

Some-one like you, _   you make it all worth-while.   Some-one _ like

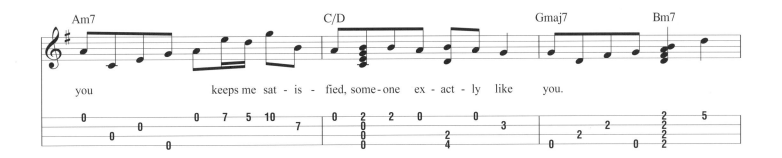

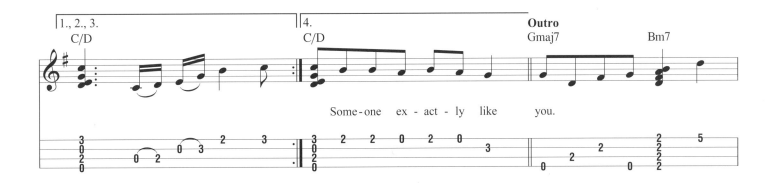

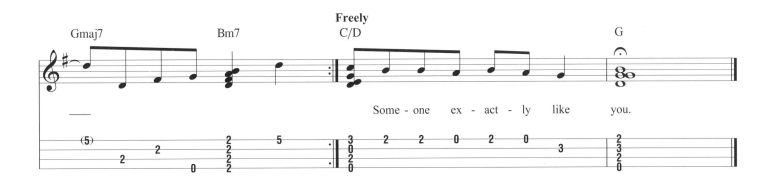

Additional Lyrics

2. I've been trav'lin' a hard road.
   Yeah, I've been lookin' for someone exactly like you.
   I've been carryin' my heavy load,
   Waitin' for the light to come shinin' through.

3. I've been doin' some soul-searchin'
   To find out where you're at.
   I've been lookin' down the highway
   And all kinds of foreign land.

4. I've been all around the world
   Marching to the beat of a diff'rent drum.
   But just lately I have realized,
   Baby, the best is yet to come.

Spanish Eyes

Words by Charles Singleton and Eddie Snyder
Music by Bert Kaempfert

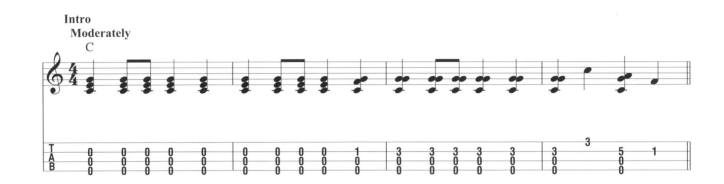

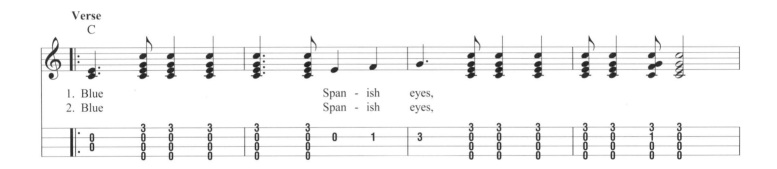

213

Stardust

Words by Mitchell Parish
Music by Hoagy Carmichael

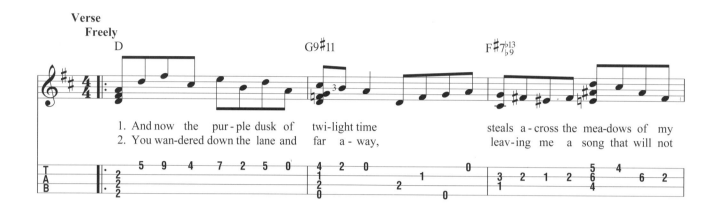

1. And now the pur-ple dusk of twi-light time   steals a-cross the mea-dows of my
2. You wan-dered down the lane and far a-way,   leav-ing me a song that will not

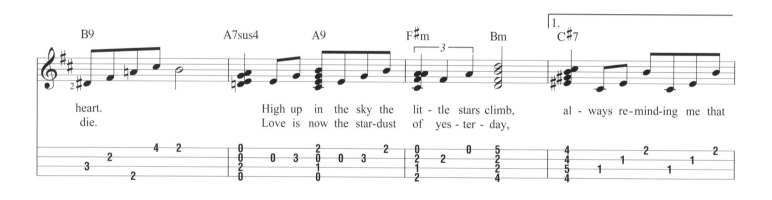

heart.   High up in the sky the lit-tle stars climb, al-ways re-mind-ing me that
die.   Love is now the star-dust of yes-ter-day,

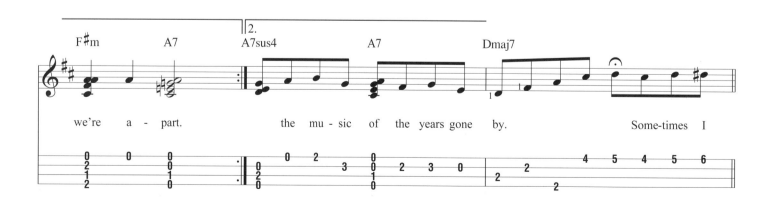

we're a-part.   the mu-sic of the years gone by.   Some-times I

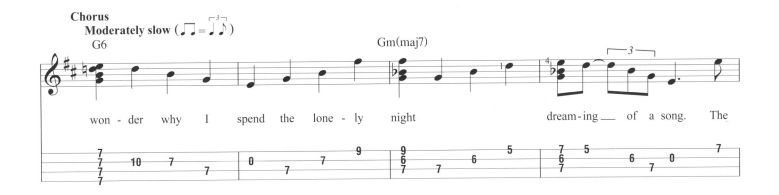

won-der why I spend the lone-ly night dream-ing___ of a song. The

mel - o - dy ___ haunts my ___ rev-er-ie, and I am once a-gain with you when our

love was new, ___ and each kiss an in-spir - a - tion. But

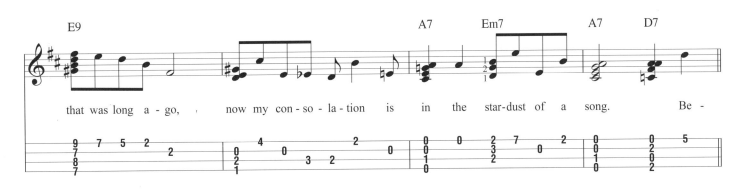

that was long a - go, now my con-so-la-tion is in the star-dust of a song. Be -

Chorus

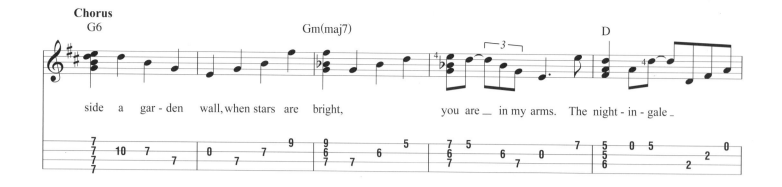

side a gar-den wall, when stars are bright, you are __ in my arms. The night-in-gale __

tells his __ fair-y tale of par-a-dise where ros-es grow. Though I

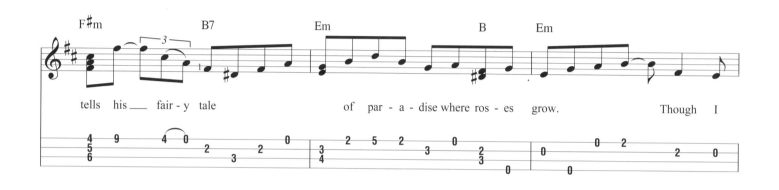

dream in vain, __ in my heart it will re-main: my

star-dust mel-o-dy, the mem-o-ry of love's re-frain.

Strangers in the Night

adapted from A MAN COULD GET KILLED

Words by Charles Singleton and Eddie Snyder
Music by Bert Kaempfert

Intro
Moderately slow

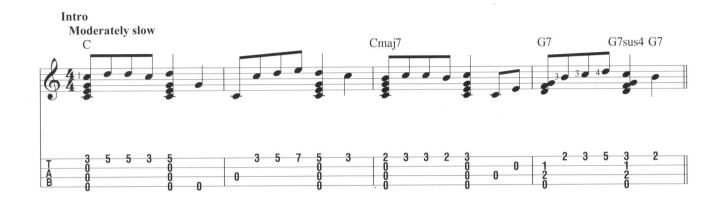

Verse

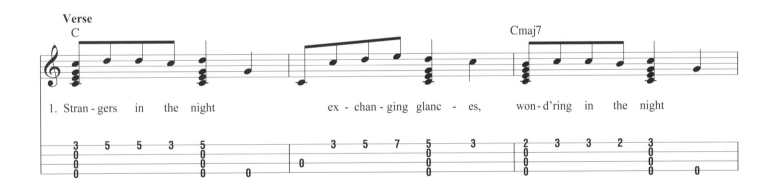

1. Stran - gers in the night ex - chan - ging glanc - es, won - d'ring in the night

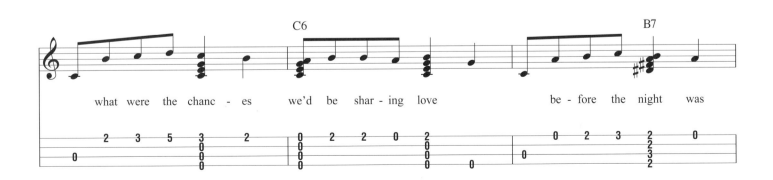

what were the chanc - es we'd be shar - ing love be - fore the night was

through.   Some-thing in your eyes   was so in - vit - ing,

some-thing in your smile   was so ex - cit - ing, some-thing in my heart

told me I must have you.   Stran-gers in the night,

two lone - ly peo - ple, we were stran-gers in the night   up to the mo - ment when we

said our first hel - lo.   Lit - tle did we know   love was just a glance a - way, a

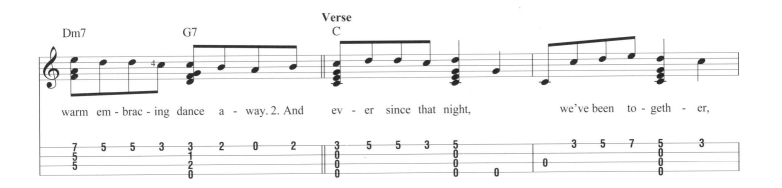

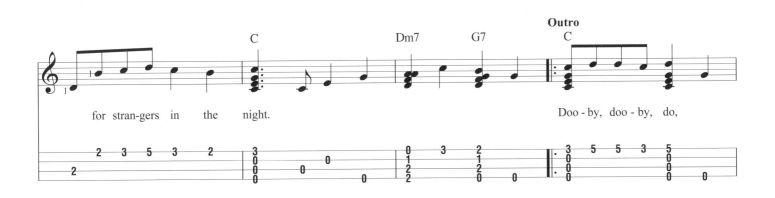

Sunny

Words and Music by Bobby Hebb

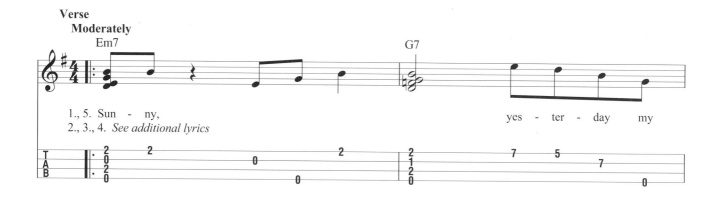

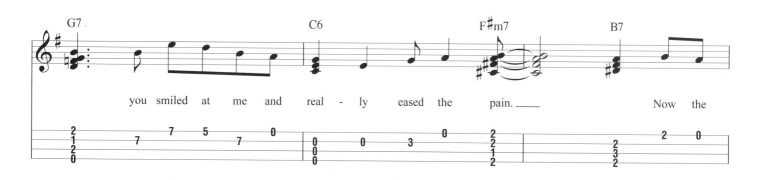

dark dys are done ___ and the bright days are here. ___ My sun - ny one ___ shines

so sin - cere. Sun - ny one so true, ___ I love

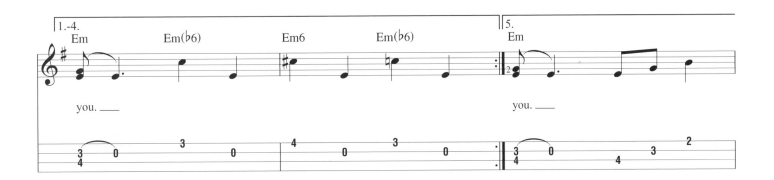

you. ___ you. ___

Outro

Repeat and fade

I love you. ___ I love

Additional Lyrics

2. Sunny, thank you for the sunshine bouquet.
   Sunny, thank you for the love you've brought my way.
   You gave to me your all and all,
   And now I feel ten feet tall.
   Sunny one so true, I love you.

3. Sunny, thank you for the truth you let me see.
   Sunny, thank you for the facts from A to Z.
   My live was torn like wind-blown sand,
   Then a rock was formed when we held hands.
   Sunny one so true, I love you.

4. Sunny, thank you for that smile upon your face.
   Sunny, thank you, thank you for that gleam that flows with grace.
   You're my spark of nature's fire;
   You're my sweet complete desire.
   Sunny one so true, I love you.

Tears in Heaven

Words and Music by Eric Clapton and Will Jennings

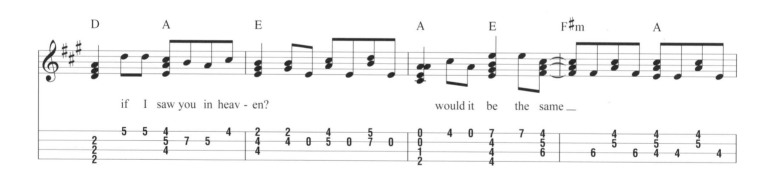

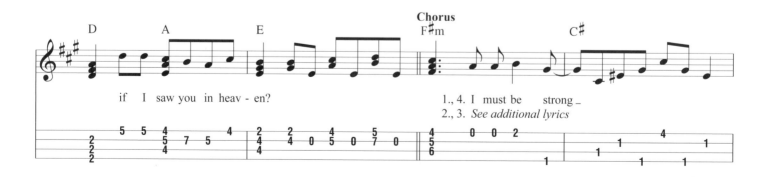

Tenderly

from TORCH SONG

Lyric by Jack Lawrence
Music by Walter Gross

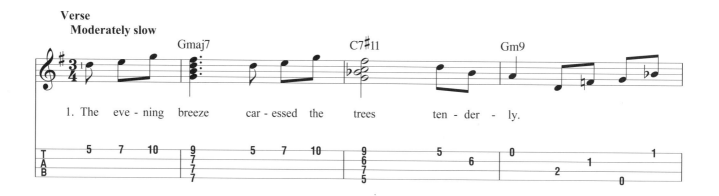

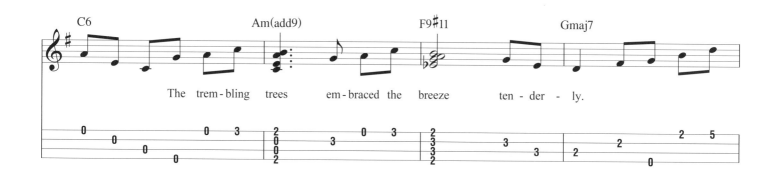

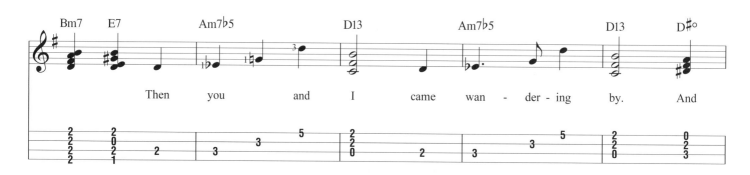

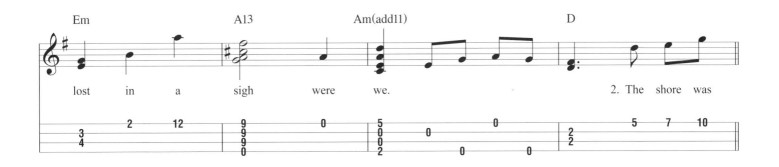

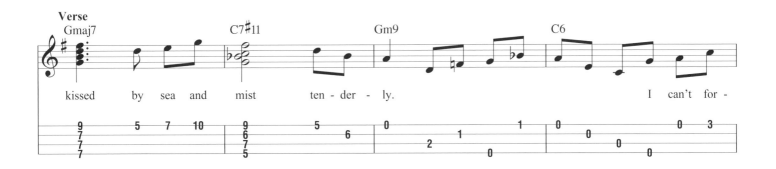

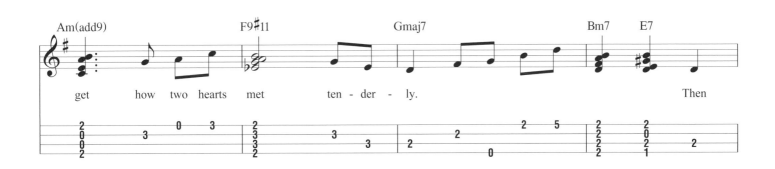

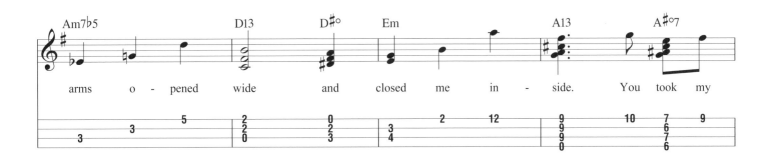

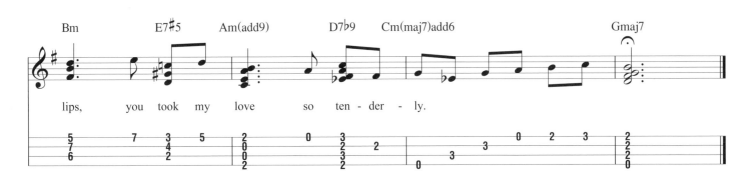

Through the Years

Words and Music by Steve Dorff and Marty Panzer

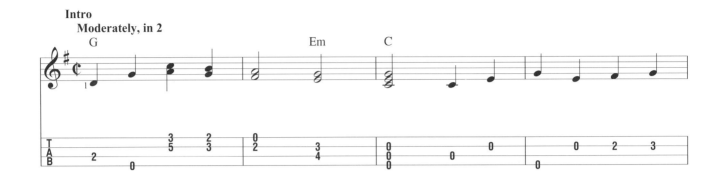

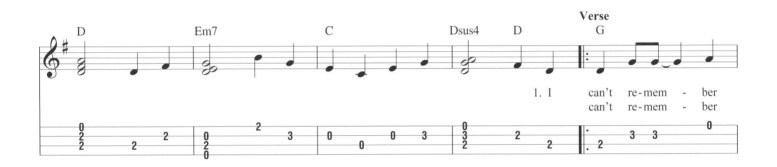

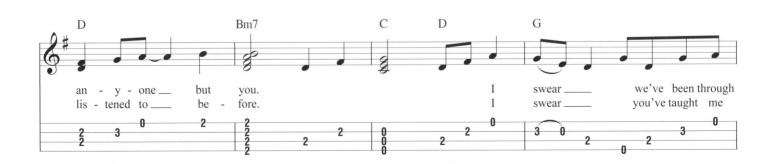

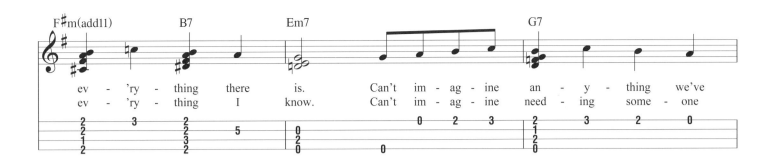

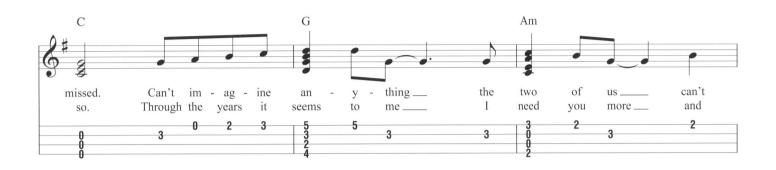

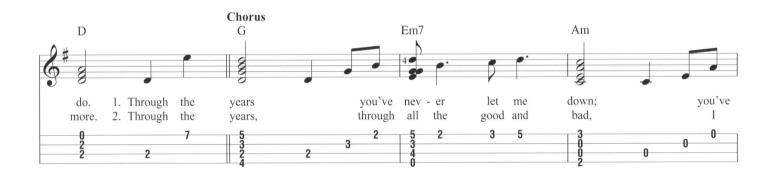

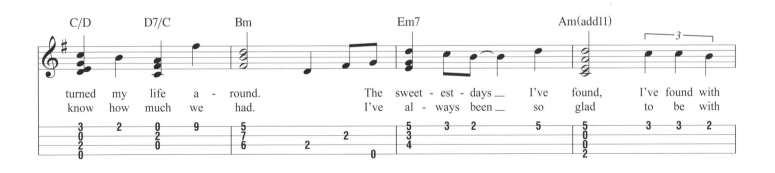

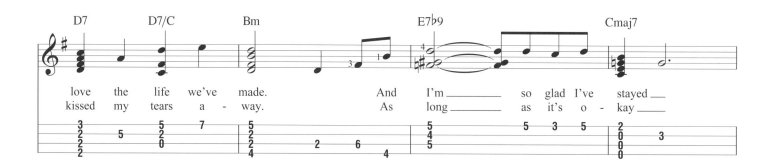

love the life we've made. And I'm _____ so glad I've stayed _____

kissed my tears a - way. As long _____ as it's o - kay _____

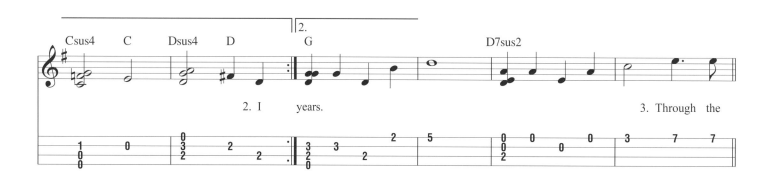

right here with you through the years.

I'll stay with you through the

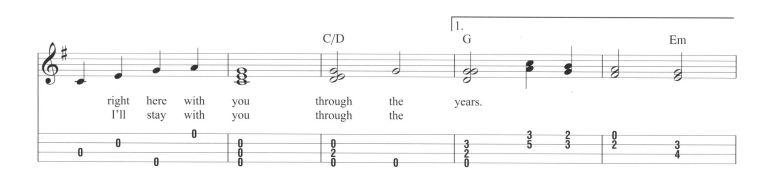

2. I years.

3. Through the

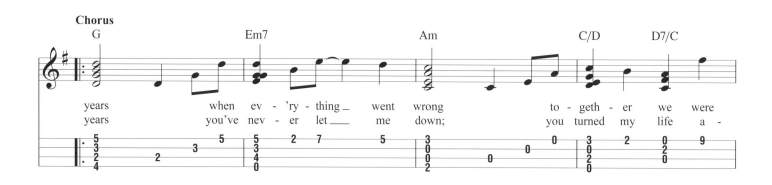

Chorus

years when ev - 'ry - thing_ went wrong to - geth - er we were

years you've nev - er let _____ me down; you turned my life a -

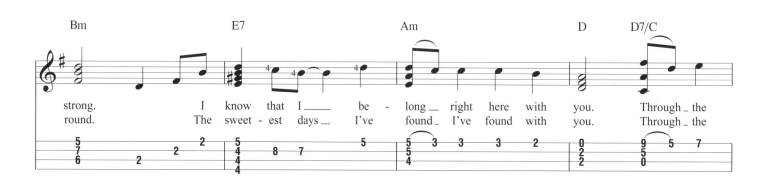

strong. I know that I _____ be - long_ right here with you. Through _ the

round. The sweet - est days_ I've found_ I've found with you. Through _ the

years   I   nev - er had a doubt   we'd al - ways work things

years   it's bet - ter ev - 'ry day,   you've kissed my tears a -

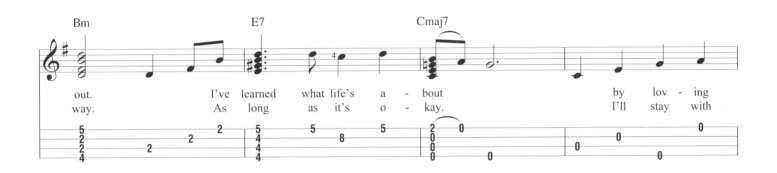

out.   I've learned what life's a - bout   by lov - ing

way.   As long as it's o - kay.   I'll stay with

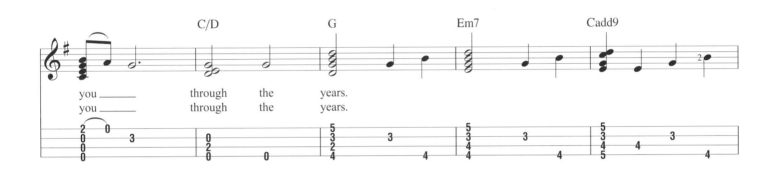

you &rule; through the   years.

you &rule; through the   years.

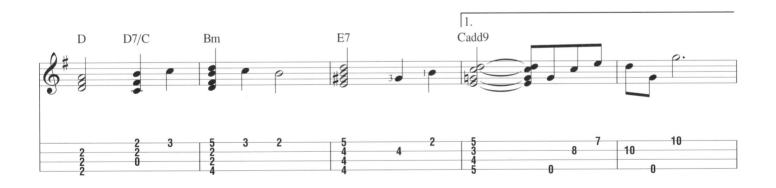

1.

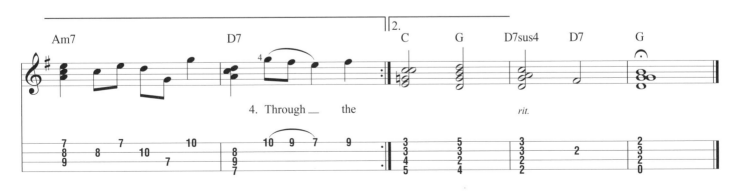

2.

4. Through &rule; the   *rit.*

Till There Was You

from Meredith Willson's THE MUSIC MAN

By Meredith Willson

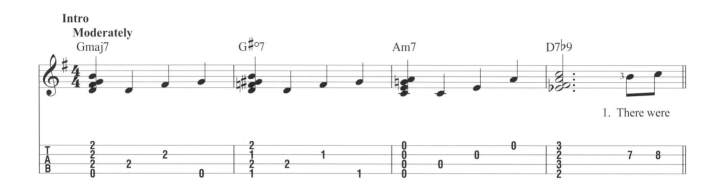

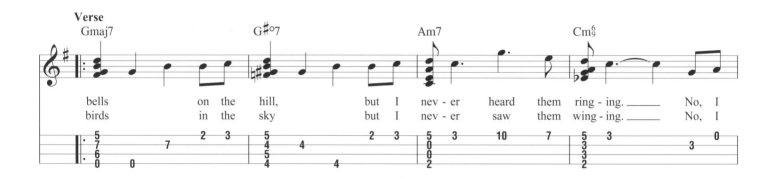

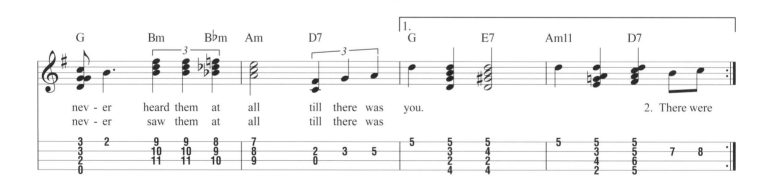

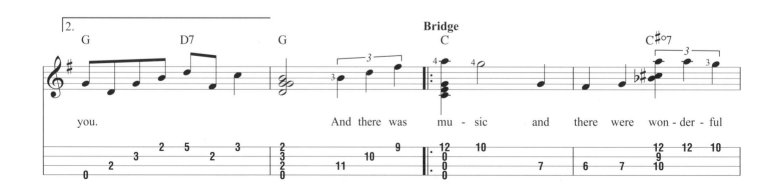

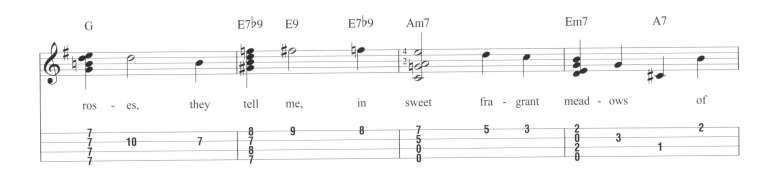

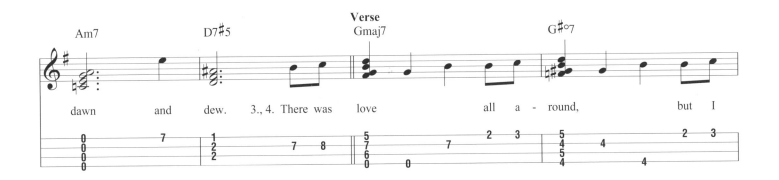

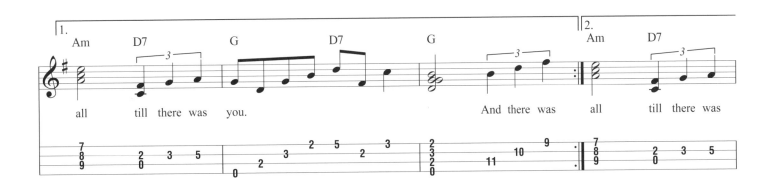

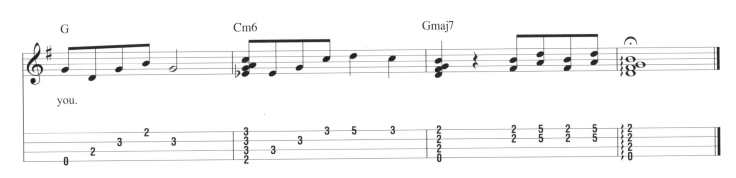

Time After Time

Words and Music by Cyndi Lauper and Rob Hyman

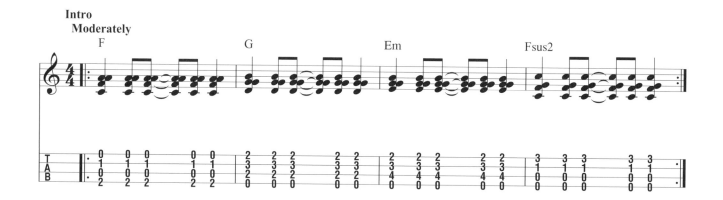

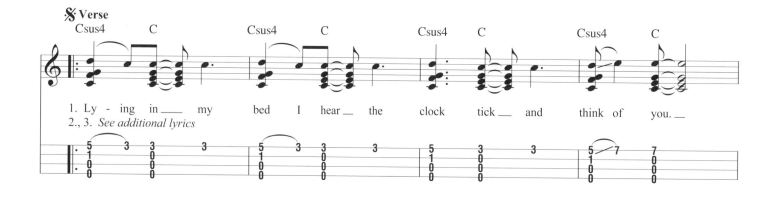

1. Ly - ing in my bed I hear the clock tick and think of you.
2., 3. *See additional lyrics*

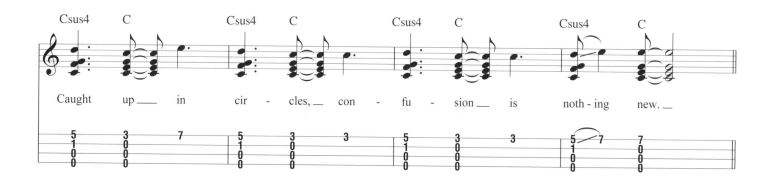

Caught up in cir - cles, con - fu - sion is noth - ing new.

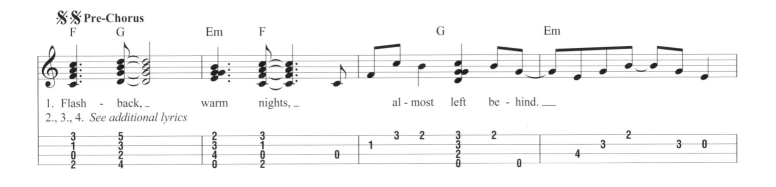

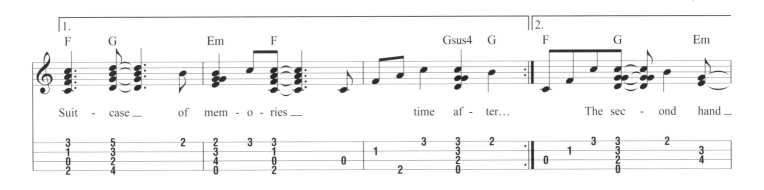

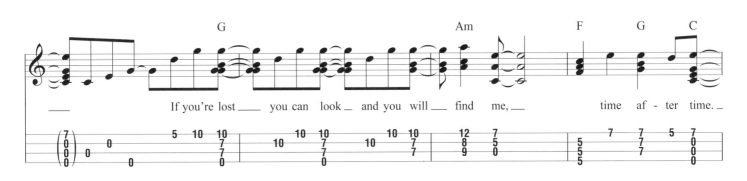

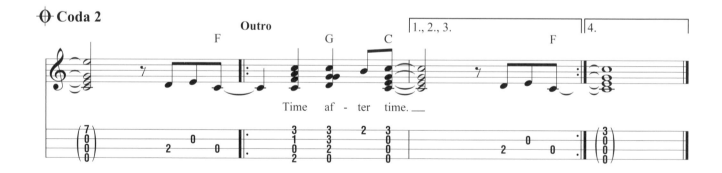

Additional Lyrics

2. Sometimes you picture me; I'm walking too far ahead.
   You're calling to me; I can't hear what you've said.

Pre-Chorus 2   Then you say, "Go slow," I fall behind.
   The second hand unwinds.

3. After my picture fades; and darkness has turned to gray.
   Watching through window, you're wondering if I'm okay.

Pre-Chorus 3   Secrets stolen from deep inside.
   The drum beats out of time.

Pre-Chorus 4   Then you say, "Go slow," I fall behind.
   The second hand unwinds.

Time to Say Goodbye

Words by Lucio Quarantotto and Frank Peterson
Music by Francesco Sartori

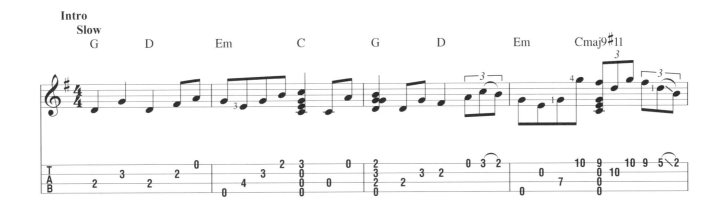

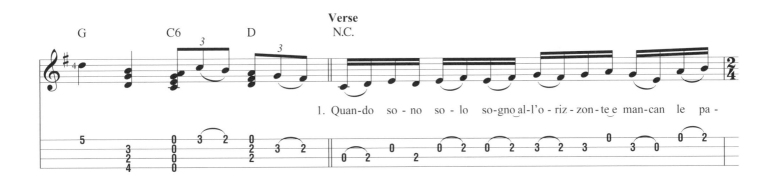

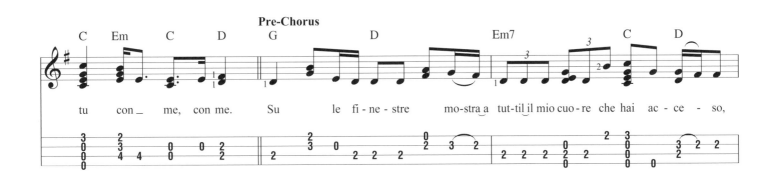

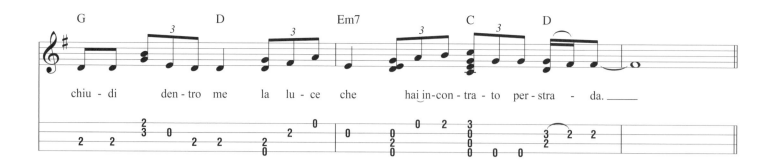

chiu - di   den - tro me   la   lu - ce   che   hai in-con - tra - to per-stra - da. ____

𝄋 Chorus

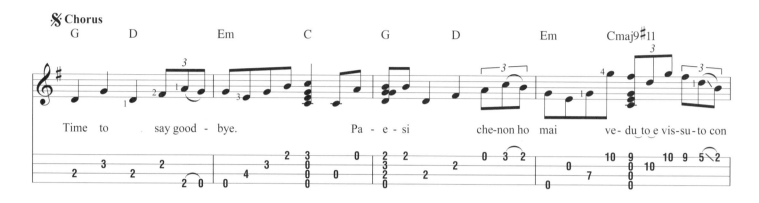

Time   to   say good - bye.   Pa - e - si   che-non ho mai   ve - du - to e vis-su-to con

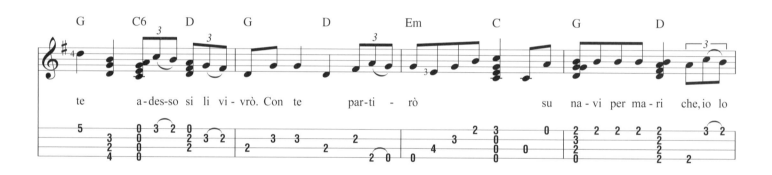

te   a - des-so si li vi - vrò. Con te   par-ti - rò   su na - vi per ma - ri   che, io lo

To Coda ⊕

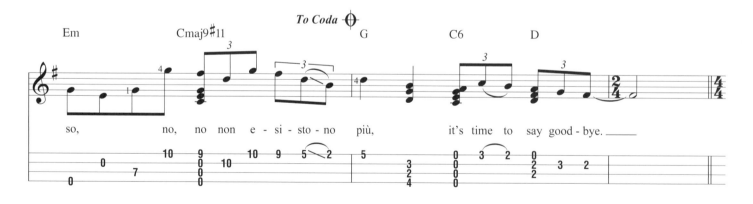

so,   no,   no non e - si - sto - no   più,   it's time to   say good - bye. ____

Verse

N.C.

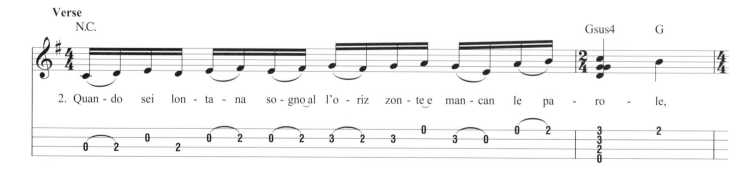

2. Quan - do   sei lon - ta - na   so - gno al l'o - riz - zon - te e man - can le pa - ro - le,

236

e io si lo so che sei con me, con me, tu mia lu-na tu sei qui con me,

D.S. al Coda

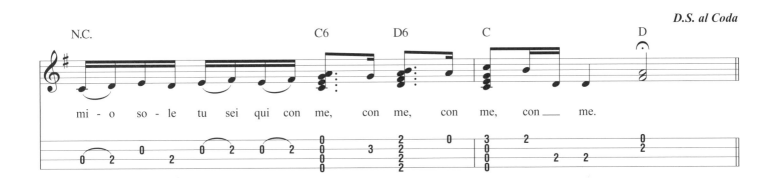

mi-o so-le tu sei qui con me, con me, con me, con ___ me.

⊕ Coda

Outro-Chorus

più, con te io li-ri-vi-vrò. Con te par-ti-rò su
Instrumental

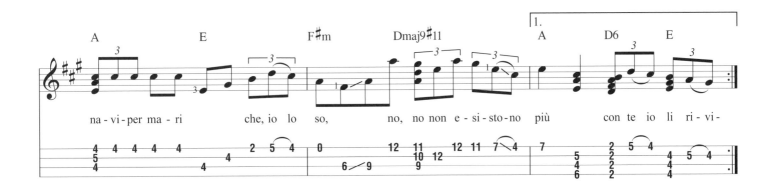

na-vi-per ma-ri che, io lo so, no, no non e-si-sto-no più con te io li-ri-vi-

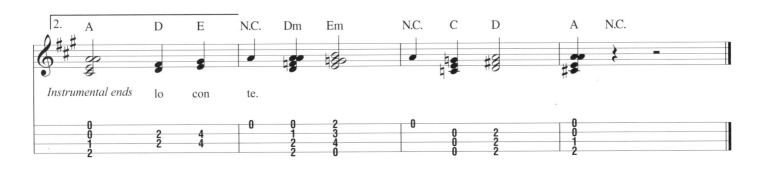

Instrumental ends lo con te.

A Time for Us
(Love Theme)

from the Paramount Picture ROMEO AND JULIET

Words by Larry Kusik and Eddie Snyder
Music by Nino Rota

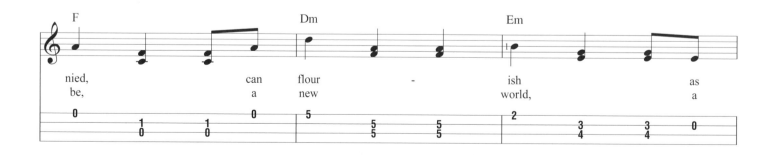

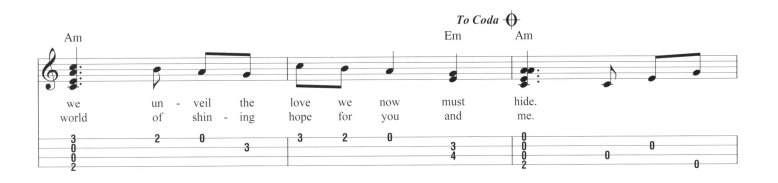

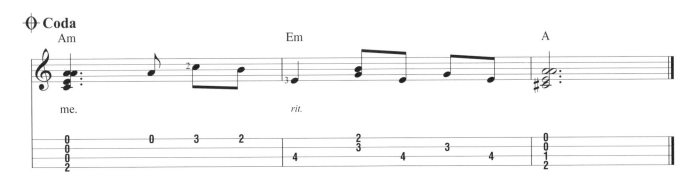

Up Where We Belong

from the Paramount Picture AN OFFICER AND A GENTLEMAN

Words by Will Jennings
Music by Buffy Sainte-Marie and Jack Nitzsche

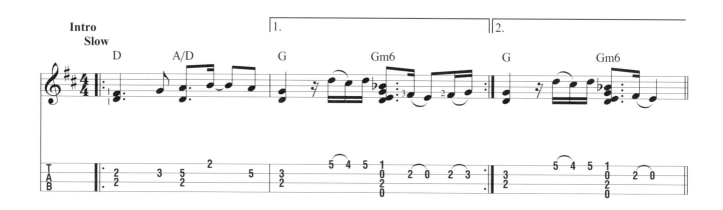

1. Who knows what to-mor-row brings in a world few hearts sur-
2. Some hang on to "used to be," live their lives look-ing be-

vive. All I know is the way I feel; when it's
hind. All we have is "here and now," all our

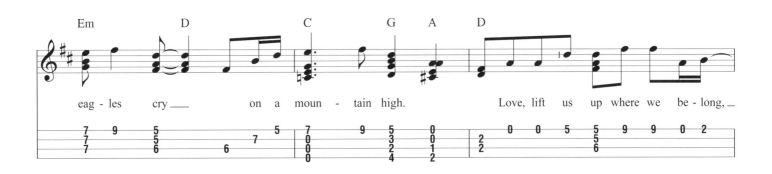

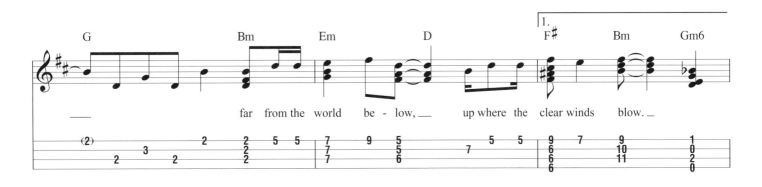

clear winds blow. ___

Bridge

Time goes by, no time to cry, life's you and I, a-

Outro-Chorus

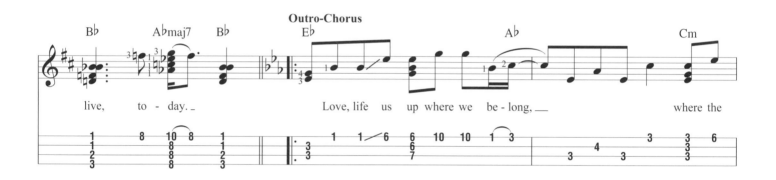

live, to - day. ___ Love, life us up where we be - long, ___ where the

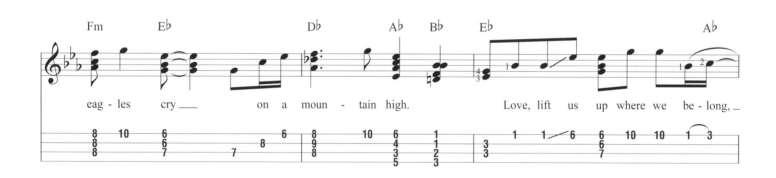

eag - les cry ___ on a moun - tain high. Love, lift us up where we be - long,

Repeat and fade

___ far from the world be - low, ___ up where the clear winds blow. ___

What a Wonderful World

Words and Music by George David Weiss and Bob Thiele

Intro
Moderately slow

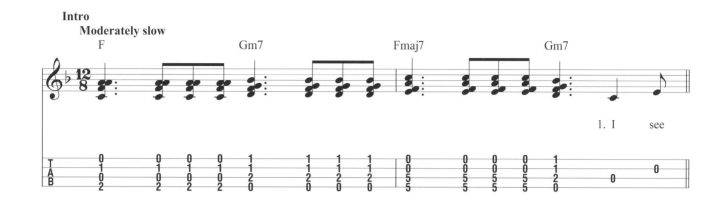

Verse

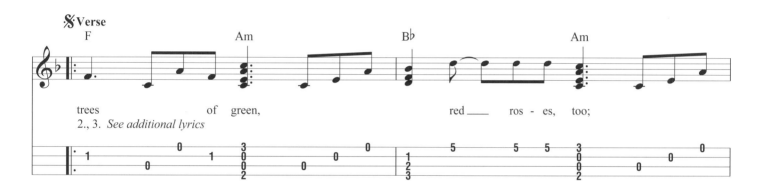

trees of green, of green, red ___ ros - es, too;
2., 3. *See additional lyrics*

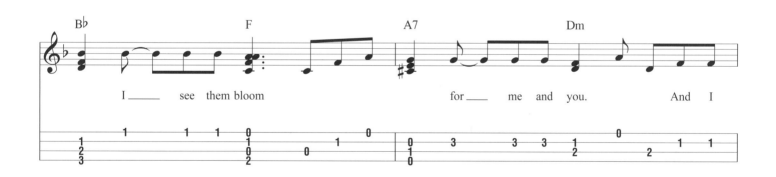

I ___ see them bloom for ___ me and you. And I

think to my - self, "What a won - der - ful

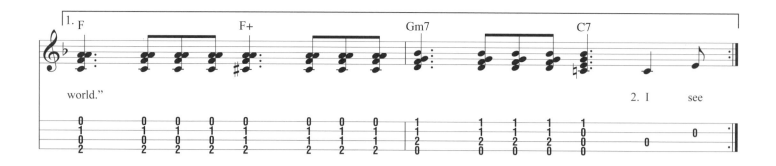

world."   2. I   see

world."   The

Bridge

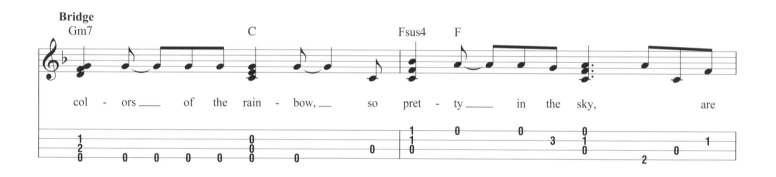

col - ors ___ of the rain - bow, ___ so pret - ty ___ in the sky,   are

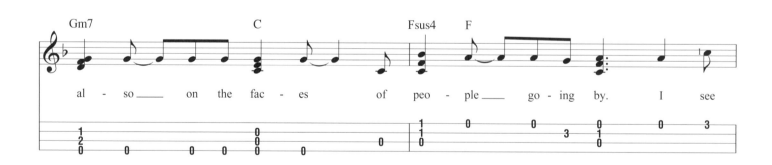

al - so ___ on the fac - es   of peo - ple ___ go - ing by.   I   see

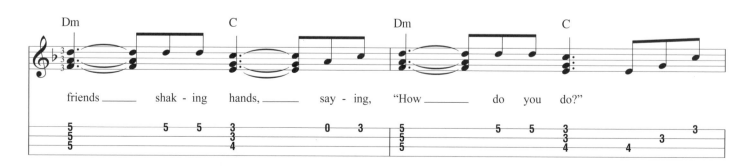

friends ___ shak - ing hands, ___ say - ing, "How ___ do you do?"

244

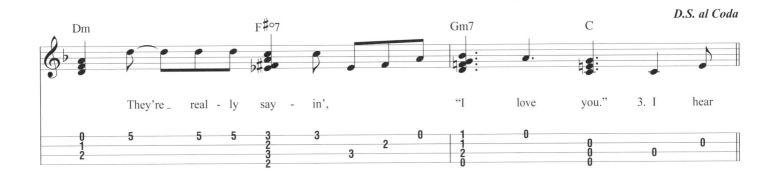

They're _ real - ly say - in', "I love you." 3. I hear

Coda

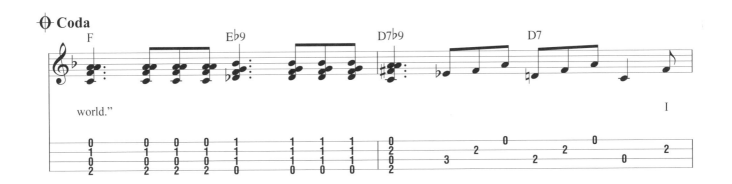

world." I

Freely

think to my - self, ___ "What a won - der - ful

world."

Additional Lyrics

2. I see skies of blue and clouds of white,
   The bright, blessed day, the dark, sacred night.
   And I think to myself, "What a wonderful world."

3. I hear babies cry, I watch them grow.
   They'll learn much more than I'll ever know.
   And I think to myself, "What a wonderful world."

We've Got Tonight

Words and Music by Bob Seger

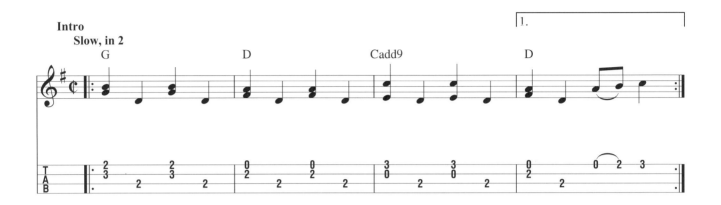

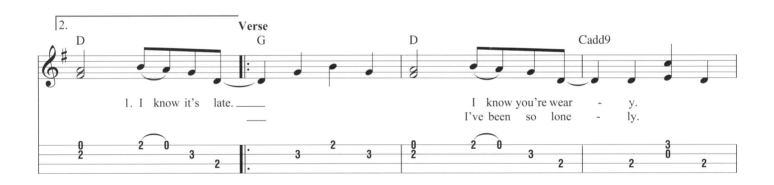

1. I know it's late. ____
I know you're wear - y.
I've been so lone - ly.

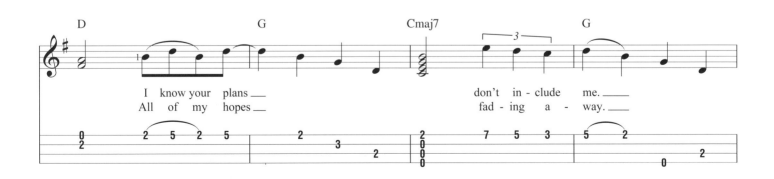

I know your plans ____ don't in - clude me. ____
All of my hopes ____ fad - ing a - way.

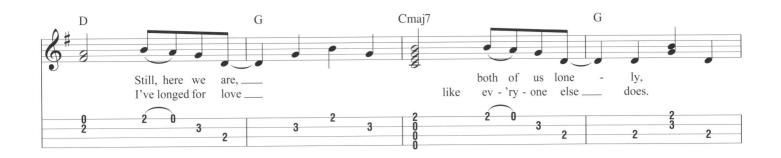

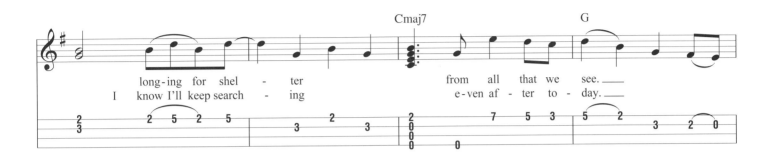

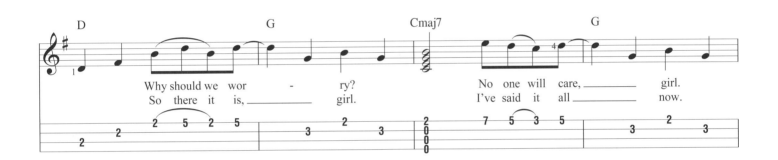

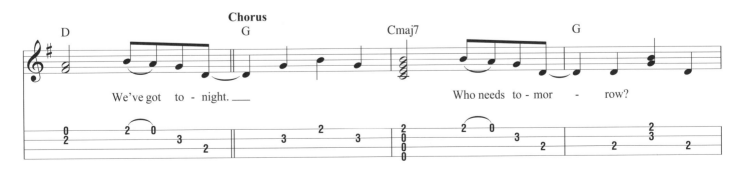

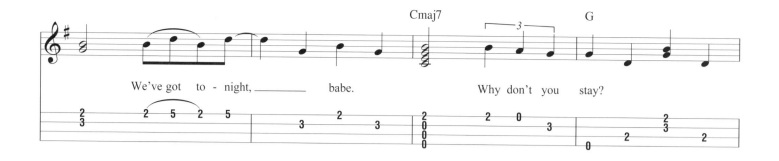

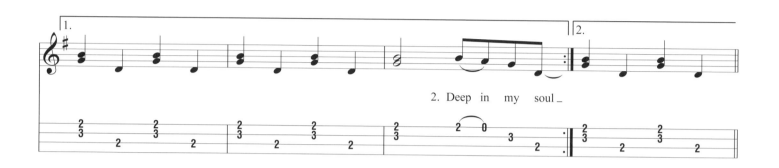

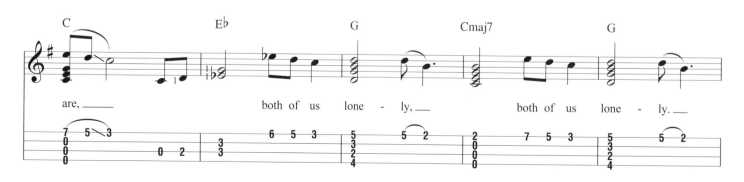

We've got to - night ___
Who needs to - mor -
Come take my hand, ___

- row?
___ now.
Let's make it last. ___
We've got to - night, ___
Let's find ___

a way.
Turn out the light. ___ ___ babe.
Why don't you

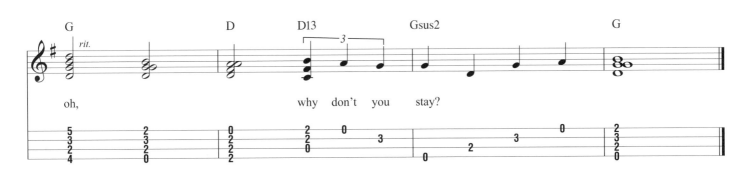

stay?
Oh, ___

oh,
oh,
why don't you stay?

What About Love?

Words and Music by Brian Allen, Sheron Alton and Jim Vallance

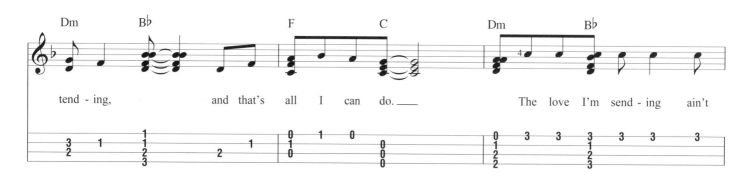

mak - ing it through _ to your heart.   2. You've been

Verse

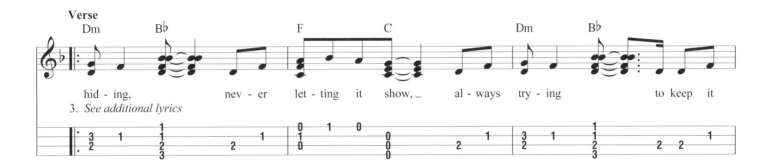

hid - ing,   nev - er let - ting it show, _ al - ways try - ing   to keep it
3. *See additional lyrics*

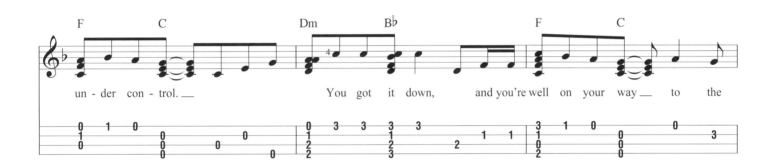

un - der con - trol. _   You got it down,   and you're well on your way _ to the

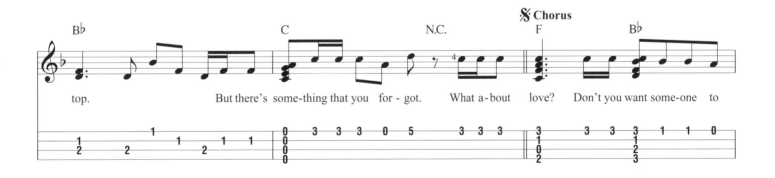

top.   But there's some-thing that you for - got.   What a - bout love?   Don't you want some-one to

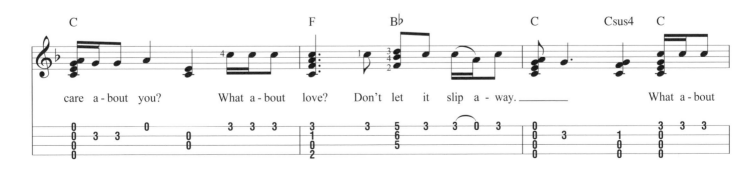

care a - bout you?   What a - bout love?   Don't let it slip a - way. _   What a - bout

love?   I   on - ly   want   to   share   it   with   you.   You   might   need   it   some - day. _

Yeah.   3. I   can't

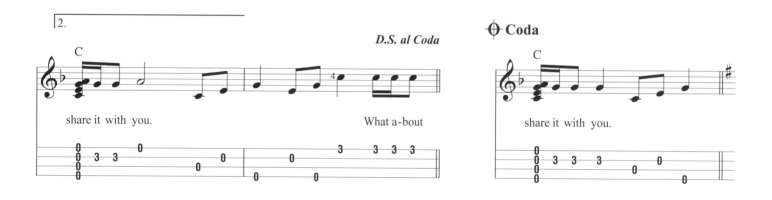

share   it   with   you.   What a-bout   share   it   with   you.

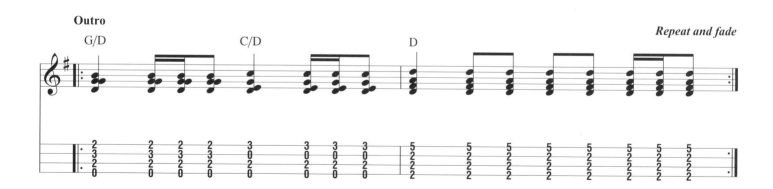

Additional Lyrics

3. I can't tell you what you're feeling inside,
   And I can't sell you what you don't want to buy.
   Something's missing, you gotta look back on your life.
   You know something, it just ain't right.

What the World Needs Now Is Love

Lyric by Hal David
Music by Burt Bacharach

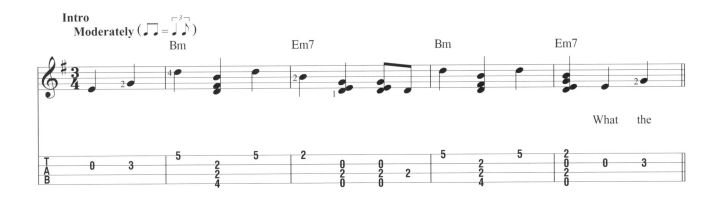

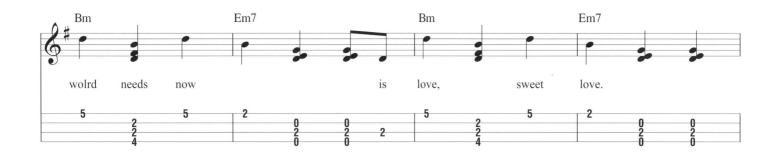

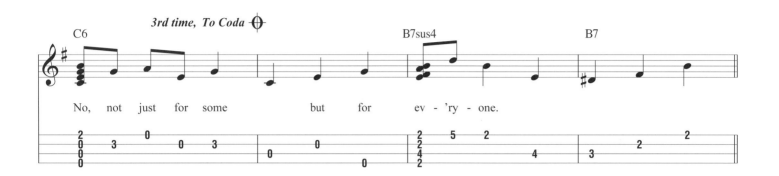

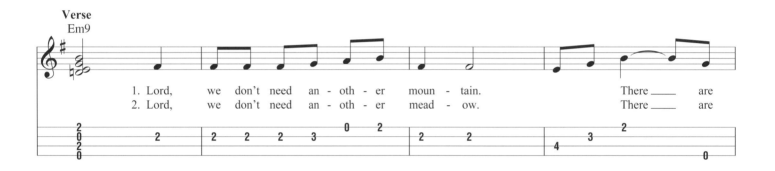

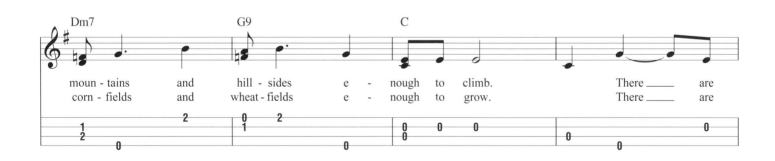

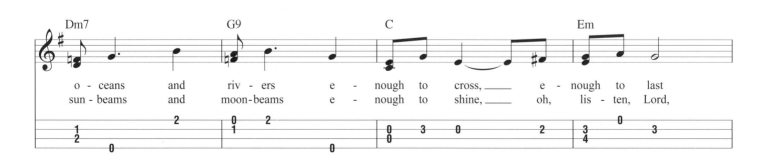

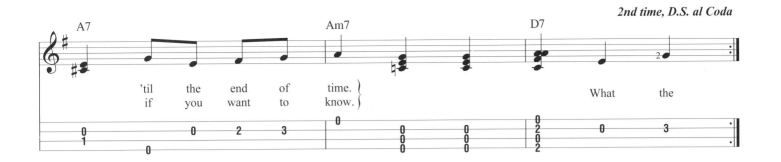

'til   the   end   of   time.
if   you   want   to   know.

What   the

⊕ Coda

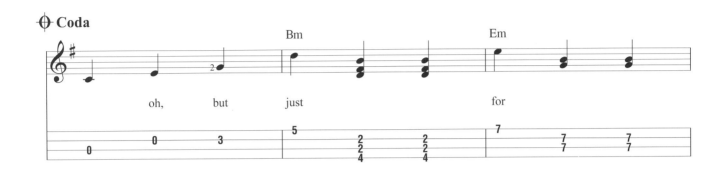

oh,   but   just   for

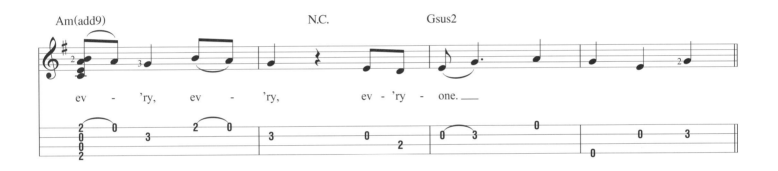

ev - 'ry,   ev - 'ry,   ev - 'ry - one.

Outro

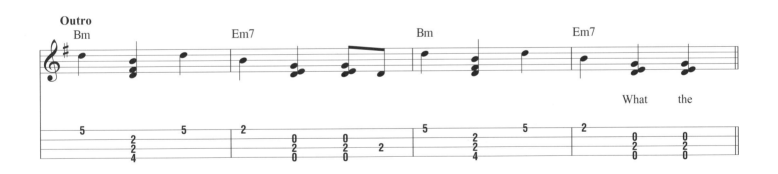

What   the

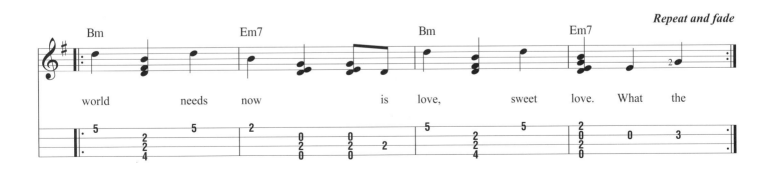

world   needs   now   is   love,   sweet   love.   What   the

When I Need You

Words and Music by Carole Bayer Sager and Albert Hammond

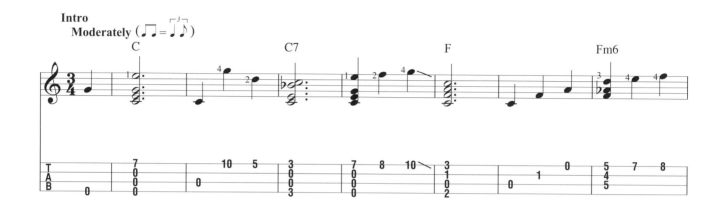

1. When I (3.) need you, I just close my eyes and I'm with
2. *See additional lyrics*

you, and all that I so want to give you, it's on - ly a

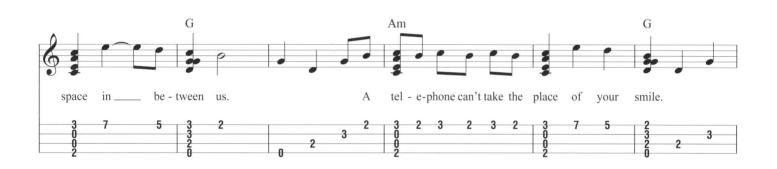

heart - beat ___ a - way. ___ When I day. Miles and miles of emp - ty
See additional lyrics

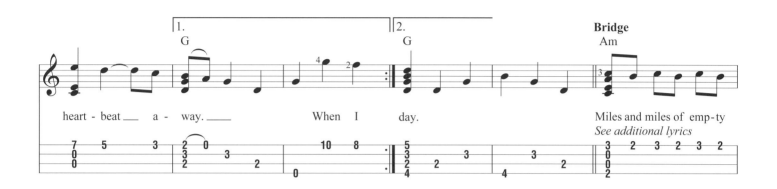

space in ___ be - tween us. A tel - e-phone can't take the place of your smile.

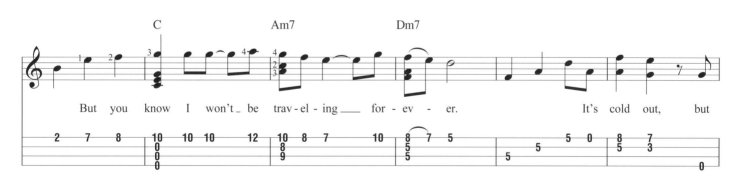

But you know I won't __ be trav - el - ing ___ for - ev - er. It's cold out, but

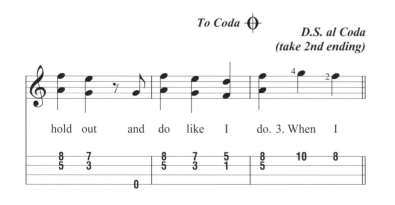

To Coda ⊕
D.S. al Coda
(take 2nd ending)

hold out and do like I do. 3. When I

⊕ **Coda**

Interlude

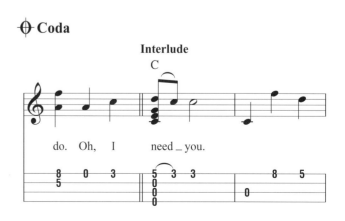

do. Oh, I need __ you.

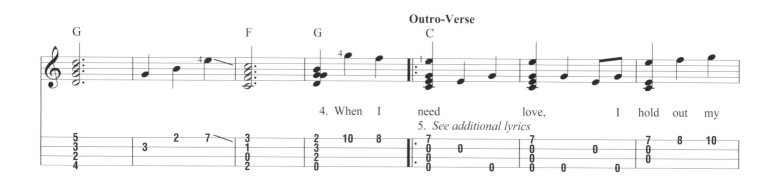

Outro-Verse

4. When I need love, I hold out my
5. *See additional lyrics*

hands and I touch love, I nev - er knew there was __ so much

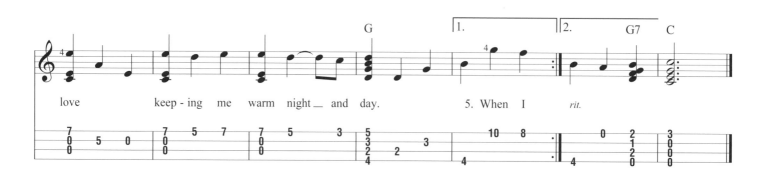

love keep - ing me warm night __ and day. 5. When I *rit.*

Additional Lyrics

2. When I need love
   I hold out my hands and I touch love.
   I never knew there was so much love
   Keeping me warm night and day.

Bridge: It's not easy when the road is your driver.
   Honey, that's a heavy load that we bear.
   But you know I won't be traveling a lifetime.
   It's cold out, but hold out and do like I do.

5. When I need love,
   I just close my eyes and you'r right here by my side.
   I never knew there was so much love
   Keeping me warm night and day.

Woman

Words and Music by John Lennon

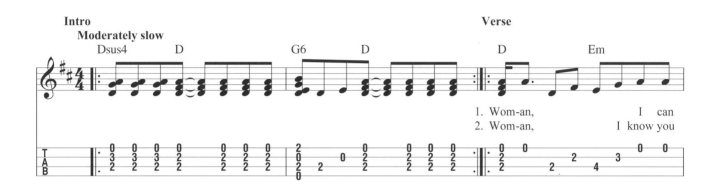

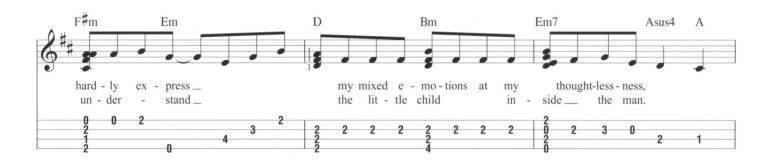

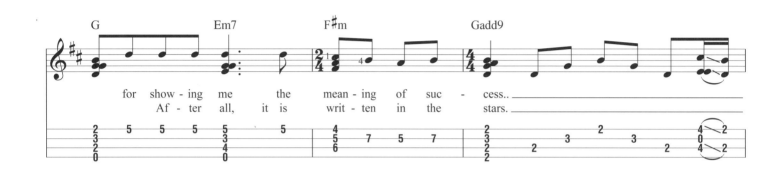

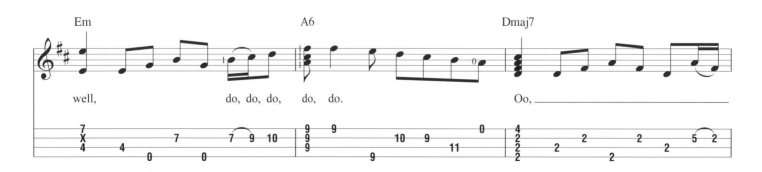

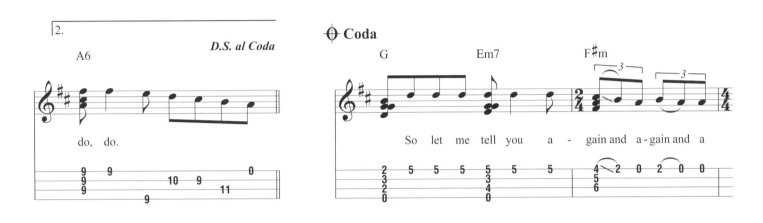

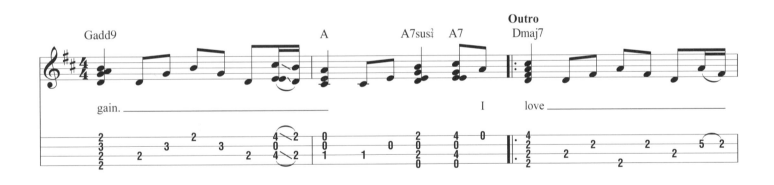

When We Dance

Music and Lyrics by Sting

loved **you** ___ like ___ I love you, ___

2.–5. *See additional lyrics*

I ___ would walk a - way in shame. I'd ___ move

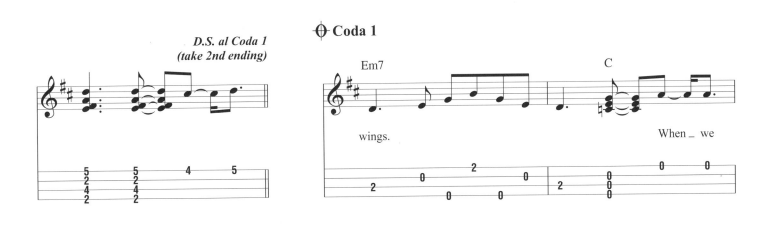

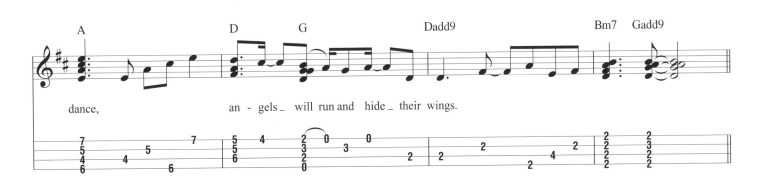

Bridge

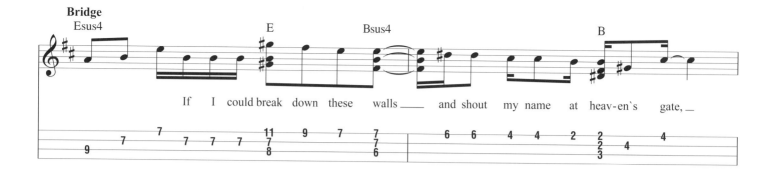

264

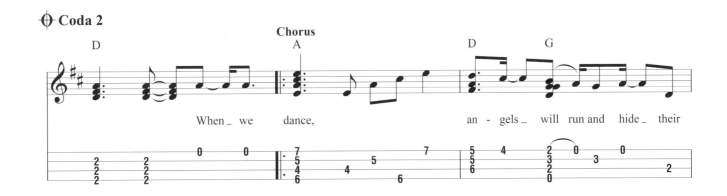

Additional Lyrics

2. When he watches you,
   When he counts to buy your soul,
   On your hand his golden rings
   Like he owns a bird that sings.

3. The priest has said my soul's salvation
   Is in the balance of the angels.
   And underneath the wheels of passion,
   I keep the faith in my fashion.

4. He won't love you
   Like I'll love you.
   He won't care for you this way.
   He'll mistreat you if you stay.

5. Come and live with me;
   We'll have children of our own.
   I would love you more than life
   If you'll come and be my wife.

A Whole New World
(Aladdin's Theme)

from ALADDIN

Music by Alan Menken
Lyrics by Tim Rice

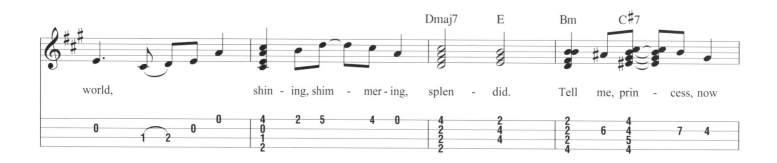

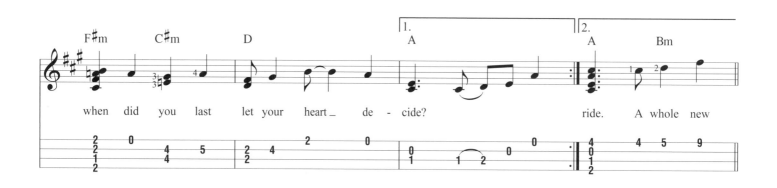

tell us, "no," or where to go, or say we're on - ly dream -

-ing. A whole new world, a daz - zling place I nev - er

knew. But now from way up here, it's cry - stal clear that now I'm in a

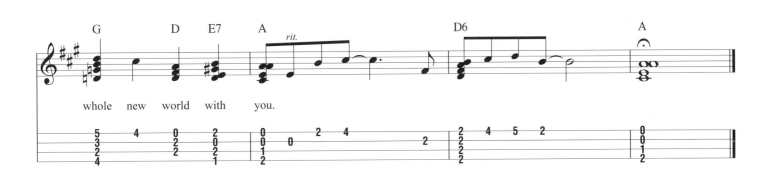

whole new world with you.

Additional Lyrics

2. I can open your eyes,
   Take you wonder by wonder.
   Over, sideways and under
   On a magic carpet ride.

You Are Not Alone

Words and Music by Robert Kelly

% **Verse**

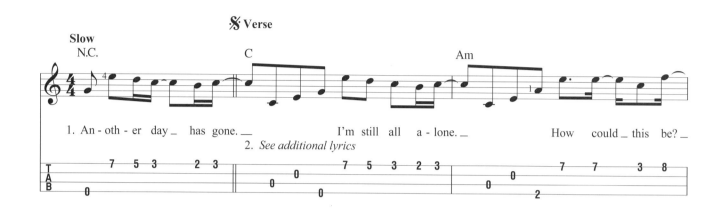

1. An-oth-er day __ has gone. __ I'm still all a - lone. __ How could __ this be?
2. *See additional lyrics*

__ You're not here __ with me. __ You nev - er said __ good-bye. __ Some-one tell __ me why

__ did she have __ to go __ and leave my world __ so cold? __ Ev-'ry

day I sit ___ and ask ___ my - self ___ how did love slip ___ a - way? ___

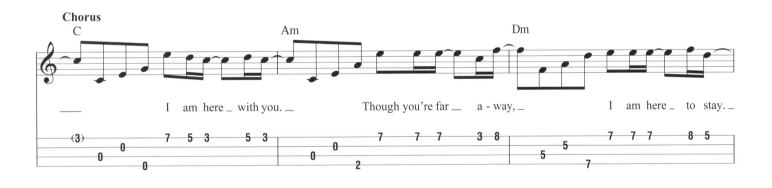

Some - thing whis - pers in ___ my ear ___ and says ___ that you are not ___ a - lone. ___

Chorus

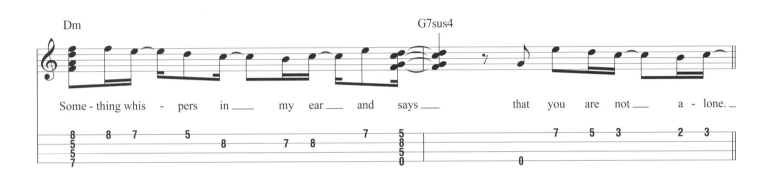

___ I am here ___ with you. ___ Though you're far ___ a - way, ___ I am here ___ to stay. ___

___ But you are not ___ a - lone. ___ I am here ___ with you. ___ Though we're far ___ a - part,

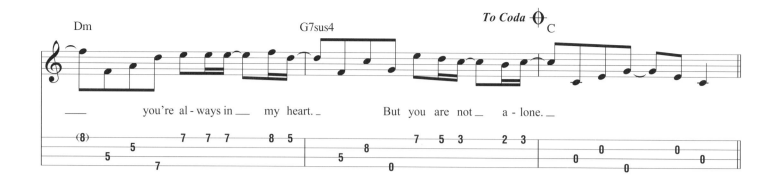

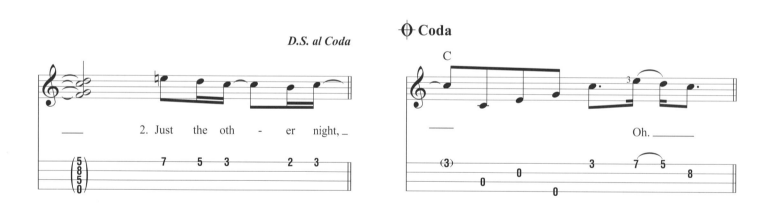

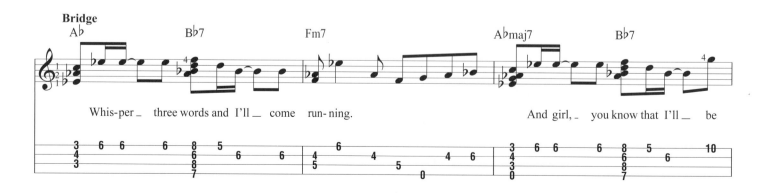

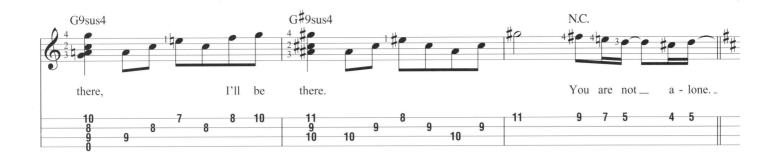

there, I'll be there. You are not ___ a - lone. ___

Outro-Chorus

___ I am here ___ with you. ___ Though you're far ___ a - way, ___ I am here ___ to stay. ___

___ But you are not ___ a - lone. ___ I am here ___ with you. ___ Though we're far ___ a - part, ___

Repeat and fade

___ you're al - ways in ___ my heart. ___ But you are not ___ a - lone. ___

Additional Lyrics

2. Just the other night,
I thought I heard you cry,
Asking me to come
And hold you in my arms.
I can hear your prayers.
Your burdens I will bear.
But first I need your hand,
Then forever can begin.

You Are So Beautiful

Words and Music by Billy Preston and Bruce Fisher

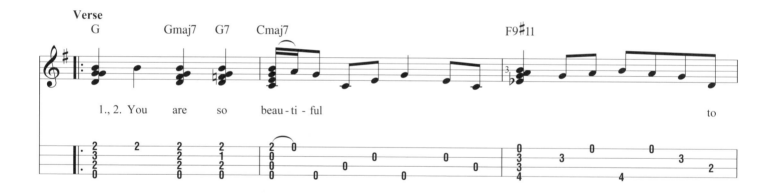

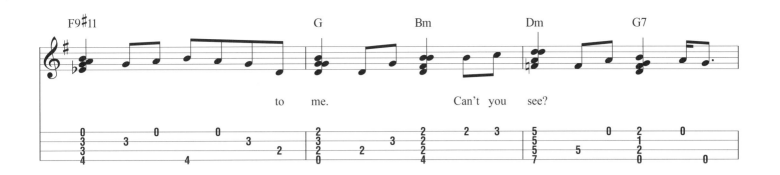

to me. Can't you see?

You're ev - 'ry - thing I hoped for. You're ev - 'ry - thing I

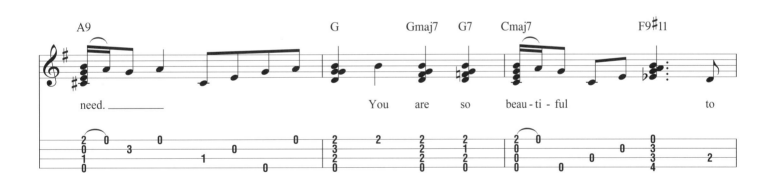

need. _____ You are so beau - ti - ful to

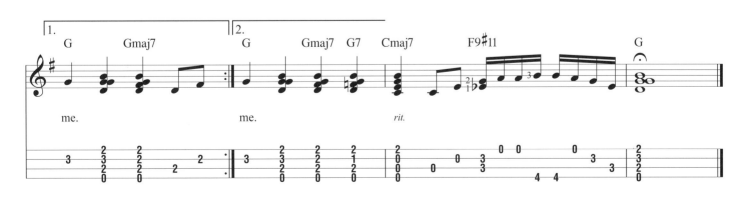

me. me. *rit.*

You Belong to Me

Words by Carly Simon
Music by Michael McDonald

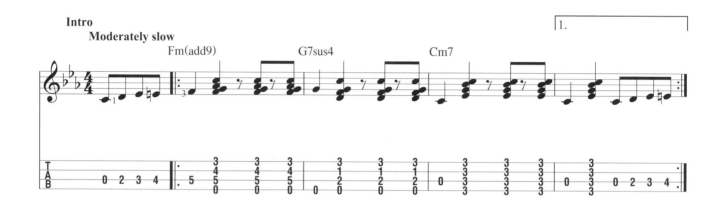

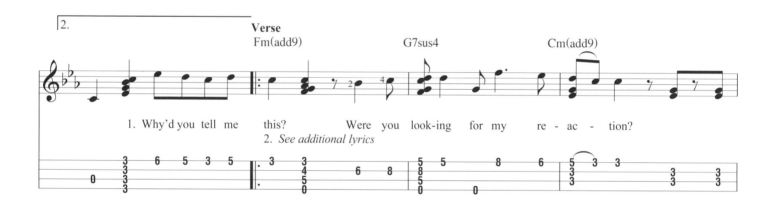

1. Why'd you tell me   this?   Were you look-ing   for my   re - ac - tion?
2. *See additional lyrics*

What do you need to   know?___   Don't you know I'll al - ways be ___ your girl?

Pre-Chorus

1., 2. You don't have to prove to me __ you're beau - ti - ful __ to stran - gers. __

I've got lov - ing eyes _____ of my __

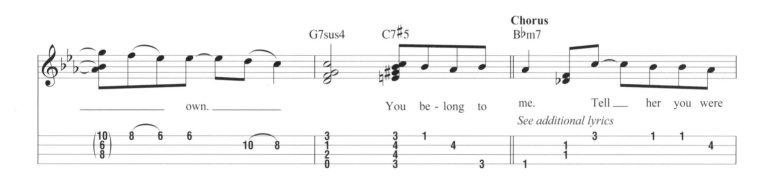

_____ own. _____ You be - long to me. Tell __ her you were
See additional lyrics

fool - ing. You be - long to me. __ You don't e - ven know __ her. You be - long to

me. Tell __ her that I love __ you. You be - long to me. 2. You be - long to

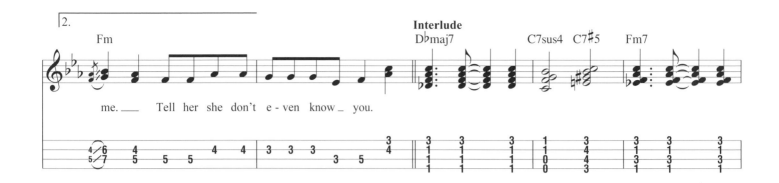

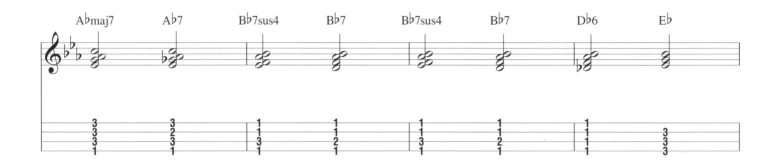

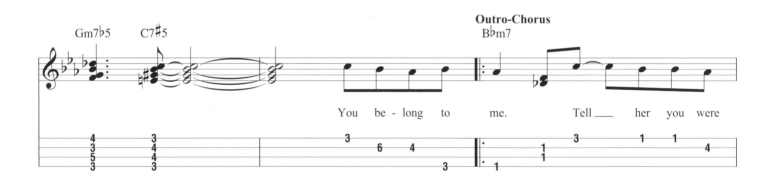

Additional Lyrics

2. You belong to me.
   Can it be, honey, that you're not sure?
   You belong to me.
   Thought we'd closed the book,
   Locked the door.

Chorus: You belong to me.
   Tell her that I love you.
   You belong to me.
   You belong, you belong to me.
   You belong to me.
   Tell her you were fooling.
   You belong to me.
   Tell her she don`t even know you.

You Raise Me Up

Words and Music by Brendan Graham and Rolf Lovland

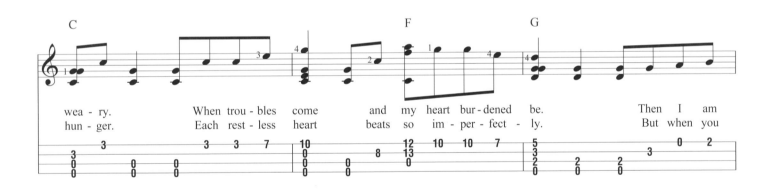

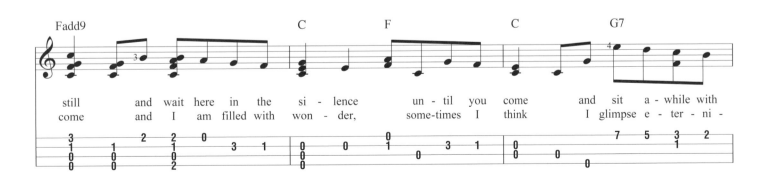

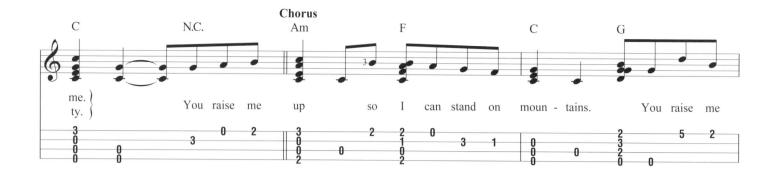

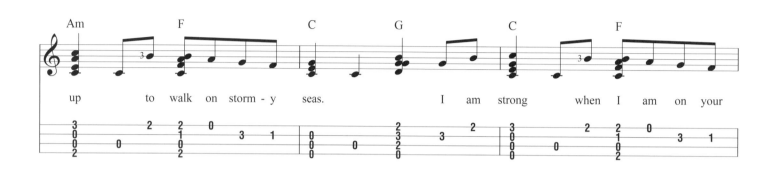

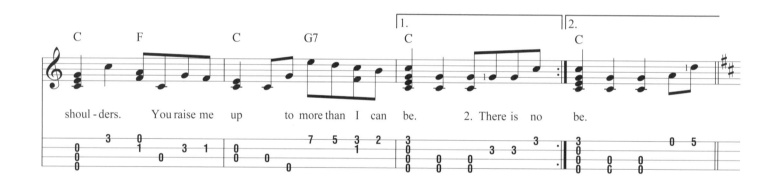

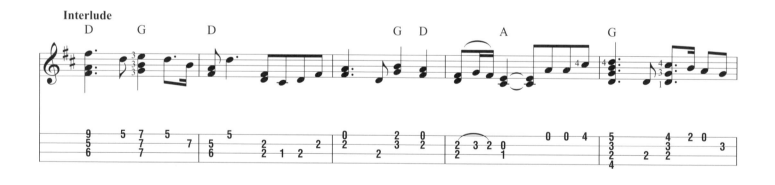

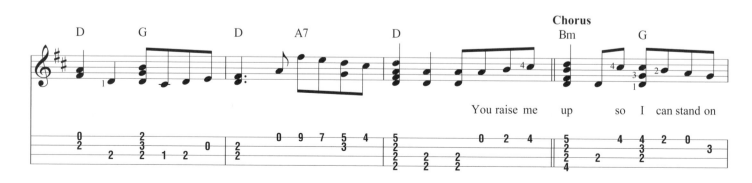

mountains. You raise me up to walk on storm-y seas. I am strong when I am on your

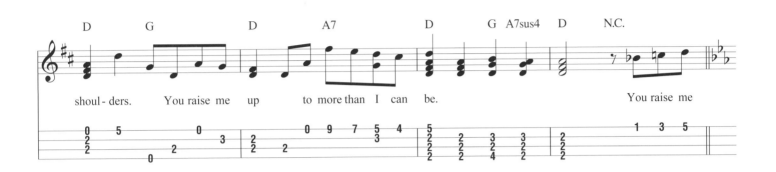

shoul-ders. You raise me up to more than I can be. You raise me

Outro-Chorus

up so I can stand on moun-tains. You raise me up to walk on storm-y seas. I am

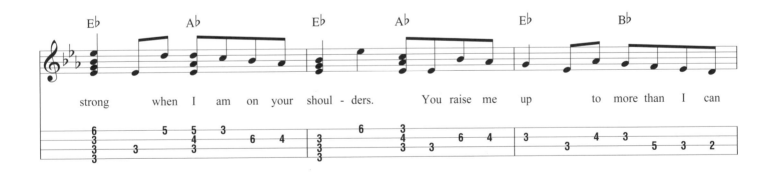

strong when I am on your shoul-ders. You raise me up to more than I can

Freely

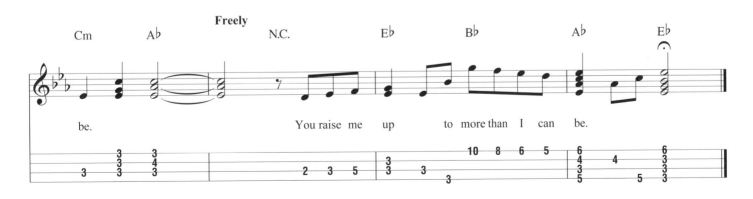

be. You raise me up to more than I can be.

You Light Up My Life

Words and Music by Joseph Brooks

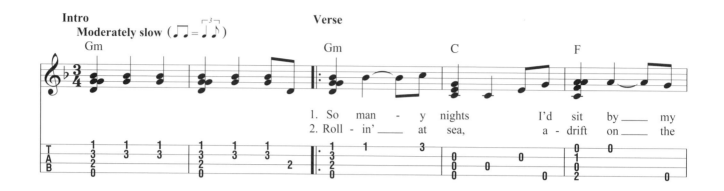

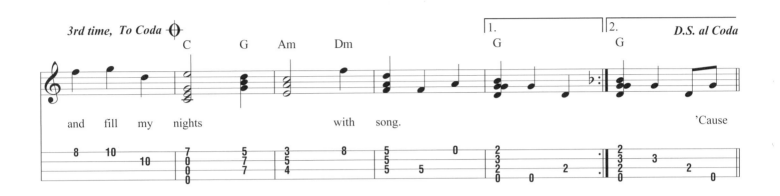

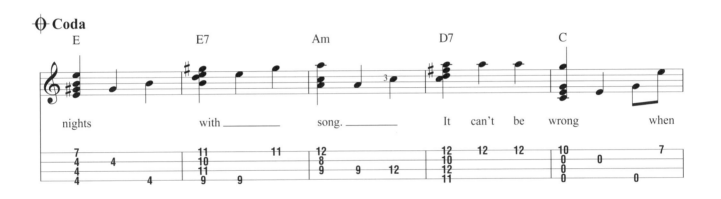

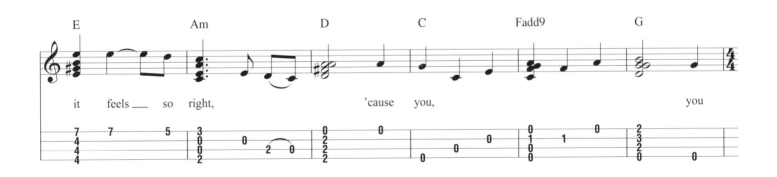

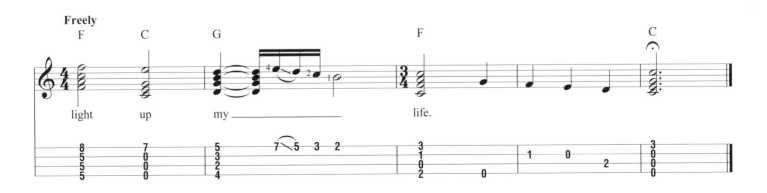

You're the Inspiration

Words and Music by Peter Cetera and David Foster

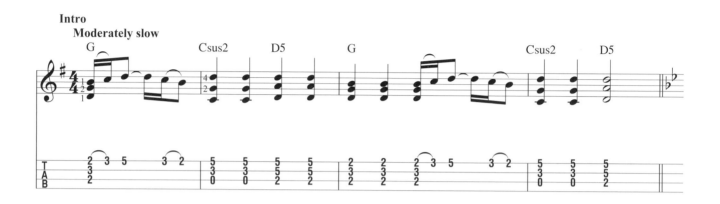

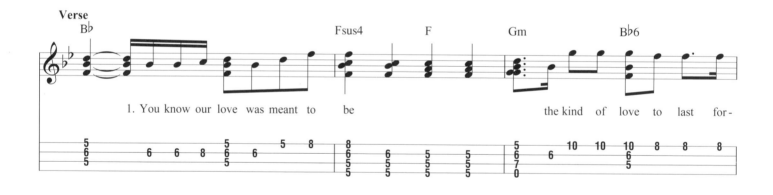

1. You know our love was meant to be the kind of love to last for-

ev-er. And I want you here with me from to-night un-til the

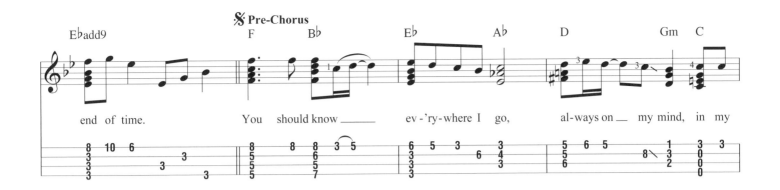

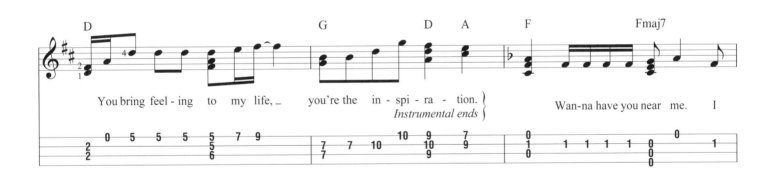

you.

2. And I

Verse

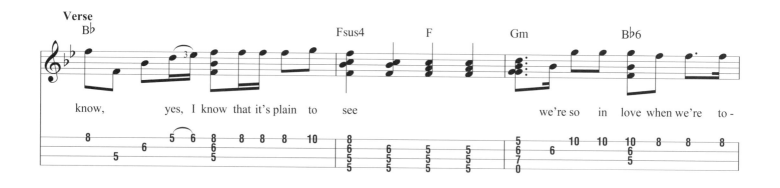

know,　　yes, I know that it's plain to see　　　　we're so in love when we're to-

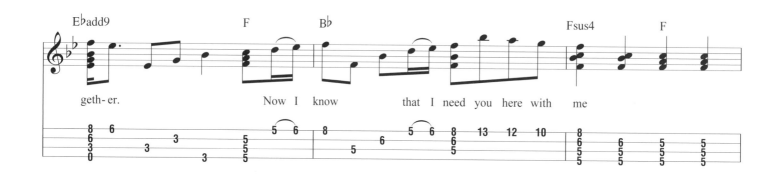

geth- er.　　　Now I know　　that I need you here with me

D.S. al Coda 1

from to-night un - til the end of time.

Coda 1

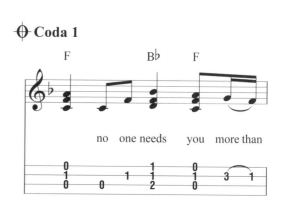

no one needs you more than

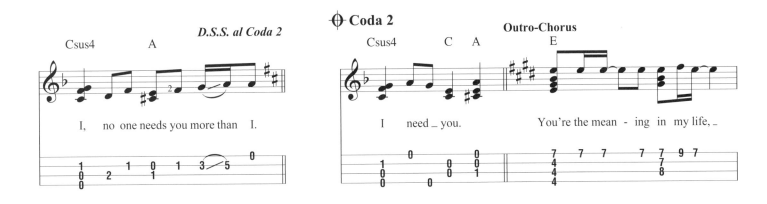

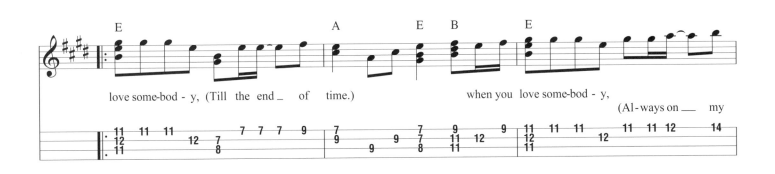

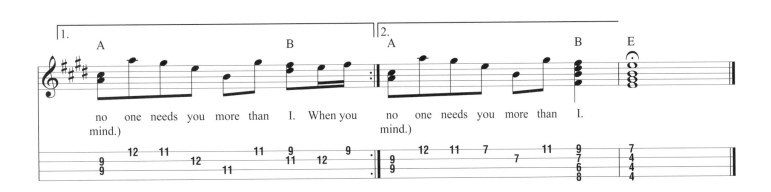

You're Still the One

Words and Music by Shania Twain and R.J. Lange

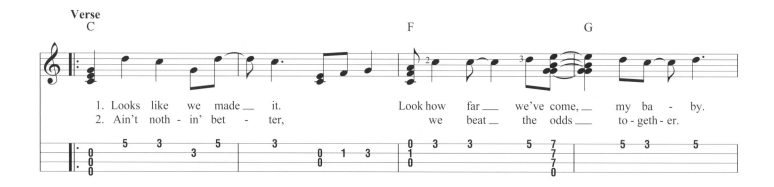

1. Looks like we made __ it.   Look how far __ we've come, __ my ba - by.
2. Ain't noth - in' bet - ter,   we beat __ the odds __ to - geth - er.

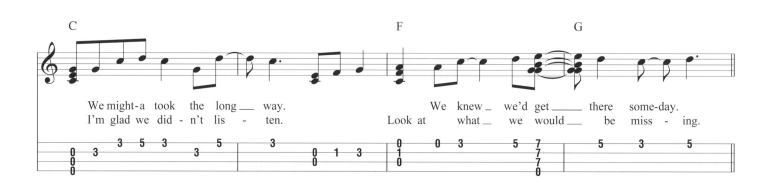

We might-a took the long __ way.   We knew __ we'd get ___ there some-day.
I'm glad we did - n't lis - ten.   Look at what __ we would __ be miss - ing.

Pre-Chorus

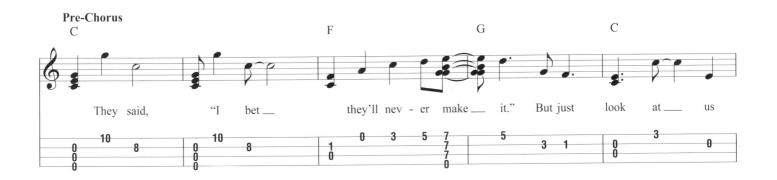

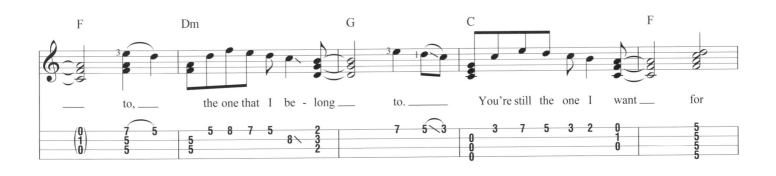

287

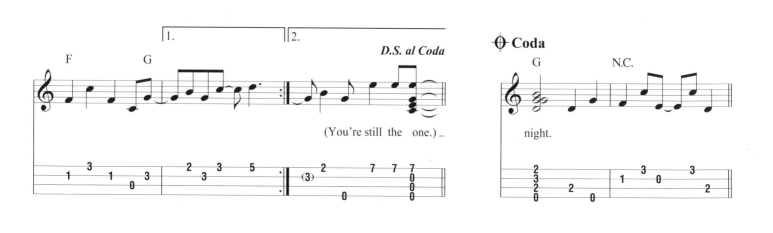